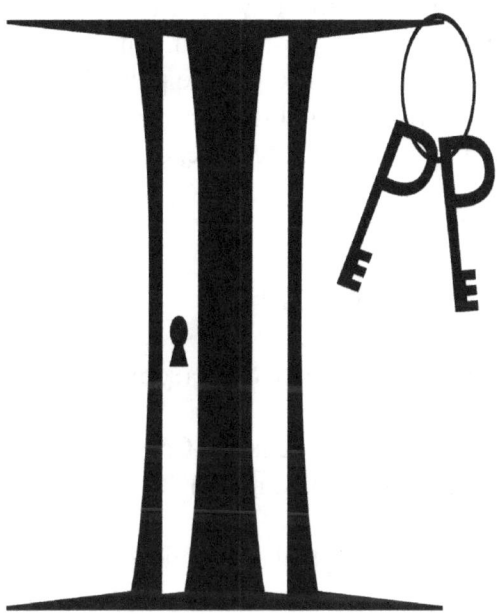

Institutionalized Persons Press

ISBN-10: 0615747019

ISBN-13: 978-0615747019

Published by Institutionalized Persons Press.

Cover layout & design: Jennifer-Crystal Johnson
www.jennifercrystaljohnson.com

Edited by Jennifer-Crystal Johnson

EMPTY-HANDED
but not
EMPTY-HEADED

The PrisonProof Project

By
John L. Hunt

Table of Contents

This book is dedicated to the Hunt family for supporting me through many incarcerations, relapses, wasted resources, and lost family moments.

This writing is also dedicated to all the men and women in the world who are visually impaired, physically disabled, institutionalized, or in an unbearable oppressive situation.

And finally, after I was released from prison on November 1, 2011, I was blessed to have some of the most generous people I've ever met come into my life. The majority of these people work at Metro Call A Ride in St. Louis, MO.

Jeremiah 6:16

"Thus says the Lord: Stand at the crossroads, and look, and ask for the ancient paths, where the good way lies; and walk in it, and find rest for your souls. But they said, 'We will not walk in it.'"

Introduction

Today, I'm incarcerated at the Federal Medical Center in Lexington, KY, and I woke up one morning with a new idea: What if I wrote a daily entry of a page or two about what I was witnessing? What if I started with the geography of this complex? Can I introduce myself as a creative writer from this point in my life? How am I going to remember all of the ideas that I've had over the years? What about all of the ideas that I've forgotten? What good could possibly come from the publication of the work? Who is my audience and why should I be the one to bring them this message? Is it okay that I write this book even though I've never completed a writing course? How beneficial is it for institutionalized persons to write about themselves and their experiences? What about all of the ideas from the newspapers, television, legal work, law books, and business periodicals? And last but not least, what about this "colorful" institution, for lack of a better word, called the Federal Medical Center, formerly known as the US Narcotics Farm?

The first US Narcotics Farm was established by Congress in 1929 at Lexington. The facility was staffed by the US Public Health Service and two major divisions: Clinical Research Center on Drug Addiction and Addiction Research Center. The facility was designed to treat those addicted to drugs who voluntarily admitted themselves, as well as Federal prisoners addicted to narcotic drugs.

The first female inmates at Lexington were received in January of 1941 and were originally housed in the Women's Building, which is now known as the Federal Prison Camp (FPC) Atwood. In February of 1974, the Clinical Research Center was transferred to the Federal Bureau of Prisons and became a low-security, co-correctional facility. Several years later, the Addiction Research Center was turned over to the Bureau of Prisons.

During 1988, the prison was converted to an administrative facility for low-security level women and women needing medical treatment. In 1989, security was increased by adding a perimeter fence. Due to the increased need for bed space for men, the facility again became co-correctional in January of 1990. The institution returned to an all-female institution in November of 1990. In November of 1991, the facility's name was changed from Federal Correctional Institution to Federal Medical Center to more accurately reflect its mission of providing healthcare to federal female offenders.

In 1993, the Federal Bureau of Prisons announced that FMC Lexington's mission would be as a medical referral center for male inmates. During 1994, the female inmate population decreased with the arrival of the first male inmates in November, 1994. Simultaneously, the Federal Prison Camp was activated at Lexington, housing low or minimum security females.

Today, the mission of Lexington is multifaceted: Federal Prison Camp Lexington for female offenders and the Federal Medical Center Lexington as a patient center for male inmates requiring chronic care for medical and surgical needs, and a nine month residential drug program (RDAP) for approximately 60-90 inmates. In addition, FMC Lexington has the capacity to provide both medical and psychiatric care to inmates with chronic long-term medical and mental health problems.

The daily operation of any correctional facility is dependent upon the relationship and cooperation of all divisions. Unit Management teams include a Unit Manager, a Case Manager, a Correctional Counselor, and a Secretary. Unit teams are located in each housing unit and provide case management services to the inmates. A full range of Psychology Services is offered, including admission screening and follow-up counseling. Religious services are available for all faiths and are provided by FMC Lexington or contract staff.

The Education Department offers multifaceted programs including Adult Basic Education, General Education Department (GED), English as a Second Language, Parenting Program, Career Counseling and Development, and US Department of Labor programs. The Recreation Department provides a broad spectrum of actives and sedentary programs.

Federal Prison Industries (UNICOR) operates a Customer Service Center, Centralized Accounts Receivable and Payable, and an Electronic Cable Factory at FMC Lexington which, along with their support functions, employ approximately 500 inmates.

The Business Office staff manages an annual budget of over $65 - $100 million including approximately $80 million for staff salaries. Three full nutritionally balanced meals are prepared and served each day by Food Service staff with a budget of $2.78 per inmate per day. Maintenance of the over one million square feet of floor space and 519 acres of land is done mainly by inmates under staff supervision. The area within the secured perimeter is 37 acres. FMC Lexington employs approximately 160 correctional officers whose role in daily operations is critical to the orderly running of the correctional institution.

This book is the first manuscript I have brought to publication and I'm working on a few more to bring to print. The courage to write was born in the guilt of not having a formal education and a discipline of reading for many hours every day. This conditioning was instilled in me by older, wiser men who will never be released from prison or have a significant amount of time remaining to serve. These men would listen to me talk about community service, starting companies, higher learning, and what I should've been doing in my community. So they instructed me to learn, and to master what I've learned I had to teach, and to teach something of substance I had to read, write, and study for a minimum of eight to ten hours every day.

As I went through these steps I came across a book entitled *How to write a Memoir* and that book was the seed that led me to produce this work.

There are many men institutionalized who have the desire to become an author, but the tedious work of getting the work to publication is a major hurdle for them. This book represents my lighthouse, a beacon of light to look toward for every institutionalized person that I told I would write back, support their efforts in rehabilitation or their efforts to financially support their families and themselves. And I'm proud to personally have the skill to transcribe this work into braille for my ex-students and visually impaired brothers.

How This Book is Presented

This book has been purposely sectioned into 30-day parts, each consisting of daily diary entries. Each month is dedicated to a special person in my life, and each chapter introduction states why this person is important to me and a little about my relationship with them. However, each person is not connected to the material in the chapter.

The reason I chose to keep the diary format is simple: to show other inmates that, in one year with a little work every day, they can also write a book. Not only will this help them to see that it is possible and very doable, but doing a project like this will also help them to look back and learn things about themselves that they may not have known before.

My author photo in the back of the book was taken while I was incarcerated. I'm including this photo in particular because I want to make sure every person who reads this book has absolutely no doubt of where it's coming from. Because I was able to do this, I hope that other inmates take the initiative to start writing down their own stories, thoughts, ideas, and plans to better their lives and the lives of their families.

This is a glimpse into my life as an inmate. May it give you perspective, teach you, or even just entertain you.

Chapter One: God, Our Creator

I was raised a Baptist, went to Catholic private school, and to this day I still believe in God as my creator. There are many instances in my life where I truly believe that I should have been killed or died from abusing alcohol and drugs. For His own reasons, God has plans for me. Moreover, I believe that it is my destiny to help people like myself who still possess the strength to do well and help others.

In the past I have found peace while studying Siddha Yoga Meditation and I found the ability to study my thoughts. I have read volumes of literature on all types of religion and disciplines; however, I have always found it comforting to rely on my mother's understanding of God.

When I was very young I was assigned to special education classes at St. Phillips Catholic School, the beginning of feeling like an outcast. However, I didn't know that God had assigned a special angel in my life: my mother, Jessie Hunt.

Today is my birthday and I'm 40 years of age. I was born in 1970, when everything was plentiful and at peace. I am incarcerated here at the federal medical center in Lexington, Kentucky. I've been at this institution for seven years and incarcerated for 15. I've always felt that it was paramount for me to write a book before I was released from prison. If you are spending this much time in prison and you have had plenty of time and opportunity to start your manuscript, then why not do it? There really is no reason for me not to get published when I leave prison, even if it has to be self-publishing; so be it.

Over the past three years, I've started working on a personal memoir about my life. I stopped that project to start this one because I have been meaning to get something like this done to show other guys how easy it really is. I preach a lot to the brothers about writing a book or keeping a diary about their prison experiences or just how they evaluate their surroundings.

How do I tell them about my past and what are some of the dangers that I see them walking into? How can I demonstrate the need to finish strong in relation to their future? I challenge them to see if they can analyze some of the younger generations of men coming into the prison system. I also challenge them to gain strength, wisdom, and understanding through the written word and come out better men than when they went in.

At this point, I have about 27 months remaining on my sentence and I frequently think about my past and the stumbling blocks I put up for myself. Three stints in prison, four drug rehabilitation centers, countless jails, and sleepless nights on some of America's deadliest streets in the state of Illinois.

I have started winding down a lot of my classes so that I could concentrate more on completing this diary and my memoir. I really do have a lot to write about since my man, Barack Obama, has won the presidency. I am a supporter and contributor to him but we don't see eye to eye on all of the issues.

Mr. President, Barack Obama, did just sign the fair sentencing act of 2010. It changed the sentencing disparities between crack cocaine versus powder cocaine. I already received a sentence reduction and was really happy about that. A majority of the guys here didn't I get the reduction for many reasons: incident reports, gang activities, and so forth. Some were disqualified because of their status as career offenders. I am hoping with this new law that they will receive some type of sentence reduction.

But getting a sentence reduction to go home to no money, no job, no support, and no family in this economy is murder. All I want from these men in this country is to try working together as a team. When you're in a situation like what is going on in America today you have to team up and make due with what you've got until you can prosper again. Sometimes it is not meant for us to make it as an individual. Sometimes we need a little help.

Everybody here is waiting to see if the new crack law is going to become retroactive on November 1, 2010. I think the sentencing commission will wait until next year to make the law retroactive.

I have gotten a lot of advice from my main man, Dr. Moon. Mr. Moon does not hold a doctorate but he has been incarcerated for so long that he has reeducated himself very well. Mr. Moon's level of experience while being incarcerated for over 40 years has come in handy more than once.

Mr. Moon is the man that introduced me to reading the *New York Times* every day. I introduced him to foreign affairs. These publications have become the foundation of information in relation to world issues and history for us. Mr. Moon made his way his entire life to provide for his family, mainly for his grandchildren so that they may attend college and get plenty of education. I have learned a great deal from him about the law, politics, psychology, and cultural differences in relation to the guys that we're all locked up with today.

I thought that I read like a madman but he reads like a madman for real. Dr. Moon sleeps with his books in his bed. And I'm talking about rows of books. I believe that he is a great role model for the middle-aged men still trying to find their way.

August 23, 2010 - Day 2

I woke up this morning at about 7:00 AM because I had to get to the open house for legal mail, about a five minute walk away from my unit. I live in the unit *Terry*. Then there are *Bluegrass, Veritas, Cornel, Tears, Maritime,* and Healthcare units. This compound holds about 1500 to 1800 inmates at a time. For a while the statistics about the population and transfers changed as the wardens changed, about every three years or so. Every three years, they change the wardens because this institution has a slot for wardens that pay a high salary. This position is used to put these wardens through so that their highest-paying three years of employment is used to calculate their retirement.

I am still waiting to get the results back from the National Federation of the Blind in regards to my exam in Nemeth Braille. Nemeth Braille is the translation of college mathematics into braille to enable blind or physically impaired individuals the opportunity to study and get a quality education. I failed the test miserably the first time that I submitted it for grading.

I have already been certified by the Library of Congress in literary transcription. Literary transcription is the beginning of learning the craft of braille transcription. I really enjoy this craft because there are a limited amount of people in this country who hold these certifications. This craft will be with me for the rest of my life.

The New York Times is full of information. Rest assured that if there's someone dying or committing some form of fraud, it will be exposed in the New York Times. We are still waiting to receive the next edition of foreign affairs.

After talking to a lot of the guys about doing something in regards to providing a product or service, they did not seem impressed by my conviction. They did not feel an urgency about their individual futures or the future of black men as a whole. They did not want to write. They wanted to drink hooch, gamble, lift weights, and have encounters in dark corners in the units. This is the very small minority versus the majority who feel inadequate when it comes to writing, or – better yet – a little intimidated.

I was asked to ghostwrite for a guy named Big Poppa. This process took about three months to complete, and I had never done that kind of work before. He wanted to write an urban novel. I would rather they write about urban life than sit and watch the TV all day long.

My cellmate just interrupted me and told me that I should call and talk to my mother. I think Mr. Jefferson is feeling a little guilty about his lack of communicating with his own mother in the past. He constantly tells me about not listening to his mother's advice and seeing it come to fruition. Mr. Jefferson's wife betrayed him by providing some secret material to the United States attorney's office that aided in his prosecution. I think his crime was money laundering. Mr. Jefferson is still having trouble accepting that he is in prison, even though it has been six months. I am sure he will be just fine.

August 24, 2010 - Day 3

The associate warden is in the unit to do an inspection. A few of these units around want everybody. I never could understand why you let a woman inspect the living quarters of over 200 male inmates. She'll probably find all kinds of bullshit to complain about. But the funny thing about women that work in corrections, whether it's state or federal, they despise working at a women's prison.

A few months ago, I found out that the high blood pressure medicine I am taking to keep my kidney disease under control has been found to cause cancer, mainly lung cancer. I have only been taking about 300 mg every day for about seven years. I have seen about four or five different kidney specialists and no one thought it was important to share that detail with me.

Even though this is a prison, it is also a medical center. I have got my own primary care physician and there is a central lab for full-blown work and other testing. I get tests done every 90 days with urine tests and x-rays. I've also been vaccinated for hepatitis A and B twice. I have taken at least 20 to 25 HIV tests in the last 15 years of incarceration. My kidney biopsy at Cox South in Springfield, Missouri, was the most fun I have had while incarcerated because I got to take Vicodin and eat strawberry swirl ice cream. I know, instant gratification, you don't have to say it out loud.

I think a lot of about the first time I walked into a public hospital with handcuffs and shackles. I used to see this stuff on television and now I'm living it in real life. It was demoralizing but after the first time, it took on a new life.

If you can survive the embarrassment, humiliation, guilt, resentment, despair, desperation, anger, hatred, impatience, attachment, loneliness, weight loss or gain, fear, lack of education, pain, headaches, and suicidal thoughts just to name a few, you just might have what it takes to finish strong.

I have completed the nonresidents drug program and we had to write a personal letter to someone in the group, which was designated by pulling names. I realize that I only have a 9th grade education, but I continue to strive to do my best. I am sitting here in the law library with some of the guys who are still fighting their cases in court, trying to get their sentence reduced by a day if they can. I remember those days of reading case law for eight to 16 hours a day, always the last one to leave the library. I needed to fight, I wanted to fight, I couldn't survive this incarceration without putting up a fight. I may not have won, but I'm still going to finish strong.

August 25, 2010 - Day 4

One of the guys who works with the inmate companion program is also an inmate companion participant. This is a job for inmates assigned to help other handicapped inmates here at the medical center. Some of the duties entail pushing outpatients to get to breakfast, lunch, or dinner. The staff rotates some of the time and it just so happens that we have got a new supervisor.

Ms. Underwood has taken over Mr. Childress' job as the coordinator of ICP's. She used to work in R&D and the mail room. I mostly saw her over the past seven years in receiving and discharge. I believe that she's going to work out just fine. It will take a little bit of getting used to the new job but she will learn the ropes really fast. Ms. Underwood has asked me to be an ICP/quarterly for a while, sort of a troubleshooter. The ICP mainly takes care of patients getting showers, callouts, and other miscellaneous everyday needs. Since I do not have a patient, she has assigned me to be a unit orderly.

A couple weeks ago I sent out 11 freedom of

information requests so that I could get records to substantiate my claims for disability when I get out of prison. There was a guy who was a triple board-certified emergency and trauma surgeon and he taught at the University of Kentucky. He told me that if they accepted my claim, I could request to be referred to him because he is also a disability termination specialist. I could really use all of the help I can find. Today, I received the first response from my request that I sent out for medical records, among other things. The first response was from Jacksonville, IL.

My cellmate just told me that the guys in the Chapel go to church every Sunday. I told him the Chapel is the first place that rapists, child molesters, and sexual deviants go to hide.

I am sitting here reading the New York Times and I'm glad that Iraq war is over. I don't believe that we should have been in this war to begin with. I firmly believe that we should use the money from the Iraqi's oil reserves to pay down the national deficit. We all poured trillions of dollars into the Middle East and we have gotten very little return.

I believe Israel is going to strike Iran unilaterally. I do say that there is enough international pressure on the Iranian president that he will sit and negotiate. The different clerics in the country should speak out more and challenge the Iranian president. They need to engage the youth because that is where the power of the future lies. If the Iranian president will not choose peace, then I think we should look at more drastic measures, like regime change. Violently if necessary!

August 26, 2010 - Day 5

It literally takes about 3 to 4 hours to read the New York Times. I will go to the library and look at the Washington Post, Wall Street Journal, or the USA Today. I do not like any of the political magazines that give you snapshots of what is happening in the world. The Times, Newsweek, the Weekly, Forbes, etc. The Economist is okay.

In the last few months I have had a lot of guys coming up to me asking my advice about challenging their sentencing or trial judge's oath of office. These guys are filling out the Freedom of Information Act request to get copies of these judges' Oath of Office and Affidavit. The law does require that these documents be on file. On the other hand, if they are successful in exposing the particular judge's lack of Oath of Office to the court then the Department of Justice has some serious legal problems inherent in relation to jurisdiction. Whether they're going to be successful or not is yet to be seen. I don't think I'm going down that road at this time. I will keep a close eye on events to follow.

The new email system is really efficient and I will save a lot of money on postage. I don't think I really want to communicate with a lot of people, so I will not be using it excessively. Besides, I do not believe that there is a person who is interested in communicating with me.

Some of the guys found out that I was writing a book about the Prison Proof Project and and they wanted me to write for them. I told them that I was beginning the project for myself, which is the foundation for my company named Braille First Incorporated. In addition to the email system, they are getting LEXIS-NEXIS law library software. The staff put in 15 terminals but they will all collect dust because the majority of people here do not want to fight their cases for whatever reason. I applied to get into a program that gives you a 12-month sentence reduction and six months of halfway house. At first, all you needed to get into the program was a drug conviction. One month before I was to enter the program I went to go over the program rules, which had changed in relation to enrollment. Now, they say that you have to have documented drug or alcohol abuse 12 months prior to your initial arrest to qualify for the Residential Drug Program.

I got a response from the social worker upstairs to help me file my disability claim two months before I'm released. These people know that the crack law has been signed into law and I may leave any day now. But who cares as long as they get to play email tag and watch porn on the internet, why would they need to do their jobs?

A lot of the guys don't like to listen to me. Sometimes I still try to tell them that the future is uncertain and it's going to be really hard to survive once you're released. A couple of months ago, a couple of the guys waited until it was two in the morning and went downstairs to delete all of the news channels from the televisions. How do you respond to something like that? Now, I have some idea – my father used to beat me with extension cords!

August 27, 2010 - Day 6

I went to my 9 AM callout to see Dr. Marrero. She is my primary care provider while I'm at this institution. I told her about my situation in relation to being destitute once I am released. I explained to her that I feel I need to be on Social Security Disability and that the kidney specialist at the University of Kentucky medical center advised me to file for it. Dr. Marrero told me that she would email the social worker and explain my situation to her. The progress you would expect from a social worker is not the same when dealing with someone behind bars.

Today was my last day of nonresidence program. Mrs. Sanborn handed back to us, among other things, our workbooks which included personal statements of change. We all pulled names and our last assignment was to write a letter to that person in the group.

I almost forgot, I brought an article about the types of

blood pressure medicine that were found to cause cancer to Dr. Marrero. She told me that I really had nothing to worry about and that even if I did, it would not matter because I still have to continue taking the medicine for the rest of my life.

I returned to my unit from drug class and, as I walked into the building, I ran into my braille coordinator. Ms. Leslie told me she has good news and bad news and handed me my grades from the second submission of my Nemeth braille exam and she said that I failed it a second time.

The person who graded my exam said that I have great potential but need more study time. I have to humble myself and overcome my failure. It will take me about five minutes to complete my acceptance and now it's time to move on to the next project. I will reevaluate my situation and see if it serves my future. Or should I take a detour? Ms. Leslie and I went downstairs and talked for a few minutes about studying braille formats. I told her that I was not planning on continuing with the braille at this time but I will reestablish myself again when I get out. I believe that the college in San Antonio, Texas has courses to learn braille.

Accepting that I failed the exam is really just disturbing. But I have got to push through it, accept it, and figure out a way to capitalize off of these minor setbacks. I have had to deal with setbacks all my life and they are never easy to swallow.

My life could be worse, I could live in Pakistan with all the flooding, hunger, and desperation felt by the women, children, and elderly. The front page of the New York Times always spotlights Afghanistan and Pakistan.

I have chosen to go back to college to get my doctorate in sociology. The staff thinks I would be a good teacher or researcher.

The majority of guys in all of the 10 to 12 state and federal prisons I've been in have hated being a resident.

The inmates that believe there is hope find out relatively quickly that the cards are stacked against them before they leave prison. This applies even more so if you are a minority and disabled. I have been released from to prisons and both times I did not have close to the education I needed to support myself or my family. Everybody in your family really doesn't want to have anything to do with you except your mother or favorite uncle. A lot of inmates at this institution have self-surrendered, turned themselves in to the prison on the date designated by the court at the individual's last bail hearing. These inmates are usually nonviolent people but the savagery of the system can turn you into an animal.

If you ever find yourself in the judicial system in this country, you will unconsciously start to develop what I like to call "iron wisdom." The lessons of what not to do, who to stay away from, the convicts to avoid, and using the staff to help you rehabilitate are some of the many actions you might take, which helps you develop this type of wisdom if you have done time as a teenager, as I have. Then there are certain lessons that are built into your DNA. Those lessons cannot be put into words but they will strike a chord and hit all your senses at once. This is not where you want to be because nine times out of ten you have just been stabbed or raped, or worse yet, witnessed such a cowardly act. The anticipation of danger is worse than the danger itself. And if you are not careful, you will have a stroke in the blink of an eye.

The impairment or handicap that prison has imposed on me is the inability to live a single day without a struggle, without complex tasks. I feel the average inmate or convict needs projects that take decades to complete.

Sometimes I listen to the late-night radio shows and some daytime shows as well. Rush Limbaugh, Mark Levin, Dave Ramsey, Ms. Ingram, Mr. Cunningham, a little coast-to-coast. These individuals in particular are very opinionated about how the country should be operated. I believe we all should understand the opinons of these individuals and the understanding of our ancestors whose shoulders we stand on. I wish Ronald Reagan were alive. Would he support the Republican party, the Democratic party, or no party?

A few months ago I had a conversation with my friend, Biscuit. Biscuit is about 64 and weighs about 375 pounds. Biscuit tried to commit suicide with a very sharp razor. These cuts were really deep. He told me about the times he was molested as a child and that there is a lot of family history when it comes to suicide. Biscuit is a serial drug user but made his livelihood from selling marijuana. It took the staff a while to clean up all of the blood in the unit. Biscuit was taken to the hospital barely alive.

The doctors put him back together and gave him tranquilizers and other mood-altering drugs. His sentencing judge gave him a choice. If he took the drugs, he would have to stay in special housing, also known as the hole. There you stay locked in a concrete room or cell. The guards like to punish you for being in the hole. These idiots turn the temperature down so low that they have to wear coats to withstand the cold. This kid told me that he gets a tranquilizer shot every two weeks. They give him migraine headaches but the attending psychologist really doesn't give a shit. I told Biscuit that he should try drinking some coffee.

Queen was a Marine and veteran hired to beat the shit out of a white guy that had supposedly jumped on an elderly man. Queen took care of business while Biscuit sat and watched in fear. I got a good look at the white guy that was attacked. I also heard that the elderly man started the whole episode. The victim wound up with a concussion. He is really lucky but I don't think he would've been if it had happened at the last joint I was at. FCI Florence is a rough joint and is all the way up in the mountains in Colorado, so medical attention, especially really bad cases, are dangerous compared to here; dangerous in terms of getting help fast enough to save a life. For years I was the staff response to medical emergencies. Trust me, the majority of the staff is not in a real big hurry. I worked in two medical centers for substantial amounts of time and I'm speaking from experience. I have seen several people die just waiting for medical attention.

The prison system is unforgiving and shows no compassion. Some of the inmates would come to a prison like this medical center and go back into society and brag or confess to their ability to navigate in prison. They need to start everybody out at maximum security, especially the staff.

I have talked to one of the interns here from the University of Kentucky who tried to finish a doctorate degree in psychology. I told him that I was interested in a doctorate degree in sociology. The intern told me that my dissertation had to be a qualitative analysis: a methodology that another person could follow and get the same results. I thought that was really interesting. I wonder how many of the students are prepared to spend 15 years in prison as an experiment? I understand that they don't deserve the harshness of prison to learn, but what an ambitious desire to study, to learn, to put your boots on the ground. Maybe this issue is due to years of community service before going to college?

August 29, 2010 - Day 8

I almost forgot I had to make an entry tonight. It takes real discipline to make sure that you log at least a page every night. I often thought about starting the Hunt Institute. This is to provide health insurance for inmates that are released from prison for two years. Obviously there are a lot of details in this type of plan that must be worked out before it is implemented.

Every Sunday I go to the barber shop to get my hair cut. I have kept his schedule for seven years. I have only had two barbers over the last seven years. My main barber, Roland, just got released after doing 20 calendars. He's the guy who gave me my first photo of the first family, the Obamas. I believe Roland may have been an ex-con out of Washington, DC . I am not certain of it. But he never denied it, either.

I woke up this morning and grabbed a cup of coffee and my headphones to go and see what was on TV. I watched the last few minutes of the movie and some of the guys started to leave. I changed it and watched Meet the Press. This is one of my favorite programs and I have been watching it for about five years.

August 30, 2010 - Day 9

After I went to lunch I was allowed in the recreation yard to get some walking in. It was about three laps around the track. As I was walking, an older gentleman was sitting because he had some swelling of the spine from an injury. Swelling caused him to be paralyzed on the right side of his body. With his good leg and the wheelchair, he pushed himself around the entire track. To me, this was a sign of not having given up no matter what.

I actually met him a few weeks ago when he told me his story. I have often wondered how difficult it is to live in the prison system in a wheelchair. His sores went unattended depending on the situation. This is one of the horrors of being in a wheelchair for an extended amount of time. I could see some sores on his legs and they appear to be really big holes that take a substantial amount of time to heal. He simply cannot feel it, and when he finds out it can be very depressing because someone has to clean them out.

There is another one of my buddies in a wheelchair who needs help from an ICP to take showers. Once, he was put in the shower with the water turned on but that ICP didn't stay to check the water temperature. The water was approaching extremely high temperatures and his skin started to come off. He just couldn't yell. He was in danger. The ICP finally returned to check on him and found him with really big patches of skin missing.

A few days ago I met a gentleman at the mail room on the other side of the compound. I asked him why he has so many letters because he had about 25 of them. He was sending a letter to as many influential people as possible to help him get a surgery on his brain because he had a blood clot. The federal medical center had a contract with the University of Kentucky to perform certain tasks for certain periods of time. Not only was his surgery unheard of in relation to inmates getting the procedure, the contract with the university medical center was cancelled. The institution will only do this type of brain surgery in cases of emergencies.

Today, I received some responses to the FOIA requests that I sent out. The Illinois Department of Corrections, St. Elizabeth Hospital, and Carbondale Police Department responded quickly. I'm starting to see that it's not only procedures and certain authorizations you must have that appear to be state-specific. I was shocked earlier when I went to mail call to get my paper and saw that they had the email terminals. They will be a new toy for a few months.

I cannot wait until they put terminals in the law library so that I can research charitable trust.

Big Poppa just changed his thoughts on the cover for the second book, however he told me to go ahead and design it myself. The Pop was getting really nervous about these books. He is publishing and he is moving too fast.

September 1, 2010 - Day 10

The law library was closed on Monday for the second day. We rescheduled to come to the new law library presentation by the Regional Director of Education and the Federal Bureau of Prisons. I forgot her name. She was very nice and efficient.

The Lexis Nexus system is very nice for finding the material and research in relation to federal law and access to the courts. Learning how to use the new system took about two hours.

My aunt Portia sent me a birthday card to tell me that she has returned from Trinidad. She travels the world every year. I can't wait until I get released so that we can sit down and have a real discussion about anything and everything.

College football starts tomorrow with seven games. At least that is what my friend Wolf told me. Wolf is a Miami Dolphins fan and we were together for years at the Accounts Receivable department. Wolf is an older white guy.

It is a real waiting game when it comes to the new crack cocaine laws. Everybody is waiting to see if the United States Sentencing Commission will make the mandatory changes for the sentencing guidelines retroactive.

I need to find someone with a subscription to the United States News and World Report, the foreign affairs publication. The essays that are written by administration officials are quite informative, especially if you are not a student of history.

There are about 200 people in this unit using the microwave, which is absolutely stupid. One of these days, there's going to be a huge riot in regards to supplying the necessary amount of microwaves for these units. Every day the institution takes another step forward in their efforts to strip inmates of their humanity. All of the staff don't drink the water at the institution, they bring in bottled water. You can tell by the way they look at you and their posture around you that they look down at and judge you.

September 2, 2010 - Day 11

Today I received a response from St. Elizabeth Hospital in relation to my request for records. They sent their own authorization form for me to fill out and return. Most likely I will go to the library and type in the blanks with the necessary information.

The weather has warmed up to 95° and I am starting to sweat while waiting to eat. My room is positioned in a way that the sun cannot beam into my room. I looked on the other side of the fence in the recreation yard and saw all types of construction equipment being used. Initially, I thought they were building under the institution, but I came to find out that they are building a firehouse.

The news is very depressing for the inmates because it is always showing and commenting negatively about unemployment. And black is a hell of a hurdle to climb over when it comes to being motivated to find a job. Getting up every morning to do something to prepare yourself is challenging. The Obama administration cannot make businesses hire unemployed workers just because they are unemployed and it's good for the economy.

I am really starting to believe that credit unions are the safest place to do business. I have not read much about credit unions failing.

My friend AC was in the pill line today. AC is black and he has been sentenced to 30 years. I am concerned that none of the new drug laws will help him get a sentence reduction. AC is in a wheelchair and has been in his chair for 10 years or more. He's an older guy, maybe 50 or so, with a lion's heart. He studies the Bible every day and the courts failed to give him a second chance. I believe that God will give him a second chance because he's given me several second chances throughout my life. I do not know what religion he believes in. I humbly believe in God, and that I'm supposed to be a servant first and everything else will take care of itself.

About seven years ago, I decided to have my bio put on the internet through a company called Pampered Prisoner. I wanted to get on writeaprisoner.com but I didn't have enough money. I have also heard of Beyond the Wall. I have always wanted to find a woman who was doing a lot of time and these opinions are all I have until I'm released. I can't find as many penpals as I need. I got some responses from women, mostly in Asia and the United States. Sadly, I am too busy reading, writing, typing, and studying all day and night. Sometimes I have got to force myself to break but while I am on the break, all I want to do is study.

I cannot wait until I'm enrolled in college, most likely it will be community college. I am not an intelligent man because I did not have any formal education. I know some people who have formal education but they're still as dumb as a box of rocks. If I spend the money for an education, I'm not returning the books... I want to keep them and study until the day I die.

Sometimes I feel as though I should not be writing in this diary with the knowledge that I might publish it because I really do not have anything profound to say. Is that because I'm nervous about publishing? I wonder if I would have more important things to say if I thought I wouldn't be publishing.

Earlier tonight I went to the shower in c-alley because the shower in my unit was occupied. The shower in c-alley looks like an alley in New York's worst neighborhood. This place and others like it can have the effect of placing undue burden on yourself. Expect the worst and hope for the best, right?

There is this blonde at the pharmacy window in the main hall of the institution and she's a real Kentucky fan. She has pretty eyes, long blonde hair, and is an older female pharmacist that happens to be a UK fan. This is one blonde I know for a fact is not stupid, even though this is the impression that is put on them in this country. I always make sure I talk to her when I come to the pill window. She is very nice and tries hard for everyone.

My cellmate, Mr. Jefferson, seems to think he can get me into the Harvard undergraduate program. I think he's crazy but you cannot judge a book by its cover.

There is a lot of food that is donated to this institution from the community around the prison. When trucks turn over on the highways with food like chicken, fish, etc., what can't be sold is delivered right here for us to eat. Sometimes we get really good food, like on holidays. We usually have beef or chicken.

The new assistant food administrator has finally shown up because the old administrator was transferred to another institution to stay close to her family. She was an African-American and really nice once she got to know you. A lot of the staff here is interrelated one way or another. However, it appears the staff is turning over just as much as the inmates. I guess this would be obvious for inmates as this is a medical center. The staff turnover rate doesn't make sense, though.

We had a town hall meeting a few minutes ago and apparently Ms. Hall, one of our unit counselors, stated that if you are caught with a cell phone you have one year added to your sentence. In addition, the individual that gave you the phone will also get one year. Both parties receive a huge fine. I missed the town hall meeting because I was taking a nap. My next-door neighbor came and woke me up to tell me about this meeting. Moreover, she was wasting her time. So I went and got on the cell phone.

September 3, 2010 - Day 12

While I was typing my diary entries for the day, I had an idea. My new series of books is going to be called *A Diary About Finishing Strong*. The plan is to do one complete volume annually until I'm 65 years of age, a major project of writing 25 volumes total. I think that this is the most effective way to turn myself into an experiment. With the type of background I have, this is an extraordinary undertaking. I realized I don't have to write about my past in the memoir because the state and federal authorities have documented, very well, all of my life as a youngster. However, I still may want to publish the memoir anyway. I am going to let society look at those public records and form their own opinions. My main concern is finishing strong, serving God, and telling the world that I do care. That we convicts do care about living a productive life but sometimes it's hard to do with The Man's foot on your neck. The fundamentals of my project will not change in regards to the format of a diary. I am sure there will be people who would do something different in relation to this project, but they need to understand that I do this for me.

I was in the law library when I overheard someone say that it is your right to request a trial by jury in a 28 USC 2255 proceeding. He also said that the court of Kentucky has put the request on the docket sheet. I am definitely going to follow this development. These guys were in the law library on the new system looking for leads.

Pop Jenkins just returned from the hospital at the University of Kentucky. I went to go and ask him what the problem was but he was sleeping. I think Pops is 68 years of age. His version of why he is here rests on what was said about some youngsters that God Himself caught giving money to purchase drugs.

Mr. Kom just came over to my door to tell me that

we've got a thief in the unit as a couple of the guys' radios and headphones came up missing. This kind of nonsense happens every year; you get someone who has a cigarette or drug habit and this is what they resort to in order to support their addiction. There are alcohol, cocaine, heroin, morphine, and pills in every federal correctional facility. And 90% of the time it's the staff that is bringing it in. The Federal Bureau of Investigations has a liaison at every federal facility called the Special Investigative Supervisor. They have the power to not only report you to the District Attorney but also the Assistant US Attorney for crimes that inmates and staff members committed. Normally, you would think that the staff in all of the facilities make life miserable for inmates - they do - but through talking to many staff members over 15 years, it is each other that they go after with a vengeance.

I keep making some bad decisions because I am letting my desire for money be the guiding factor in relation to making smarter decisions. I've got to get my head wrapped around this because it is great wisdom when it comes to being idiot proof around con men.

One of my associates stole some loaves of bread from the kitchen and sold me two loaves for 16 stamps for commissary. The medium of exchange is stamps, commissary, drugs, etc.

Male prostitution is a thriving business in prison. If your core values distinguish you from this then you really should not have a problem. I do not really understand why, but I have never been approached in a situation where I had to explain myself to the office. I'm just lucky because these things were in the cards for me.
Earlier in my life, the courts had shown me I was supposed to go drag racing in a 1978 Grand Prix in mint condition and crash the car with the firm intention of killing myself.

My other buddy, Johnson-Bey, a member of the Moorish Science Temple, is about to get off of work in a few minutes. I usually take the New York Times to him on Wednesdays, Fridays, and Sundays. He then passes it around to some of the other brothers so they can review a bit instead of watching the TV and videos all day.

Some of the women will wear tight fitting clothes because, maybe they are not getting the attention they crave at home. I honestly believe this place is really a mental hospital labeled as a correctional facility. Everybody here is crazy: the staff, the inmates, the birds, and we cannot forget the spiders. They paid me a visit in the news tonight. The white guys like to catch the Brown Recluses and feed them other insects to eat. I know that society cannot wait until these upstanding citizens are released to the community.

September 4, 2010 - Day 13

I was at dinner eating some really bad pesto with one of my friends from Seattle. I asked him how he was coming along with his urban novel. He said it was *this close* to being complete, it just needed a few minor changes. He asked me about my memoir and I told him that I have stopped working on it but started a diary that I wanted to publish. So he asked me what I was going to do with the memoir and I told him I really don't have a clue. He said, "Well, why don't you make it part of the diary?"

I got to watch live rounds of football and I almost had a relapse. I was about to start gambling again. I try to justify it to myself by saying I'm going to try a mathematical system of picking the top five teams. The plan was to do this for the entire season. However, now that the game is over, I see I would've lost my money, as usual, and start examining again. This is the next vice I have to get rid of.

The guards are walking around giving breathalyzer tests to different guys. They know they are not going to catch anyone drinking. As soon as they came into the unit with the gray box and a folder, the word was all over three floors within seconds.

I walked by one correctional officer last week and he smelled like he was still smoking marijuana. His eyes were really red and he was apparently hiding from the Lieutenant. This guy is still within his first year of employment which is a probationary period. I have seen a lot of people come in as a new hire, and you can tell that they are really struggling. I do have disdain for correctional officers but I realize that they really need these types of jobs, especially the benefits. When I get out I want to find all those systems and have them clean themselves up.

I have had some of the most beautiful, smart, outgoing, loving, caring, sisters I have ever seen in my life. My moral compass was clearly blurring with these women and I wish I could talk to every single one of them to apologize and ask for forgiveness for my behavior.

I have listened to a radio show on AM radio called Handel and Law. This is the funniest show I've ever heard. Mr. Handel is a no-nonsense lawyer. I have been listening to the show for years and I have learned a substantial amount of information in relation to small claims.

September 5, 2010 - Day 14

The violence in the state and federal prisons is on the verge of exploding. The gang problem in this country is getting worse and the Mexican drug cartels and Mexican gangs are gravitating to this country at an alarming rate. It is already in the urban areas and will continue to rear its ugly head in the suburbs. I believe they're going to start building more gated communities and schools.

The women here at the federal prison are required to wear a radio on them that has a little button that they push in case of an emergency. I have witnessed on several occasions staff members moving within the assigned areas without it.

What we have is experimentation by carelessness. The United States government is not proactive when it comes to averting crisis in its prison systems. As long as they like getting their feathers ruffled and their paycheck shows up on the first and 15th of every month, they don't care.

Why isn't every inmate given a mental examination at the time of - or shortly before - his release? Liability is the hidden weak link. The programs of psychology and psychiatry would be held accountable if they deemed an individual "normal" and he goes into the community and commits an abnormal violent crime. If a psychologist or psychiatrist allows himself to be used in a court of law as an expert on human behavior in relation to a crime, then he would have to admit that the patient's time spent institutionalized may have further damaged the person.

What about the staff? Do they need to be evaluated to work around institutionalized people? Are they being observed, evaluated, or tested for the preemption of abnormal behavior in relation to the position of authority they possess in an environment in which abuse, discrimination, and neglect are all accepted as the norm? When their main goal is to take a substantial amount of your good time and the job security is excellent, why would they want to see any inmate rehabilitation?

What about the men that are raped and don't alert the staff? Incidents have happened, and if a man is not a homosexual, sodomizing another man is abnormal behavior. Should this be diagnosed and treated?

None of the guys here are interested in going to college, trade school, or independent study. Their ignorance is similar to how I was for many of my younger years. Is it more painful to walk around blind or watch others walk around blind?

Around the years 2030 to 2050, institutional prisons will be a thing of the past. Home confinement will become the new era of detaining and monitoring felons and people who require federal and state controls.

Should ex-felons be allowed to be judges later in life? Are all abnormal versus normal people considered peers of one or the other? Should nonviolent offenders be allowed to pay a fine instead of receiving jail or prison sentences?

When I die, want to leave something behind that benefits humanity. I have to express, care, love, help the community, and protect children and senior citizens. But the main goal is to help the convicted felons regain their place with God and the community. Forgiveness and giving will be married after that happens.

The insight that I possess in relation to this type of life is quite unique and overbearing at the same time because it is hard to find a way to start. But it has to be done; I need to forge a way for change in regards to the rates at which men return to prison. I know the prison could be used as a laboratory. If you are able to see the elements that have been put in place for you, that time can be used wisely. I will finish strong and be an example.

September 6, 2010 - Day 15

I woke up this morning with a slight headache and I probably slept the wrong way. Some of the guys and I had a lunch talk about Mississippi. One of the guys at the table was Kelly. Now that he has done some time, I am sure he will have much better judgment than before. I have faced racism before, but not on the level as in the 40s and 50s.

I have not talked to my mother because I do not have any money to call or email right now. I finally wound down all of my classes except Mr. Jay's class. I hope I am able to get a good night's sleep tonight without a cramp in my neck tomorrow morning.

I hope to hear something from the United States Sentencing Commission. I just want to get out so I can take a long walk somewhere, eat some really good food, and find my future wife.

September 7, 2010 - Day 16

Many of the men that are imprisoned behind bars or concrete walls don't have a passion for writing their thoughts. I understand how they feel because this diary will be cascaded among some intellectuals as not really being substantive in nature. They are right. I do not have a formal education, but the education that I do possess cannot be learned from a book.

President Obama just announced his $350 billion economic plan and he is getting criticized for it. It's okay to to disagree with someone but why all the hate? For some people, politics has nothing to do with it.

September 8, 2010 - Day 17

I went to mail call and got my papers in a package from the Morgan County Sheriff's office. The sheriff sent me all of my records on the bookings from back in the day. They also said that all of my medical records had been destroyed.

Every day for the past 30 days or so I have not been put on the callout. I love that this commission on my job requires that I do absolutely nothing every day except Wednesdays. On Wednesdays, I have the go to the healthcare unit and get hygiene bags for indigent inmates.

A lot of the guys here do not have a lot of money being sent to them on a regular basis and that is really a bad feeling. When you are in a place like this and you don't get mail or have any family or friends showing support, it really hurts. Most of the guys here would not admit this, but they show you just how resentful they have become.

I've got a friend who is a serial bank robber and he's

the most pessimistic person I have ever met. He has total disregard for people's feelings. I am guilty of this misbehavior sometimes.

September 9, 2010 - Day 18

There is still a good amount of racism in prison, and this one type of barrier will remain forever, among others. Today I saw some guys that were my age giving each other handshakes and representing a gang that they belong to. The future of the black man in this country is bleak for lack of education. For all of these guys in here, it's so different to try to get help to get an education. And in the years that graduates cannot find a job, they are saddled with huge amounts of debt because society tells us that education is the key. Just like the economist Paul Krugman says, somebody has got to be the mechanic, social worker, painter, plumber, bricklayer, teacher, and so forth. It appears they want to keep you in the prison system with no education, no family ties, and a ripe environment for homosexuality. A lot of the black men in this country today would not have conducted themselves in this manner if they had played it straight and supported their jobs, businesses, and families.

I know my mother is tired of waiting for me to come home. And sometimes my eyelids feel like boulders and my mind like spaghetti, but my struggle is in line with developing character, integrity, levels of caring, and respect for my community.

I have lost all confidence in the stock market as a safe haven for investing in my retirement. Especially with my background, I've got to be more creative with finding ways to start my own enterprise along with change for myself and my family. I believe that you should invest your money in producing a product or a service. I am interested in being a lender, on some level. I am definitely going to be writing books and this may be an area in which I do a lot of my initial investing. I'm still working this angle as I type this diary. At my age of 40, I really don't want to go to work in the traditional sense. I am interested in being a micro-lender as well as an accredited lender.

September 10, 2010 - Day 19

It's 1:50 p.m. and normally I would wait until 9:30 or 10:00 p.m. to do my journal entries. I have just watched president Obama give a news conference on Fox TV and he seemed very confident in his ability as commander-in-chief and as a leader in foreign-policy.

It is quite extraordinary how the press continues to think that there are questions the president can be boxed-in on or incited to anger with. What have they been watching for the past four years? Reporters are trained to ask questions in which the president's answer could create headlines. All of the so-called Republican pundits, obviously, are willingly blind to the hatred and anger that their baseless assumptions vibrate to the media and airways. Some Republican strategists for the last two years have been trying to obstruct this administration's policies, and the losses are to the American people.

Why is it that there have been only a few black senators and congressmen? Why aren't there more African-Americans in the Republican Senate and the House of Representatives? Who benefits from illegal immigration? How does America stand to lose if a president doesn't embrace Islam in this country? Where did baby boomers' retirement savings go to? Why is it that liberals don't listen to talk radio to get more information?

September 11, 2010 - Day 20

It's 9:00 am and I am reading Friday's New York Times, and all I see are crooks and everybody crying about what 9/11 families should mean. The Wall Street bankers and financiers and brokers are getting away with stealing billions and billions of dollars from their clients and shareholders. There is absolutely no way I will put up any money at this point. If you invest in the United States treasuries or bonds, the more money that gets sent to the treasury, the more the interest that is paid to the holder. A lot of Americans do not understand that if you put too much money in the treasury, the interest room turns negative and you will be paying them to hold your money. This is not a good plan. The majority of Americans already give the government formal tax returns. You need to tell them that you want to match investing in a one-year CD certificate of deposit. When the year concludes, cash the CD and reinvest your money in lending. The money is working 24 hours a day and you have a more stable answer as opposed to the stock market. Moreover, your long contracts can be insured for any losses, especially non-repayment. Here, you don't have to be wary about the money men of Wall Street stealing from you under the bounds of the law. This is what real redistribution of wealth is all about.

Starting small is my reality for now, but I shall build an empire slowly but surely over the years.

My cellmate started a pity party last night so I had to remind him about the wisdom and philosophy of the east he attributes himself to. We had a short conversation about Taoism and ego, placing blame, attachment, aversion, gossip, contentment, anger, revenge, and temperament, just to name a few. What is the philosophy behind the way of knowing?

It's about 10:00 am and I have just finished watching Meet the Press and it was quite interesting. One of the guests, Mr. Reza, just published a book called *The One God*, and he basically believes that Americans are exhibiting the behavior of the bigot in regards to the 1 1/2 billion Muslims in the world. Americans are painted with a broad brush, and of course we have good and bad Americans. Moreover, some Americans treat each other worse than terrorists treat Americans. The only difference is we use phrases like, "it was a clean shooting," and, "the officer thought he was armed." Just because the media doesn't brand your actions as being terrorist in nature does not mean that you do not incite terror in the community.

The prison population would deftly explode when and if we have a Republican president and Republican Congress. The job security for the unemployable and the Iraq and Afghanistan war veterans will be met by an increased prison population and a building prison complex. The new media constantly displays military veterans having breakdowns, unemployment, and violent domestic behavior in military commanders.

One of the most fruitful and dangerous things in prison is ambition and what I sometimes refer to as caged ambition. Every day you wake up to think about your goals, dreams, and ideas. However, there is the lack of money, lack of resources, lack of support, and smaller hurdles on the street, which translate into major hurdles in prison.

Iran is contemplating whether or not they should release the three American hikers. David Axelrod has stated that the administration has been through repeated start and stop scenarios with the Iranian government. I believe that the pressure that needs to be applied should be in the form of tactical political assassination of the president of Iran. We should have permanent military bases in Iraq and

Afghanistan with a minimum of 150,000 soldiers. Maybe we should invade Iran and dispose of its leadership. The women and the children in these countries are the real victims of greed and corrupt politicians.

I made a really bad decision about two years ago when I closed my brokerage account at T. Rowe Price. Now, I do not have any money and this book is the only asset that I possess at this time in my life. This book probably will not become a New York Times bestseller, but I believe that if you can read and write, every man should write at least one book in his life. I have watched the commentators and the politicians and they have all published books on a one to two year basis. I plan on publishing one book a year until I am 65 years of age.

September 13, 2010 - Day 22

I was in the law library and a young man approached me about subject matter jurisdiction. When I went to the printer in the back room to print some labels, he wanted to ask me some questions. This guy was facing 20 years to life because of the section 851 enhancement. This enhancement is applied by notice to the defendant charged in the indictment.

The Prime Minister and the elected party are not interested in stopping the building in Palestine territories. If for some reason these people are able to come to an agreement, Abbas Glavine will have his hands full. There are elements of both governments that will do everything within their power to develop the Middle East peace talks. The Obama administration has chosen to address the issue. These governments can agree to whatever they want, but the people will have the final word. Turkey is flourishing with Democratic policies and they are on their way to joining the European Union.

September 14, 2010 - Day 23

I made a really stupid decision today to chase jobs and go back to the vocational education Department. I put myself back into the line of fire in relation to dealing with the braille coordinator. I can't wait for November 1st to get here.

For some reason I cannot get the email system to work for me. I don't know if I am forgetting to do something or not. Asking people for assistance really gets on my nerves. I will probably just continue to write letters until I get out of prison and send my home email address out.

Meditation is the key to alleviate my frustration right now. I swore to myself that I would never return to vocational education, and now here I am, back in the department. Mrs. Lombardi was the first one to ask me what in the world was I doing back working down in education. I explained to her that my supervisor told me that she was not happy paying guys for not doing any work. Mrs. Underwood told me that I should find another job. The job was okay because it did have its perks. I really needed to convince my new boss, Mr. Hammond, that I only wanted to work half days.

It seems North Korea and South Korea are making progress in not trying to start war with each other or destabilizing the region with nuclear weapons.

I got word from my aunt Portia telling me about the possibility of going to college under my father's G.I. Bill.

September 15, 2010 - Day 24

Today I spoke to my case manager about going to the halfway house. She basically told me to stop listening to all of the people on the compound, staff included, and commented about my transitioning to the community. I think Ms. Hoskins was really upset that I sent a letter to the

United States probation office about being a pre-release prisoner.

I sent mom two emails and should be hearing something from her or Christine probably tomorrow. I'm glad I haven't got a way to contact her very fast.

It would really be nice if I could get into Harvard, Yale, Princeton, Columbia, or any really good private college. I will probably be lucky to get back into college at all. I think it is going to be absolutely brutal trying to get employment, but I have been preparing myself for this for years.

My Aunt Portia seems to think that I will be just fine when and if I am given an immediate release. She wants me to let her know the second that I am released from prison. I feel that I have got to prepare more for pre-release classes. I'm ashamed that I have not saved enough money to get an apartment or home. I am 40 years of age and I do not want to live with anyone. I need my space and I need it to be quiet. Very quiet! I am probably going to have to live in an efficiency apartment or something like that. I really should not be worried about what is going to happen. I need to just let it happen and enjoy the ride; it is better than prison.

September 16, 2010 - Day 25

I sat back today and thought about being released from prison without any halfway house or a job lined up. I believe that I can survive in this new environment because of the way I have been trained in prison. 15 years have passed and knowledge and wisdom saturated my being. It'll surface on its own once I am put in a situation to bring it to fruition.

Today I exercised the power of being nice to a person who seems to find joy in treating people really bad. When I asked this staff member to print copies of documents I was working on for my supervisor, I actually made sure that I said please. So she said, "Next time, when you ask for copy, you shouldn't tell me what to do." I replied, "Anytime I have come to you for copies I have said please."

I have not gotten a response to any of my emails that I have sent to Mom, but I know she's probably sleeping. I wonder why Angel is getting sick all the time. Dale has not been in contact with me for a long time, at least in the past 12 years.

September 17, 2010 - Day 26

I received a letter from my probation supervisor in response to a letter I wrote them about having 12 months of halfway house or RRC placement. Mr. Gandy told me that I could always get a modification to my supervised release and that there may be some other assistance available to help me with my circumstances. My plan is to write him back and tell him how much I appreciate his response and his candor. Mrs. Hoskins, my case manager, was highly upset that I wrote the United States probation office about being released immediately without any assistance. I am sure I will be all right once I am released. I have done 18 months in a halfway house, but back then I was not as knowledgeable as I am now. I didn't have my head screwed on correctly. I had a really good job at a place called the Pasta House in Carbondale, IL.

I got tricked by a girl saying she was pregnant and needed money for an abortion. I wasn't supposed to give her the money because I was suppose to turn my paycheck over to the staff at the halfway house. This was a state halfway house. I have spent exactly half of my life – 20 years – in prison, drug rehabs, and the streets. Now I can't stop reading and learning. I have finally realized that continuity in age is using your mind constantly, especially in middle age. I can feel my days behind the wall are leading to a final chapter in my life.

September 18, 2010 - Day 27

I wrote the United States probation office a letter explaining my situation. They responded and I decided to share the information with some of the guys so that they could teach themselves to make better decisions. They don't want to listen and don't really appreciate any help. This one guy listened to me but he was kind of an idiot.... I told him the night before to bring me my letter from the probation office before he went. He didn't realize that this was his first mistake. He went upstairs and sat in his room and started copying in his letter what the PO wrote me. I really wanted to slap the shit out of him but instead I took my letters and left. I am tired of trying to help people that do not want to be helped. It is time for them to start suffering as I did in the past and as I still do sometimes.

Hunt International Incorporated or Hunt Enterprises Incorporated sound really good right about now. I'm still debating whether to start this company is a sole proprietorship (a one-person private corporation), charitable trust, nonprofit foundation, or international business corporation. I would have to hire an attorney to establish a business license, bank account, and registration with the small business administration and digital services administration as a small minority-owned business. I want the company to establish primary micro loans, and to be a purchaser of commercial paper, for example commercial loans, residential mortgages, and commercial leases and bonds.

My diary, which is published annually, will contribute as the start of this company and during its entire existence. It appears that my business model may be unorthodox but I created it and I want to see if I can make it successful. The average person wouldn't go with this plan and would be scrutinized by the public about the type of history that I have. I cannot change the past and I would never run for elected office. But I do believe I have the makings of a good businessman. There will be people who will tell me not to do this, that this is not a good business model. The average American is raised to be a consumer, not a creator, even though 90% of Americans are employed by small businesses. I will probably have to take the initiative to establish this business on my own. Learning as I go is the key. I do not want to hire anyone to do work for me; I need to have them teach me what it is. I cannot do or know what I am not aware of.

There is a lot about my life that would not be written about in this book because it puts lives in jeopardy. I have never been taught how to fight but I'm very good at survival. I believe that your life is what you make of it and you will have to make tough decisions and take real chances to succeed in your goals. You have got to have the patience and endurance to be something over the years. Success is measured at the end of 30 years of sweat equity in your company. I read about these women suing Walmart for fraud and discrimination and they had been making $10 an hour over 10 to 16 years.

A dollar bill is an employee just like the book *Rich Dad, Poor Dad* articulates so well. You cannot spend away employees because at the end of the day, you have got to go to work to support yourself if you plan on eating. I believe 50% of income should be kept to build your home business.

Hispanics are so successful once they come to America. They starve themselves to succeed to establish something. How can five people share a bowl of rice and be happy knowing that is the day's only dinner? It is because they are trying to build something. Why can't black men get it together? Simply put, we lack integrity. We need to be re-educated that your word is your bond. This concept should be the most valuable core value in a man and in any person's life. This is why I did terrible in school! This is why I lied to my parents! This is why I committed crimes!

This is why I've been in prison for more than 20 years. This is why I'm not married with my own family! This is why I am uneducated! This is why I am poor! This is why at 40 years of age I am destitute! This is why: I have lacked integrity.

Today, my word is my bond and this core value means more to me than my life. I have known all my life what it feels like to be looked upon as nothing and this may continue but it'll never be said from this day forward that I broke my word.

I have read books about JP Morgan, in particular the House of Morgan. The writer never talked about particulars in relation to how the family went about building their family company. I am going to write about more particulars in regards to how my company is built and maintained.

I have got to go in the back of food service tomorrow at 7:15 am to see Ohio Red about some typewriter wheels and ribbons. You may not believe it but it costs money just to write and type this manuscript. But the capital to start this book, which is the foundation to my company, is very little compared to the potential long-term profit.

September 20, 2010 - Day 28

I forgot to put Mom's email in the book, but she sent me Angel and Christina's email. I thought Christina was still a baby. I have been incarcerated so damn long I am starting to miss gaps in time. People are growing up out there even though the bankers on Wall Street just stole a big chunk of their pensions.

I am going to have to travel a lot to promote this book internationally. There is the remote possibility that I might have to actually publish this book in concert with a printer. The return sales and paperwork will probably be voluminous. That is okay, I will be in my apartment building collecting rent receipts and building my company.

I am really not interested in the stock market, but I am interested in building a strong financial company that eventually becomes a trusted lender worldwide.

September 21, 2010 - Day 29

The supervisor of visitation, Mr. Hammond, gave me a template to catalog all of the reentry classes that the institution offers. The catalog I built for him was flawed in its original creation. The new template that I created is more user-friendly and he can enter and delete information easily without compromising the template.

For some reason I cannot get the custom margin to be activated for me in this Excel application. I have tried all types of things and they are not really cooperating. It will probably take a little while, but some things will come back to me about the margins that I have forgotten and all will be well. I have been thinking about whether I should go to community college or try to get through the entrance application process of the major universities. I really would like to talk to some of those people at the colleges so that I can get a better understanding of my options in relation to attending school as a resident student.

My yearly subscription to the newspaper is almost expired and I really do not want to ask my aunt to renew the subscription when I could be going home soon.

September 22, 2010 - Day 30

I just stopped reading my paper to watch Bill Trading from the Dominican Republic teach a black state judge from Mississippi the Tango and Salsa. There is a class here in the recreation department that is geared to entry-level and advanced Salsa dance classes. I know what you're thinking: how can men dance together in prison? They are not dancing together in the sense of a couple. They are dancing standing alone. I really did not understand the concept until I went to the class to observe and found it quite interesting, especially the music. When I get released, I'm going to go to dance school and learn the Salsa and the Tango. I'm not a very good dancer as it is, but I am willing to learn as much as I can and I believe I will really enjoy the process.

I slept a few hours after lunch so I will probably stay awake for a while until I am able to fall asleep. It's count time, 10:00 p.m., and the guards are surely on their way to count. I got another email from Moma today and she sounded very busy helping my sister take care of her family. I wonder where Corey is? Is he in school? Is he in the ROTC program or what? I'll be glad when Angel and Portia answer their email.

We are all still counting down the days to November 1, 2010. I talked to my case manager today about the letter I received from the probation office. Mrs. Hoskins is a challenge to say the least.

September 23, 2010 - Day 31

I got a little rest today when I came back to the unit from lunch. Some of the staff wanted me to come back to education to work on some of their projects.

For some reason I really don't like it when someone doesn't return what I give to them in the same condition I gave it to them.

There were no email messages for me in the last few days. I can't stop thinking about the possibility of the law being changed in my favor in less than 40 days. Everybody is on pins and needles. Even the case managers are wanting to know what is going to happen in a few weeks.

I am still undecided whether or not I should still go to college. My residence is still up in the air until I find out what will happen in November. President Obama said that the Republicans will be really upset come November 2. I do not know if he was implying the Fair Sentencing Act of 2010 or the elections being held on November 3, 2010. Obama is about to change some of the people in key positions in his cabinet. I think Rahm Emmanuel should stay his chief of staff. I really did not dig Larry Summers too much and Christina Roma gave her best according to reports in the newspapers.

I am still overweight and I need to start running. My belly is starting to bulge really bad and I am at 230 pounds and rising. I will have to get off my fat ass and run sooner or later. My face is a little puffy and that happens when I start to gain a lot of weight.

Chapter Two: Jessie M. Hunt

My mother worked her whole life to provide for me and my two siblings and she was not rewarded with the American dream. My mother spent her retirement writing me in prison and grasping to hold a family together. Every time that I was released from prison, she was there with her love and support.

She really enjoys visiting our extended family in Mississippi and traveling with her brothers and sister when she can. She is an avid reader of books of all types and regularly gives away boxes of books to charitable organizations helping children and the elderly.

The other day she asked me if I was courting anyone, so that statement pretty much lets you know what era she has come from (she is 70). She is in great shape and exercises daily, walking up and down flights of stairs at home. Also, she walks several blocks to pick up her grandson, Alex, from school during the week. Her mother, Willie Mae Washington, and father, Leroy Washington, represented the backbone of the family and we all miss them to this day.

September 24, 2010 - Day 32

I sat and talked to a gentleman who convinced me to change courses with this diary. He told me that he was tired of African-Americans writing about their problems and crying. I felt we shouldn't write about prison and how tough it may have been. He is a lover of history and he reads a lot of history books. Obviously, he has read about individuals having greater suffering than us and does not want the comparison to be exposed, I guess. I contemplated his position and concluded that my diary might fit the crying scenario he described. So, for the next two days, I did not write entries into my diary and I started back with my entries on the 27th because I came up with a new idea about my old plan in regards to the diary. This is when I noticed that what he had to say really did not matter to me. I know this is not a best-seller and it is not highly or remotely intellectual to academics. This diary is a part of an ongoing experiment of myself and prisoners in this country. My project has been reinstated effective immediately.

There are times when you can have a constructive conversation with an inmate and allow yourself to be influenced in such a way to accept defeat or alteration of your project or agenda and not hold true to your own plan because of the fear of looking really stupid or having a frivolous idea. I have decided that, no matter what, I am going to finish my project that I have planned and it will take the rest of my life to complete this work that I have designed to do multiple things and meet multiple goals. This will not be the first time that what I believe and want to do will be challenged.

September 27, 2010 - Day 33

I got to page 60 in this book about Hitler and Stalin. These guys were – in my view – renegades, political scientists, and great actors. They apparently disposed of millions of people through murder, suicide, mental illness, and attrition, among other things. Hitler was asked why he didn't play sports in prison and he replied that a leader doesn't allow himself to be seen beaten at games. I believe and know this to be very true. I've got about 600 more pages to go and a lot of studying on these two guys in the future.

Mr. Moon asked me which of the two are the smartest. I told him I could not answer his question until I finish reading the book. I am inclined to say that Stalin was the smartest. Hitler appeared to have lost his bearings along the way and operated with a mental defect. His inner circle was not able to detect his illness, whether it was physical or mental. None of his inner circle knew his behavior. They also didn't know that he contemplated suicide for many years. Hitler may have been remorseful for the actions often under his control. Was he able to forgive; did he ever express forgiveness?

This is the first book, *The Dictators*, by Richard Devey in 2004 in regards to Hitler and Stalin. I am sure that I will encounter several books and questions in relation to the significance of their era and the state of mind of their followers. It looks as if something was put in the water supply and everyone drank it and it had a structural effect on everyone's DNA. Crazy? Maybe not?

After reading the business section of the New York Times, it appears that the Chinese want to engage in a trade war. I believe that China has more to lose than America if trading were stopped between the two countries.

September 28, 2010 - Day 34

I got some of my medical records yesterday and a lot of the reasons I was there I vaguely remember. I remember the dog biting me. I remember taking a lot of pills when I was about 12 or 13 and being taken to the hospital.

I remember a time when it was raining really hard and Terry, Herb, and I had to get home from the YMCA. I took off first and crashed into an oncoming truck. The truck was on top of me and my bike and I had to stay there until the paramedics arrived. I went to the hospital and they informed me I had broken my left ankle. Herb's parents came to the hospital to make sure I was okay. The Connors where very decent people and the best friends I have ever had.

They are getting ready to court martial some of the soldiers who served in the war in Afghanistan. All of the foot soldiers are very young and they did not really sign up for the extra tours of duty.

Some inmates posted some new rules the case managers have to abide by and by the end they did not like it very much. They have town hall meetings for everything else, and here are these changes. Why? Job security? Vindictiveness? Arrogance? Contempt?

Mr. Jefferson is starting to feel the pressure and anxiety of fighting the prosecution and dealing with family issues at the same time. From what I have experienced and observed, this state of mind changes your body composition. You start to move slower, your shoulders appear to hunch forward when you walk, and sleepiness overcomes you. You can hear the disappointment in his voice and see the urge to want to get out of prison. I grabbed my newspaper turned off the light and left to watch television.

It appears president Obama is in full campaign mode in regards to visiting all of the colleges. I have read in the papers that he is trying to encourage all of the young people to get out and vote. The president has not been able to keep all of his campaign promises but I believe he has put forth one hell of an effort.

I have been thinking about college a lot lately and I

have concluded that when I receive my doctorate in sociology, I am sure the federal prisons will want me to return and speak to the guys as a success story, maybe even some drug treatment centers.

My subscription to the New York Times is about to run out in the middle of October and I've gotten accustomed to reading it every day. I have found that reading the newspaper while doing time is a good way to occupy yourself. I remember reading a book entitled *Long Walk to Freedom* by Nelson Mandela and one thing that they long for was not food, women, or recreation, but newspapers. The prison system in this country is really bad depending on where you are and how long you have been there.

President Karzai and his brother are going to find themselves in the crosshairs of a sniper rifle. It appears that these guys are very corrupt, not that the United States is that innocent of these types of activities.

September 30, 2010 - Day 35

There is so much corruption in the state and federal governments. I mean at all levels of government. I believe that more jobs will be lost in the future and a lot of millionaires will move to other countries for safe harbor. Places like Singapore and Hong Kong or Taiwan, with no extradition treaty. The Obama administration is trying to pass a new tax law that gives corporations a tax break for returning the companies to the United States. It appears that the CIA and the Pakistan government have extensive ties to each other. More and more, day after day, it appears that the Taliban is coming around to reconciliation.

International currency is a phrase that we will hear more about in the future. China does not want to bow to Western pressure but the United States has trade deficits with more than 90 countries. I wonder how long the US currency will be the world reserve currency? But right now it appears that it is the default international currency. This is why corrupt governments, renegade government militaries, sovereign wealth funds, drug lords, politicians, and others counterfeit United States dollars in massive quantities.

Some visitors from Lexington came to visit the institution and they walked by the braille room while I was reading the New York Times. Mrs. Lombardi, the guidance counsellor, was walking them around when she spotted me. She came in with the visitors and asked me to tell them about the braille program.

October 1, 2010 - Day 36

We arrived at work around 7:50 am and the entire hallway was flooded with water. However, the water came from the showers, washers, and dryers from the unit near the education department. This is one day that these federal workers really wished they were not at work and some of them finally realized where they were.

This black lady that works in the Accounts Receivable department is very healthy and has curves in all the right places. Today she was wearing a pair of jeans that looked as if they had been painted on her. It appears she had just arrived back at the institution from her lunch and she had about 15 or 20 inmates following her. Obviously she knew this was going on and that is why she did not wear a jacket around her waist. But the funniest thing that I have ever seen in 20 years of doing time was how the guys following her literally bumped into Warden Hickey.

Sometimes I find myself in these situations because my natural instincts kick in. Since I have not had sex in a while, I'm very interested in women at this point. However, I believe that you can still remain respectful and speak without being rude. Masturbating gets really old after the first few years.

It appears that president Obama will still be hounded

that this was the biggest government intervention in American history. But what a lot of people don't realize is that everything he does is history. The history books will be rewritten based on him and his administration.

The guy down the hall just lost his one-man room because the unit manager saw a couple of pieces of paper on the floor during the inspection. I am next in line for the one-man room. Finally, after 15 years!

I have been writing these diary entries since August and longhand doesn't hurt that much anymore. If you don't use it you will lose it, right? I have got to stop drinking coffee so late, if not I'm going to be up all night in the dark, half-asleep, looking for the bathroom to urinate.

October 2, 2010 - Day 37

It is 6:02 am and I woke up earlier because the guard came to tell my roommate, Mr. Jefferson, that he had to report to the kitchen for count and duty work. Mr. Jefferson has had his job changed three times within the last three days to the same detail: recreation. I told him this morning that these people are having a good laugh at his expense. I told him to ask for the operations lieutenant and the duty officer and put this situation on the record. He might finally listen to me. Even if there are things he said about the CIA contact and his life that are true, he still needs to realize where he is. As far as the staff here is concerned, you're a piece of shit, a parasite of the community. Being African-American makes it even worse.

I just saw a centipede about 2 inches long down the hall. This institution is infested with black widows, since it was built in the 1930s. Wolf spiders, ants, and cockroaches that are as big as your thumb. The brown recluse spiders are here also. And these insects you do not want to run into. These bad boys will hurt you really bad and the medical staff does not understand emergencies.

My buddy, TJ, was adamant about court. He said another guy fell to the ground and was having a heart attack the staff took their sweet time to walk to his location but he died before arriving at the University of Kentucky medical center. Something like this happens every year.

It's 7:00 am and it has finally come to me what I want to see in regards to the publication of my diaries. I'm going to establish a 529 education account with my websites to accept donations pursuant to a doctorate degree in sociology and maybe a juris doctorate. I want to stay in school throughout the years without a vacation. This would be a good way for me to get help with my education expenses: through donations and book purchases. I think I will call the website the Hunt Education Initiative.

October 3, 2010 - Day 37

It is 1:49 p.m. and the Pittsburgh Steelers are playing the Baltimore Ravens and the score is 7-7. I'm a little disappointed that the game is not on television, but it really depends on what region of the country you are in.

One of the guys named Gemini has rediscovered this hardback book and I cannot help but wonder what it was all about. I asked to review the book and he handed it to me. The name of the book is *The Stuff of Thought* by Stephen Pinker. ISBN 978-0-670-06-327-7. I need to put this information in the diaries so that I can remember to get it for reading and my library.

I was listening to the Dave Ramsey Show on 590 AM and Dave usually talks about finance. I have been very lucky to have had the opportunity to watch a lot of Dave's videos and read a lot of his books. Dave has been a real inspiration in my life and he is the real motivation behind this book in relation to paying cash to go back to college. When I graduate from college I will be debt-free because of studying Dave's principles on debt-free living.

The unit was fourth to be called to lunch. They served pork sausage, scrambled eggs, oatmeal, and pancakes with a carton of milk. I guess if you are in prison in China or Russia this would be considered a five-star meal. I think we are having chicken fried steak for dinner but I will probably have a mackerel with some saltine crackers.

My barber will be waiting for me when they release our unit for dinner. It appears I am starting to get a little gray hair.

October 4, 2010 - Day 38

I looked at the examinations for college mathematics and decided not to try and rush my education. I want to take my time and enjoy the college courses. I have been imprisoned a long time and there aren't many things in my view left to enjoy. My life has changed from my younger years of recklessness. Now, I love reading, writing, and studying.

I lot of the staff is starting to rotate out of the facility to other prisons or other jobs. Staff members are finally going into retirement, which is a good thing. Some of the staff that have been here for 10 and 20 years need to move on with their lives.

I believe that the suicide rate will increase and that it's inevitable in this occupation. I read an article today that talked about how men have to reconstruct their lives and become more employable. To be able to do that, they have to realize that education is the key to change in regards to the future. Just because you have worked construction all your life doesn't mean education is out the door. It is an advantage to realize that there is nothing wrong with going back to college.

October 5, 2010 - Day 39

From my point of view, a lot of individuals often attempt to measure themselves against some belief, whether it is quantity or quality. The fear of being uneducated or perceived as such fosters the traditional late-in-life self education using comprehensive textbooks that are available. It should be a prerequisite to maintain a diary every year through high school and that they be your written essay for the ACT or SAT.

It is 9:35 p.m. and I talked to one of the GED tutors in the unit about study and some of the prep books for science, social studies, math, language arts, reading, and writing. He told me not to be worried about the ACT tests because it is just a requirement that is part of the process of admissions. How good you are only matters if you're trying to get into a really good, prestigious college. For some reason I just can't get motivated here to study a little bit more. I want to go to the classroom and not only learn the subject matter, but learn how to teach. The tutor told me that he'll help me as much as I need and I'll probably take him up on his offer while we are at work. We both work education, Mr. Kelly and myself.

October 6, 2010 - Day 40

It's about 1:00 p.m.. I stopped by the community unit to report for staff search. They want to make sure that you have the correct amount of sheets, blankets, pillows, pants, and shirts required to be assigned to you. Some of the guys kill themselves to hide all of their excess sheets, clothes, and contraband. The unit secretary was the one that searched my two-man room. I did not believe that she even knew what some of the stuff she was looking for looked like. The majority of these people are pencil pushers. I cannot wait to get to the university to study and learn what they have been taught.

I am starting to study some of the ACT and SAT tests. If the laws are made retroactive in November, I will have studied really hard for the SAT. I have started skipping the movie as of today, but as time goes on I will start to study more and more. I will probably start to cut back on watching football on the weekends. I cannot wait until I get out.

I am eating ice cream and I know that it's really stupid, but I don't think about how stupid it is until I eat the damn thing. I will do something about it one of these days.

I thought I had lost all of the copies of my certificates and that had me really upset. I even called the court clerk that I sent copies of my certificates to. I found out today that she did not make copies for the judges; that is okay because I still have people helping me out.

October 7, 2010 - Day 41

It's 9:00 p.m. and I just finished taking one of the tests in the SAT study guide and I only answered 50% of the 25 questions correctly. I'm starting to think it is better for me to start slow and at the bottom, the community college. That way there's no question that my education is now appreciated a lot more. I want to be able to take a sentence and identify the parts of grammar for it. I should be able to deconstruct and reconstruct the sentence based on the rules of American English. Or whatever the national standard is currently.

Some of the people in third world countries must really go through some suffering that we are just unable to comprehend. I read about the Congo, the chemical spills and hunger. The Haitians living in trailers and fields owned by church organizations, trying to survive. Tent cities in other places. It seems that there is so much fraud in some of these countries that insurgents are causing the governments to fail. As soon as the money shows up everybody starts plotting for themselves.

October 8, 2010 - Day 42

At 12:30 p.m. I got called to the mail room for legal mail. It was my ex-trial attorney, Mr. Philip Cavanaugh, who is now the federal public defender for the Southern District of Illinois. He was responding to a letter I sent to the probation office in regards to establishing a pre-release plan in accordance with the second chance act of 2008.

One of the guys was telling me how he wanted to finish his apprenticeship as an electrician and then join a union to save money for his release. I cannot remember his name, but he was very, very receptive to my idea that he should publish his own book. We sat back and watched CNN and he made comments on the radio show interview. I personally do not like the show on CNN, but they are trying to come up with the format to bring in more viewers.

The news television stayed on news programs and there was always some breaking news. The foreign correspondents were particularly special because their take on the boots on the ground was really informative. Sometimes I get to watch 60 minutes of the Discovery Channel or the Learning Channel. I am sick of everything else on cable because I've seen it all a thousand times. Ever since I started reading the New York Times and foreign affairs every day, my taste for television has diminished.

More and more articles are appearing detailing scholars who have forged their credentials and committed outright plagiarism. This goes back to the notion that people in academia should make their education records and transcripts public. That is exactly what I am going to do with my diaries: I'm going to publish my associate, bachelor, masters, and doctorate degree grades along with my juris doctorate grades.

I told my boss that he did not have to pay me, but this month he paid me $40. I was really surprised because I had been working every day, all day. I think she realizes that I really don't want to be down in vocational education all day.

My Siddha Yoga lessons arrived today. I remember when these lessons arrive because it is a reminder of what really matters. It's really easy to get caught up in my issues... or someone else's, for that matter.

I cannot wait to witness what President Obama will bring to the world in the next two years. He has got Michelle campaigning for him and this should be very interesting. Michelle has a very short fuse and she's not inclined to bite her tongue for anyone. She is raw and sometimes maybe too honest. How in the world can you be too honest?

October 19, 2010 - Day 43

At about 11:00 am I went and got a football ticket to gamble on the college football games because Tim told me that Chi-town was taking food as currency and you would get paid in food so I took the bait.

I've finished my Nemeth Braille course, which took me about 18 months to complete. I took the exam twice and failed because I was not prepared. I needed to take the Braille Formats course for certification to be able to navigate the Nemeth exam successfully.

My cellmate's attorney is screwing him around with his appeal, but what he doesn't understand is that this is the normal course of business. Once you get behind these bars, you are no longer a priority. If you somehow keep sending the attorney money, then you may get your phone calls accepted, *maybe*. A little advice about attorneys: don't ever pay an attorney a lump sum of money. Always pay by the hour, always get an itemized bill. And always remember that their hourly rate is negotiable. Every time I see someone's paperwork in relation to their case I start having flashbacks about all the lawyers and judges I have dealt with over the last 20 years. The justice system in this country isn't fair sometimes, but its better than China, Congo, North Korea, Abu Dhabi, Afganistan, Siberia, Columbia, and many more around the world. I may have a little resentment in my tone but it is well-earned.

It's 9:13 p.m. and I just finished watching Karate Kid with Jadan Smith and it was really good. I love Kung Fu and I always wanted to study martial arts when I was a child. I wanted to run away to Japan but I didn't have any money and I didn't know how to get there. I like watching Jet Li, Jackie Chan, Chow Yun Fat, and all the masters.

October 10, 2010 - Day 44

We just watched two really good movies, "Courage Under Fire," and, "Proof of Life." However, I don't think that we are going to be able to finish Proof of Life because it is count time and we have to wait until after this count.

I was in the law library the other day and I noticed that there were a lot of Danielle Steele's romance novels in the library. I have never in my life read a romance novel until I was in segregation for a year in a federal correctional institution in Sandstone, Minnesota. I got into it with the staff.

October 11, 2010 - Day 45

My cellmate told me that he had to take a guy over to the lieutenant's office because of the way his eye was swollen shut. I told Mr. Jefferson that the institution is not interested in his medical opinion, especially on the weekends. When I worked on the cancer floor at the Federal Medical Center in Springfield, MO, I witnessed an older gentleman refusing treatment for cancer. He had stomach and prostate cancer, if I remember correctly. This guy was in such pain that he often screamed so loud you could hear him through the walls. These walls were built back in the 1930s. There were so many inmate deaths on this floor that correctional officers refused to even come to the floor.

I don't know what I'm going to die of. It really doesn't matter, but I refuse to be a pain. Just because my life is ending I absolutely refuse the notion of being a burden on anyone, especially my family, and it is paramount for me to be secure in my finances to be able to pay someone to help me in my last days and help make me comfortable. However, I might get lucky and go very quickly.

October 12, 2010 - Day 46

This afternoon I talked to my buddy about private versus public colleges. I did not understand that private colleges are not accredited by the entities established by the United States Department of Education. This is one thing that causes problems when you transfer or try to get a masters degree in a public institution with a private college undergraduate degree.

I thought about writing an essay on federal prisons and have started working on an outline. There is a starting point, but I'm going to take my time and work on this project.

I found out yesterday through a newsletter from this law firm that solicits criminal casework from incarcerated individuals that the crack law is not scheduled to become retroactive this year due to a procedural rule established by the sentencing commission. This means I will probably remain in prison for another year at a minimum.

I have got to get my subscription renewed and start a new subscription for foreign affairs. My subscription for the New York Times has expired and I'm having withdrawals as I write this entry. I am reading Danielle Steele's *Mirror Image,* which is a romance novel.

I am overweight at this time but I have had a better diet in prison than I would have had on the street for the last 15 years. But my health will improve once I'm released.

October 13, 2010 - Day 47

At 5:30 p.m. I went to mail call and there were four New York Times newspapers waiting for me. I have encountered strange turns with reading this newspaper for years and how it changes your perception of other reading material. Any subsequent material is rated during this course, it is not up to a reasonable intellectual standard and your mind rejects the material.

I have started reviewing more college material about admissions and I see that the state college is a much better choice for my interest in sociology. The doctorate in sociology is really appealing to me, but I have got to be patient because this is quite an undertaking. In addition, I have discovered that I am not proficient in math; I have not been taught the arithmetic required to pass college math. I received my GED in 1993 and I passed by one point. I guess smoking a joint before the exam did not really help me, either. That was the first GED test I took before going to prison the first time, I think.

My supervised release officer may be a hindrance to me being a resident student at the state college because I am an ex-felon.

October 14-15, 2010 - Days 48 and 49

I took an ambien today to help me sleep. The food I've been eating has been making it hard for me to get any sleep.

It is 9:00 p.m. sharp and Wisconsin is beating Ohio State 21-3. Everybody was going with Wisconsin to win hands down.

I got some really good sleep last night and I probably will tonight. My cellmate told me that his appeal bond was denied. I explained to him a while back that the court of appeals believes that if you had a trial, then you've been given your constitutional rights.

The double major seems interesting to me but it may require a lot of studying and writing. I don't have a problem with it but I do not want to overload my plate.

There have not been any real big fights in awhile. They only occur about once or twice a year at this institution. The government uses this place to hide people who are vulnerable to gangs or extortion. They usually are police officers, stock brokers, lawyers, judges (state, not federal), and politicians, among others.

While walking past the sports televisions on the second floor, I saw a book entitled *Hinduism*. It looked pretty old and I was curious about its content. I wonder who left this textbook just laying around? It must have come out of the leisure library. After I finish reading it I'll return it. I need to go get Mr. Moon's book, *How to Read a Book*.

October 17, 2010 - Day 52

It is 8:30 am and I have had a good night of sleep. The Pittsburgh Steelers are playing today, so this should be another victory for us.

Today I found out from Mr. Lawrence that I have too much time remaining on my sentence to enroll in the WIN classes. This course is developed and accredited by the American Council of Education. The software is designed to teach you in three specific areas which are basically cognitive skills. It was almost like taking the ACT or SAT. I wanted to enter the class because I need the practice due to my firm intention of going back to college. I have 24 months remaining on my sentence and the class requires individuals to be at least six months shorter.

After 15 years of imprisonment, I still have ambitions to drive to work, to start a business, to write a book, to have hope, to listen, and to give sound advice. And what about the outlook for ideas on how to use my past as an asset to the community, myself, and my family?

October 18, 2010 - Day 53

It's 3:52 p.m. and it's getting close to count time. Today was filled with doubt about a lot of things. Will I remain relatively healthy? Is 40 years of age too old to start college again? Are my plans too optimistic? Is it even worth it to try and educate myself? Doubt seems to be the seed to depression, despair, and delusion, among other things. Every time your curiousity or ambition drives you to seek out information for an idea, you shut down because of the barriers of being incarcerated. Mr. Moon told me that you can achieve at different levels in life, but it all depends on how ambitious you are. My ambition stops when it comes to me compromising my integrity.

One day a while back some of the guys were sitting

around shooting the shit and there were some homosexuals standing around amongst them. However, one of them named Jim used to be a good friend of one of the guys talking with us named Pitt. So Pitt called the homosexual over to us and asked him, "How can you take another man's dick in your ass?" Jim told Pitt it really doesn't hurt, it's like taking a shit but only in reverse! Everybody started laughing and falling on the ground holding their stomachs because they couldn't stop laughing. One of my buddies told me that he couldn't understand why white people hated us because of the color of our skin. I told him sure you understand it because it is the same as you hating homosexuals. Ignorance! Intolerance! Lack of compassion! Lack of education!

Mr. Whitfield is about to go back to court to resolve some issues that the court of appeals ruled in his favor. Now these issues have to be resolved and I want to give him some advice but he's a judge and I may be out of place. So I won't say anything.

The Monday night football game should be very exciting and I can't wait to have a beer and watch a game. Oh yeah! I am in prison and they don't serve beer here... or do they?

October 19, 2010 - Day 54

I just got back from the library typing journal entries and I finally ran into Paul, who is a board certified medical doctor. I asked him about my elbow and it just happens he has the same symptoms. He told me I should put in a cop-out to physical therapy to see Dr. Benner. A cop-out is an institution-created form for inmates to submit staff requests. Paul said to tell the doctor that I have an ulnar nerve compression at my left elbow. I made two copies so that I could put one under his door and I will send the other through the institution mail system. Every time I even think about leaning on my left elbow I cringe at how bad it really hurts. I went to sick call to see if they could help me and they scheduled me for an X-ray. However, Paul has told me that the X-ray will not show the damage.

The New York Times for today is reporting that the blacks in the country are upset with President Obama but they will still vote for him. If I were out, the president would surely get my vote and volunteer work also.

Wall Street and the big bankers have made me more resolute in finding ways to invest in myself and I think I have found a way with my books and endeavors in college. Everybody knows California is willing to pass laws for recreational use of marijuana because of their financial problems. I have learned through my past that making decisions based on prior decisions gives fruition to more bad decisions.

Families Against Mandatory Minimums (FAMM) has sent out their quarterly periodical and everybody's talking about it. I usually get a copy but it didn't come today. It will probably show up tomorrow.

I just talked to an old man named Jenkins and he said, "I'm tired and I am giving up! The people in the government are not going to let us out!" I told him I am sorry and I understand. I felt like a real asshole today for telling him that there may still be hope for him. When you really want something and you're denied after hoping and wishing for years, it really crushes your soul. Pop Jenkins said, "I am just gonna do the rest of my time and forget about that law stuff!"

"Scars are the thread that sews hope together, but fear is a scar that won't hold."
- John L. Hunt

October 20, 2010 - Day 55

Today was a good day for me. I had an appointment to see Dr. DiBiase, the psychologist, about why I have not been taking my psych meds every day. I told him that the pills made my appetite increase. He told me that the way to take these drugs should be in accordance with the way they are being prescribed. Furthermore, he said that to receive the therapeutic benefits of these drugs they need to be taken every day. I informed him that I have found out that I've got nerve damage. I think it is called ulnar nerve compression. Just hurts so bad that it will wake me up. We talked about me being able to get Social Security disability when I am released, but I have got to wait until I'm released from prison.

I might have to waive the halfway house. I have to really think about this before I make a move. I think I need to wait until the end of 2011 to start thinking about halfway house placement. I'm trying to be prepared for direct release; however, I have learned from the past that sometimes I need to be more patient and let things develop on their own. I didn't have to do anything for things to work out for me. But sometimes it's hard not to think that you need to help things along.

October 21, 2010 - Day 56

While I made it to work on time, I forgot to look at the call out to see if I had any appointments. I was hoping that physical therapy wanted to see me about my elbow. If I don't get it taken care of I may lose the use of some of my fingers on my left hand.

Another day at work doing nothing, so I started taking the New York Times to work more often to use the time.

The perfect place to study is in the career resource center. The guidance counselor and an inmate run the center.

I overheard she is retiring in December and it is a mystery who's going to take care of the place. She was quite helpful when she wanted to be.

An inmate named Mr. Blythe, who is 77 years of age, finally talked me into taking a class called Public Speaking and Business Development. This class supposedly covers corporations, business plans, articles of incorporation, bylaws, and majority of shareholders, among other things. Mr. Blythe is from Jamaica and sometimes it's hard to understand his inconsistency when he gets really excited about an aspect of a corporation. The class had about 15 people joining today. Mr. Blythe chased me for weeks to come to the class and I feel that it will work in the long run to attend once a week. I can say that I learned something today about the elements of corporations.

October 22, 2010 - Day 57

When I was a young teen I was sneaking into my father's dresser drawers and stealing some of his marijuana. Whenever we did something bad, my father would beat us with an extension cord. Sometimes he would make us face the wall for four or five hours. This was not as frequent as the beatings. My brother and I contemplated killing our father, but we let it go after we told our sister and made her really upset.

The first thing my father did was grab his extension cord. He started swinging and I caught the cord and wrapped it around my hand. Next he dropped the cord and grabbed me by the throat and pushed me to the bed. He pulled his fist back as if to punch me in the face but Mom came running down the hall and grabbed his arm and then he stopped. A while later I left and never came back. At that point I was a teenager living on the street.

My father died a few days after I spoke with him in 1998, while I was incarcerated in Greenwich, IL, and after our conversation, I hung up the phone without saying I love you. I guess I still harbor some resentment after all those beatings.

The medical staff at the institution made rounds to the units today to offer flu shots to anyone that wanted one. I have to get the flu shot because of my kidney disease. I cannot afford to get the flu or a cold.

October 23rd, 2010 - Day 58

It was 9:00 am when I finally woke up this morning. The first thing I wanted was a cup of coffee. I've been thinking about whether I should file for physical and mental disability with the Social Security office. I do believe that I'd be a fool, with my background, to leave prison after doing 17 years and say I'm normal and sane. I don't believe that I'm normal and I don't have any hangups about seeking counseling. I'm starting to feel a lot better since I've started taking my psych meds on a regular basis, except they increase my appetite... but I think I can keep that under control.

I've got acid reflux and it sucks really bad because every time I belch it hurts. I take a lot of meds for this also. And now I think I've got what my friend told me that I had and that's ulnar nerve compression. He also told me that if this is left untreated it could disable my left hand and arm.

Since we've found out that the retroactivity is going to happen next year I might just forget about the halfway house. The case manager coordinator doesn't allow the paperwork for halfway placement until they get ready. The change in the crack law was just the beginning of the process for the guys previously incarcerated under the old draconian drug laws. A lot of the guys here are career criminals and they're screwed if our current situation is not remedied. These guys need the federal criminal statute to be retroactive. I've left some really good guys back in the higher security prisons.

October 24th, 2010 - Day 59

President Obama is about to go on a trip to visit several countries and he has to choose which would be the most appropriate. The president has plans to visit India but he has chosen to bypass the Sihk Temple. Many Sihks in this country are upset because of the decision and they blame his decision on being personified as a muslim. I understand that the many Sihk that are US citizens were looking forward to the president's visiting their holy site. However, the tradition of placing a cloth on your head before entering the temple gives republican strategists the ammunition to forment the impression that the Sihk are Muslim. Moreover, the Sihk are not Muslim, just as the president is not a Muslim.

I believe that the administration made the right choice. You must balance not only the consequences of the choice but the benefits. The president needs to consider being re-elected. In his second term he can make a visit to the temple. We take the chance of alienating voters even though they're misinformed about the president's religious beliefs. I also believe that in his second term the leaders of the Sikh community will be asked to pay a visit to the White House.

Americans are being fed a bill of bad goods when it comes to the media, radio, periodicals, and so forth. I read an article about how none of the tea party candidates have an idea about foreign policy.

October 25th, 2010 - Day 60

On the front page of the NYT was an article entitled, "Employers' Test For Drugs May Catch Prescriptions, Too." To me it seems that if you're prescribed a psych med – or any meds that are narcotics – then to some extent you're effectively unemployable and disabled. At the very least you're going to be restricted in regards to the type of work you can do. I wonder what happens if you've been taking these drugs for years? The article went on to question the restriction on employees in relation to the Americans With Disabilities Act. The employees in the article filed suit and so did the Equal Employment Opportunities Commission. The company randomly tested 500 employees and 40 of them came up positive for narcotics. But these employees were prescribed these drugs and need them to cope with their health conditions.

The people of Haiti are suffering from an outbreak of Cholera and it's getting worse. Some of the photos that are taken give you a cold feeling of guilt because there should be resources to help these people. Black people are always shown in their worst light in the newspaper. I've never seen any countries in Europe showing caucasians in dire situations or depressed living conditions. If this country has another earthquake it's going to destroy the morale throughout the country. It just doesn't seem to be getting any better even though President Bill Clinton is overseeing the restoration of the country. But if there's anyone that can do the job it's President Clinton. President Obama has asked President Clinton to be his ambassador to Haiti.

October 26th, 2010 - Day 61

For some reason I started thinking about lawsuits and I remember the civil suit I filed against judges, lawyers, and prosecutors who never asked if I was mentally disabled. No one thought to check if I had a mental defect. It cost me a little over $400 to file that suit and I got a denied order as soon as they received all of the money. I also got a strike under the Prison Litigation Reform Act. Under this act, judges can deem your filing frivilous and allocate the petitioner a strike. Once you receive three strikes, you're barred from filing another lawsuit in federal court indefinitely. However, if your health claim can show that a dismissal would be detrimental to your health or safety then you may proceed.

Today I contemplated having a ghostwriter help me with my book. I really want the book to be of good quality writing because it will represent my resume and life experiences in detail and with vivid description. From what I've read, a ghostwriter usually charges from $125 to $175 a page. Now that is really expensive and I don't have a quarter to my name. When I'm released from prison, I'll find a job and save the money to make sure the final product is just what I want it to be.

Chapter Three: Dwight L. Hunt

My father served two tours in Vietnam and died in May of 1998. He was a certified master electrician, a hard worker, a great provider, and he walked great distances to work and in life so that my siblings and I would have the best chances to excel in the future. His extended family was from Chicago, IL and he visited them at least once a year. His mother, Ethel Hunt, was very strict and his father, John Hunt, was a lovable man. My dad's friends called him Thunder because he was a hard puncher.

As an older adult, I do understand his frustrations over the years with my lack of work ethic and reckless behavior towards education. Sometimes I wish that he could see me today but I am sure he's looking down on me every day wondering what took me so long to open my eyes. I am sorry dad! May peace be upon you!

October 27ᵗʰ, 2010 - Day 62

This is the first time I've taken my meds for at least a week. I'm on an even keel. The side effects are slowly going away and I'm going to start losing weight.

I'm still interested in getting into the WIN class so that I can brush up on the basics: math, science, social studies, language arts, writing, and reading. It's been a long time but I'm ready for the challenge. I've decided not to write the book and self-publish. I'm going to start archiving documents and diary entries to assist the ghostwriter for my book once I acquire my PhD in sociology or a law degree.

My temper is not quick to come while I'm taking my meds and I'm much more relaxed but not high, even thought elavil is a narcotic. The only frustrating part about this process is that I've got to walk to the pill line. They scheduled me for a blood test to determine if I've got an ulcer causing my acid reflux.

October 28ᵗʰ, 2010 - Day 63

At 1:50 p.m. I headed to the unit. As I was arriving at the front entrance, I heard gun fire. The gun fire came from the officers' firing range. I don't know that much about guns but I can tell that they have hand guns and automatic weapons. That's just my personal observation.

Mr. Blythe wants to teach and share his knowledge and experience with the young blacks that are incarcerated. He learned business and finance in London by attending college. In today's class, Mr. Blythe concluded with a little personal information. He told us that he went to see the doctor for his eyes and the doctor said right now it's okay. We'll check it again in six months and you may need eye surgery. He said, "I couldn't believe it, one doctor wants to take one of my balls and the other doctor wants to take my eye!" Everyone burst into laughter.

October 29th, 2010 - Day 64

I finally got enrolled in the WIN class. It's developed by ACT (American College Test). I'm going to do well with this program. The software is designed like it is a tutor and it shows you where you made mistakes. Applied Mathematics is the first section and I can't move any further until I pass the test for this section.

The institution movie for Friday was Michael Jackson's *This Is It*. Some of the white guys along with the Mexicans are making fun of Michael, whispering that he is a child molester. I grew up listening to the Jackson 5, so when they snicker and laugh I don't like it. All of the brothers are not paying them any attention and they're enjoying themselves.

I got a new cellmate today and his name is Mr. Kelly. He's an older gentleman and he's a GED tutor. I need some real work on my math and all areas of college freshman academics.

October 30th, 2010 - Day 65

This morning I awoke wanting to study some information about building credit. It's fairly complicated and effective as well. I got to watch a little football and can't wait until Sunday night for the Steelers game.

I think Mr. Kelly is studying theology. I'm studying now to take the ACT exam through WIN software.

I still haven't received an email from my mom or Angel. I see everybody's not paying me any attention. When I'm released we'll see people change their views and I won't be able to get rid of them. My mom, aunt, and lil' bro are the only people who have tried to keep in touch with me. Now I believe that my mom is getting tired of communicating with me over the phone. I know she's tired but I'll be home soon to help her.

October 31ˢᵗ, 2010 - Day 66

I spent most of the day reading some material on finance that was given to me by one of the students. I don't believe he was very interested in the class because he didn't show up the next day. Actually, I had originally thought the class was not worth going to, but I told the instructor that I would come and check it out. So Thursday of last week I went and just listened to what was taught. I learned a few things about credit management that could assist me with my plans for the Hunt Institute of Sociology or the law firm. I'm sure it'll take a lot of research and sweat but I feel that it is my calling to help these guys.

I think the Hunt Institute of Sociology should pay for SAT and ACT tests. I'll have to make sure that 75% of every dollar is spent on inmate support. I think I'll have the employees work for my for-profit. There will be no restriction as far as who is qualified to participate in relation to their criminal records. This is part of my brainstorming process and I may come up with an entirely different plan to help these guys out.

Mr. Kelly is a really good guy. He studies the Bible all day long and pretty much stays in the room reading religious material.

November 1ˢᵗ, 2010 - Day 67

Today I found out that the National Federation for the Blind is temporarily not grading manuscripts for the literary certification.

I've got to start studying the GED workbooks so that I can be sharp once I enter college.

The election is tomorrow and I'm starting to see some white guys quietly celebrating that the republican party is about to take either the house or the senate. I do not believe that the democrats are in the position to lose both houses of congress. However, being an independent is about the individual and not the party, I believe. I got a feeling that Sarah Palin is going to run for president in 2012 and split the republican party right down the middle.

November 2nd, 2010 - Day 68

Today is election day and the republicans are confident that they'll take the House or Senate in this election. I wish that they would take both so we can see their leadership in this economy. The president has planned a press conference for tomorrow at 1:00 p.m.; it will be interesting to see his tone. Being in Kentucky is almost like being in West Virginia: a large portion of the staff don't really care for President Obama.

I went outside to the courtyard in the cold to watch the pundits on MSNBC and CNN because the guys were watching their normal television shows and they could care less about this election. It was a little chilly and windy so I went upstairs to my room, got a sweater, skull cap, and coffee, and went back to watch a little more coverage of this election.

I got a callout to the diet tech about my weight gain and I'm up to about 230 pounds. The lady didn't have room to put me in the diet kitchen but she told me she would if it opened up.

I've gotten zero emails and I'm starting to understand why; I've been incarcerated for too long. And that's okay... I understand.

November 3rd, 2010 - Day 69

I've finally decided what path I should take after conversations with different people and some of my elders. I've always wanted to go to law school because of what happened behind my case. I'll start my career off by doing a lot of pro bono work with legal aid and probably a little work from some other attorneys. I've always tried to think of ways to give back to the community.

One of the guys named Skeet that I was locked up with in the St. Clair County Jail in 1996 found me in the library this afternoon. Skeet said he told Mrs. Hall that he had about four or five years left on his sentence. Mrs. Hall appeared to have told him that's not the case and he'll be leaving soon. I will be monitoring his situation very closely because we both have the same attorney representing us in our 3582 motions in which we both got sentence reductions. I really hope there's some veracity to what he told me. However, Skeet isn't the most credible person around.

I had stopped doing legal work and typing for people when I received my diploma as a paralegal, but it's time to change. I may help a brother, especially if he's got a lot of time. So I did a little typing today for one of the guys.

November 4th, 2010 - Day 70

It really felt good being at my own desk with my own typewriter. The staff in education doesn't have a problem with us working on our manuscripts.

I haven't talked a lot about the election results because I'm disappointed that the American people don't realize what they have done. President Obama is the answer to our future. I know he was really upset about the election results but he's got to move forward and make progress with the time remaining in his presidency.

The Federal Reserve is about to push $600 billion into the money system to boost the economy. The American people aren't spending; there's no consumer activity. At least not on the scale that would bring 10% unemployment down to 5% or lower. The economists at the Federal Reserve are split on the issues of buying treasuries to push down the interest rate to induce consumers to refinance or seek cheap loans or credit.

I'm probably going to start ghostwriting again so I can make a few dollars. Big Papa told me to let him know when I'm ready and I think it's a perfect opportunity right now. He might not like my offer or he might be willing to negotiate. I should hear something from him tonight or tomorrow. I sent a note through one of the guys to give to him. However, I did catch him leaving the mess hall on his way back to work.

Roland sent me some pictures of President Obama while he was at a Washington Redskins football game. I guess he was in DC. Roland did about 18 years and was finally paroled this year. I'm glad to see him enjoying his life.

November 5th, 2010 - Day 71

It's 9:27 p.m. and I've just finished writing down some ideas about my company. I can't believe the conversations that I'm hearing about the president. I really don't believe the prejudice against President Obama has anything to do with politics. A lot of good people in the Democratic House had to be sacrificed for the greater good. 80 seats were taken by the republican party. I know that the president is really unhappy about this outcome. I still believe he has all Americans' interests at heart, even though from time to time he has expressed his views inartfully.

The Hispanic community and the young population did not turn out for the president. It appears that by not showcasing his efforts for job creation, it really hurt the image of this young administration. The president will learn from this experience and rally to give the American people exactly what they've asked for: jobs and security and an end to the wars.

I finally got my own desk and typewriter so I'll probably start ghostwriting again. I took a little time out to write to a few relatives because I have not heard from them or they from me.

I don't have to worry about having friends when I'm released because I don't have any friends right now. Over time you come to realize that people may only be interested in you for certain reasons and when your back is against the wall, their true colors will shine. It's really not fair that you've got to be put in a position of being with your back against the wall to find out an individual's character. Unfortunately, though, that happens a lot.

November 6th, 2010 - Day 72

It's 10:00 p.m. and it's time for the guards to come around and count so we all have to be in our rooms. The temperature is dropping and it's starting to get very cold. The heating is not working well as it breaks down every year right after they turn the heat on.

I'm very confident about law school and hiring the ghostwriter as the days pass toward my release. While I'm a student I will build my credit and study how trusts work and the fiduciary responsibilities of the trustee. I think it's time to look at some case law to really learn the elements of an irrevocable trust or a business trust. The business should be more suited for the plan that I've developed over the last few weeks. Making these business trusts a franchise is possible, but I believe you've got to be a master at writing trusts and at being a trustee.

I've signed up for the math class starting December first. I need to study the basics a little bit more since I have not looked at math, science, social studies, writing, and reading lessons for years.

I read the NYT every day but I need to switch it up between the non-fiction books and other periodicals. My next goal is to acquire the course catalog from SIU-Carbondale so that I can see the curriculum for pre-law.

I believe that these classes may or may not be relatively easy for me but I'm sure that I can handle them. After being a jail house lawyer for so many years, I should take to the classes like a fish to water.

November 7th, 2010 - Day 73

I had to get up at 9:30 am and close the windows because it's starting to get really cold. I've straightened my room up a little and started with my coffee and a little candy.

The NYT has covered the November elections very well and they've broken down all of the races, especially the ones with the Tea Party. I believe that the Tea Party is going to split the republican party inside of congress. Some of the Tea Party winners are adamant about not compromising with President Obama on anything. I can't wait to see how they try to derail his presidency.

I think the president should've addressed the healthcare issue first while concentrating on unemployment. Some of the jobs that were lost are not coming back and a lot of men need to realize this and go back to school to learn another trade or profession. Just sitting around waiting on the government to create another job for you isn't going to happen. This mass exodus of jobs to other countries was bound to happen because of the cheap labor in the other nations. The jobs that are labor intensive will disappear more and more. It will come down to having a college education; you might as well leave the country if you don't. Especially ex-cons who are not educated. Going back to school is a must.

November 8th, 2010 - Day 74

It's 8:30 p.m. and it's time to watch Monday Night Football. I've been waiting for this game for a long time.

The Bengals really think they did something last year when they beat us twice. I just sat in my room with my cellmate deciding how I should study to pass the ACT or SAT with scores that would get me a scholarship instead of getting out and filing a claim for mental disability. I shouldn't strive to diminish myself but strive to improve myself. As the Chinese proverb states, "To be great you have to take yourself to the point of destruction."

I can't make my mind up about what profession I want to pursue but I guess that's okay because one of these days, I'll have to make my mind up. We've decided on a program to get me ready for college and it's quite simple. We have five different GED books: Science, Social Studies, Math, Language Arts, Reading, and Writing. I need to complete one lesson first thing in the morning once I arrive at work in education. I then take the workbook to my cellie and he'll grade it and bring it back to me. Whether I got the answer right or wrong, I must explain my answer in writing. He also told me that I need to go back to lesson one in the applied math section for my WIN class and redo every lesson until I receive a score of 100%. Once I receive a score of 100%, I should proceed to the next lesson. If I do this, he guarantees me that I'll do well on any type of test that I'm given.

November 9th, 2010 - Day 75

Well, today was not remarkable in any way. The institution didn't post our pay so I wasn't able to get my coffee. I just found out at 6:57 that all the inmates were ordered to return to their respective units because they were about to initiate a bed book count. The bed book count is done with photo cards of inmates categorized by room number in a book that looks like a menu from Red Lobster. This process usually takes a while to complete. Usually they're looking for someone and haven't been able to locate them. I don't know who the LT is tonight but this had to have been ordered by that person or by a phone call to the captain. People have escaped from this prison but they were always found eventually.

My cellmate just informed me that I might not be interested in a ghostwriter but maybe a biographer.

President Obama has written an op-ed piece in the NYT about how exporting is the building block for the future of this country. I believe that his article makes the NYT more prestigious. I'm sure he also writes essays for the Foreign Affairs publication by the Council of Foreign Affairs.

My sister's birthday is coming up and I should send her a Mother's Day card and one for her birthday all in one. They were supposed to send me some money but I have not heard from them. That's okay, though; it's not their job to take care of me. They have a big responsibility to take care of themselves and the children.

November 10th - 14th, 2010 Days 76 to 80

The US Treasury Secretary and Alan Greenspan are having a disagreement about getting the US economy in fiscal order, but they don't seem to care about the effects of their comments. It appears that the free trade agreements with some of the Asian countries (South Korea, Japan, Indonesia) are not going forward as the president planned this week.

The people wanted change but they didn't expect there to be this much change. I believe that some of the American citizens are not well-educated on the subject of what the president has done to make our lives better.

I talked to Mom today and she told me that she has been waiting to hear something from me, but I've been waiting to hear something from her. I'm glad I called her – she sounded really good. My Uncle Eddie Earl died, he's my mom's sister's husband. Eddie Earl was a really cool guy. It's just crazy out in the streets and everybody's out for themselves. I don't want Momma to live in a nursing home, so I'll hire some nurses to live with us and keep the place together.

November 15th, 2010 - Day 81

When I woke up this morning I felt really sluggish and tired. I went to work and I was not really ready to type or work on my GED workbooks, but somehow I managed to get it done so that I can stay on track with my plan to study and write until I reach college.

I've been thinking about what type of program I could initiate for inmates when I'm released. I've come up with some good ideas but I know that I would probably come up against some fierce opponents of the program. For some reason I feel that I'm responsible for the birth or creation of a new type of advocacy for inmates. I feel that I was predestined to go through all of the trials and tribulations that have befallen me and go from there. Sometimes I think about being a professor or assistant professor.

I thought about having the inmates write essays about making bad decisions. This would prevent them from thinking it's okay to write fraudulent material because, even though they may make up a story, they still must articulate a process to deal with the bad decision. I may still be able to use the material to show what not to do. Plus, even though you used a bad example, it can still be an example of what to do or not to do. However, it really shows your thought process and how you see the elements of approaching a problem.

November 16th, 2010 - Day 82

Big Papa caught me this morning on my way to work and asked me to accept some stamps as payment to begin his book. I had to remind him that the compound stamps are not good; therefore, he'd have to go through all of the books of stamps before he gives them to me. I believe that it's in my best interest to demand commissary instead of stamps. These guys around here are con artists and they try all types of nonsense to get you to part ways with your money or property. It's just that I am not one to give something for nothing.

Ghost writers make about $125 to $175 a page and I'm not a professional; however, I still need to be compensated for my efforts with reasonable pay. Believe me, one dollar a page just doesn't get it for this type of work.

My cellmate is working on his manuscript and he needs a few extra tools to accomplish his goal of 80%, which is passing. The Braille coordinator doesn't allow the guys to talk to one another or help each other with the Braille lessons. I can't deal with the headache of listening to her nonsense. I did find out that Braille lessons are given at a college in Texas named Northwest Vista College. I don't think I'll be able to go to Texas upon my release, but anything is possible if you put your mind to it.

November 17th, 2010 - Day 83

A lot of the older guys are telling me I should get married. If I can find a good woman to marry, I do believe that I will get married. I'm still studying math, science, social studies, reading, writing, and so forth. My cellmate talked about marrying a professor at the college that I plan on attending.

Mom still hasn't sent me an email about Eddie Earl's funeral.

I want my studies at the university to extend for at least 8–10 years. At present, I believe that I'll enroll in SIU-Carbondale. I sent a request for their course catalog and I hope that it shows up soon.

I'm starting to get more sleep and time to relax. My studying is coming along very well and I'm starting to learn some of the rules of grammar. I can't wait to attend college because that's where all of the knowledge is kept hidden.

My health is doing very well for the time being. I think that it will remain good but I may need another kidney biopsy in the future.

I read an article in the NYT about how the Russians are luring people to give up vital organs for money. However, when these people allow the procedure to move forward and wake up afterward, they are not paid the money that was promised to them. The market is very lucrative because the people who want these organs are very rich and don't care about the well-being of the individuals who they receive the organs from. These people may be on a waiting list but are told that the chance of them actually receiving a donor are slim to none. The really bad part about it is that the doctors doing the surgeries are real, certified medical surgeons.

November 18th, 2010 - Day 84

The chapel had visitors for the revival and it was held for a couple of hours throughout the week. I was invited but I chose to decline the offer. I know who's really using the chapel to hide from other inmates finding out what they've done or who they are. I also like studying the Siddha Yoga materials I've been receiving for over 12 years.

Secretary Hilary Clinton is becoming a real lobbyist for the president, especially dealing with the New Start Treaty. I wonder if the secretary is contemplating running against President Obama in 2012? When the next presidential election starts, I promise it will be a circus in every state. There will be some states that pass new laws saying you've got to be a naturalized citizen. For some reason a third of the country doesn't believe that Obama is a citizen, but really that's a facade for the prejudice they have for his skin color.

I can't wait until he writes his memoir.

I want to go to college and take all of the regular courses that all of the freshmen do. I'm not in a hurry to get a job. I want to try and start my own company while I'm in college. No more drugs or alcohol will be in my life.

Victor Bout, the "Merchant of Death," finally got extradited to the United States and there's a good chance he will not be leaving the US for a long time. The US believes that Mr. Bout has substantial intel when it comes to trafficking arms and other Russian information.

November 19th, 2010 - Day 85

I'm learning a lot about black history by reading the NYT. Today in class I learned how to use some formulas without any help and this was a real accomplishment for me. I'm still interested in being a sociologist but I want to study history and anthropology. It feels so good not to walk around with your eyes closed about society and your future.

It's 9:00 p.m. and I just finished watching the movie *Lottery Ticket.* It was a good plot but some of it I felt a little offended, particularly the scenes in the church. I really don't think the producers pay attention to the subtext they create to try to make the movie funny, entertaining, or more appealing to the African-American community.

The white boys at this institution and everywhere I've been pass gas and laugh. I don't understand the way these guys think and process being in a society. Some of the brothers have bad habits and questionable ways about themselves, too.

I just finished talking to my cellmate about getting a teaching license or whether I need one to teach at a college. He told me that a Bachelor of Arts or a Bachelor of Science is not the same thing and that a Bachelor of Science and Education would be the better choice. I need to take my time and learn how to teach. I'll be able to go outside of the country and teach.

November 20th, 2010 - Day 86

I started cleaning the room around 10:30 am. Normally, I'd clean the room on Sunday but I need to get it done and do laundry. I'm glad they haven't pulled all of the washers and dryers. A lot of the staff have been spreading rumors that all of the washers and dryers are on their way out of all federal prisons. We told some of the staff that this being a medical center should represent a special waiver if in the future this idea should be put into policy.

I'm reading a lot of periodicals and they're going out of their way to show the prejudice that a lot of people in this country have for my president. I love him to death and I hope that he is re-elected in 2012. Major portions of the independents probably will not vote for President Obama but I think he'll win by a small percentage. I believe that some of the political pundits ought to stop faking and will slip and call him a nigger. I wish I had his temperament and cool demeanor.

The Federal Reserve Chairman, Bernanke, has shown support for the president's economic policies and his efforts to control unemployment. I don't think he'll be able to turn a major part of the unemployment around. However, he will be able to turn around the 10% unemployment if re-elected. I'll be out of prison when Obama runs for re-election to the presidency. A lot of republicans will not appreciate or like the President no matter what he does. I wish Michelle would speak out against the bias towards the

Office of the President. And to think they voted to elect Sarah Palin as Vice President. I think I need to leave this country.

I'm starting to see why people hold their assets in stocks. The value of stock equals the total amount of assets minus the total amount of liabilities divided by the number of shares issued.

November 21st-22nd, 2010 - Day 87 and 88

The NY Giants played the Eagles and Michael Vick showed his extraordinary athletic skills as a QB. I sat and watched about two hours of the game before I came back upstairs to go to bed early. I wound up talking to my cellmate for a couple of hours. We talked about some of the trials and tribulations of a superstar QB.

Kelly and I discussed whether I should pursue speech pathology and sociology as double majors. He thinks that I should Clep as many of the first year credits that I can, up to 30. And if I can't get all 30 then I need to get as close as I can. Tomorrow I'll draft another letter to the University of Southern Illinois Edwardsville to request a course catalog. The one I requested from SIU-Carbondale has not arrived and it really shouldn't have taken this long to send the course catalog. I've read a lot of material about the level of success you will experience once you've learned how to become an excellent communicator. I looked at speech communications but that's not what I'm looking for.

I love to help people with disabilities and impairments and these are the reasons to pursue these two disciplines as a double major. I don't know how successful I may be but I want to be a very successful student.

November 23rd, 2010 - Day 89

It's 9:39 and I just finished helping Kelly with some of the rules in Braille. The Braille manuscript is very difficult to do and you need a good instructor to teach you the tools to proofread very well. I think he'll be alright when he starts to study more in the computer room.

Some of the guys said they saw on the news that South Korea fired a missile into North Korea because the North Koreans are being used by China to entice America into another war. There is a reason that no one ever fucks with Kim Jong-il. His son is scheduled to take over and I think they want to bring him in with military experience; a war would bring just those results.

I've decided to help my man, Big Papa, with his third book and this will be a better book than the second one I wrote. I am glad he wants to start book three and I plan on doing a good job. I've got my own desk and typewriter and a lot of quiet time.

I'm starting to understand more and more about getting admitted to college. I believe that there are a lot of grants and scholarships available if you score very well on the ACT or SAT. I'm ordering the course catalog and the study guide for the ACT so that I'm better prepared for the test once I'm released. I'll take it as soon as I'm released or when the first opportunity presents itself.

November 24th, 2010 - Day 90

Today is the day before Thanksgiving and I'd rather go back to work. When you're at work it really makes your time go by. Sometimes I wonder if I'll ever come back to the prison to tell my story to the guys. I guess I'd have to complete my goals with honors. I believe that there are many different types of institutions and organizations that could use my assistance in regards to consulting, teaching, and maybe some kind of employment.

I just came back from going to the guard's desk to get a commissary list and I wound up getting a lot of envelopes. Sometimes the counselors get tired of us asking for envelopes and they'll put all of them, all three cases, out in the guard station for anyone to take. I took a small amount but Kelly took a good portion, which I don't blame him for. There probably will be a time when you will really need them and they will not be available.

I just discovered that my pen is running out of ink. So it's time for me to go buy some more pens. I need to keep working on my diary even though I'm studying for the ACT. I've got a good amount of time remaining on my sentence to study for the college admissions exam.

November 25th, 2010 - Day 91

It's Thanksgiving Day at 1:38 p.m. and I just realized that I haven't called anybody. I don't think a lot of people are really interested in me contacting them.

We had turkey breast, cranberry sauce, dressing, ham, and dinner rolls for lunch and box lunches for dinner. We watched a movie called *Air Bender* and I absolutely loved it.

I received some money from my Aunt Portia but she didn't write me back for some reason. I probably said something stupid or unacceptable. She has been with me for a lot of years and has shown great resolve. I believe that her example of living her life on her terms is very courageous. Her example of going to college and staying there was a good plan. I really wish that I would've finished school when I had the chance, but there's no better time than now.

I wonder how many parts of grammar there are? I think this will be my next goal: Identify all parts of English grammar and study them to memorize the definitions for the different parts. I need to check Bargona Books to see if there's a reference book to study and learn about all parts of grammar.

Chapter Four: Angel S. Hunt

My little sister really didn't have the time to write me letters because she had a family to take care of while I was in and out of jail all the time. While she was fighting to stay in college and take care of her children, she had the resolve to stay the course and keep her family together. She filled the void when I went away to drug treatment centers, jail, and prison.

After many of my failed attempts to rehabilitate, she was always there to support me but safeguarded the family from me until I got my life together. Once I was released, she jumped into action by asking her friends, co-workers, family members, and anyone that would listen to help me if they could. She called in old favors and put herself in debt to give me a fighting chance at a happy life. She only had one demand: no drugs, no alcohol, no lies, and no bullshit. She demanded 100% integrity or stay out of her life. I've keep my word and she has keep hers.

November 26th-27th, 2010 - Day 92 and 93

It was late yesterday when I started to read the NYT and all I found were stories about fraud. The department of justice is starting to use wire taps on white collar criminals to get convictions on insider trading on Wall Street bankers. They're all helping each other stay on top and very wealthy. Why would the rich let their friends go into the poor house when all they've got to do is tell them a little information? This behavior goes on every day between bankers and their clients. The broker-dealer hears things and they call their investor clients and advise according to information that may or may not be accurate. The broker-dealer's livelihood depends on results, credibility, and commissions. They say money is the root of all evil. But I say evil is the root to all people. A minor discretion is the doorway to a criminal life which could turn out to be a very disastrous thing if you're not careful.

I believe that all convicts getting out of prison should go back to college full-time as a residential student. What kind of society would we have if all of our felons were released and obtained a Ph.D? They'd probably pass a law that says that Ph.Ds were not any good anymore. Maybe the institution of higher learning would not accept the convicts through some new and arbitrary admissions process.

November 28th, 2010 - Day 94

I'm constantly thinking of ways to try and give back to the community. Some of the brothers get to acting really strange when award shows come on television. They sometimes get a little loud in the TV room and the whites start mocking the loud noise. It's really easy for those guys to show their bias when they're in large numbers. I don't understand how African-Americans can be so merciful except with their own race.

Big Papa told me that the people doing his book are going to use the cover description that I submitted to them for the second book. He told me that they've pulled both books down to switch the covers because they should keep sales going. I believe their relationship, their business relationship, is getting better.

It's time for me to really start studying for the ACT college admissions test. There's no pass or fail, it's just a requirement for admissions.

November 29th-30th, 2010 - Day 95 and 96

At 6:00 p.m. I started a socioeconomic business development plan. A lot of the material I had already covered over the years but I learned very small bits of information from the instructor, Mr. Blythe. The class was overcrowded and the staff in control of the library didn't like it at all. However, I believe that she is going to let us use a larger room on Thursday of next week. The classes are being held on Tuesdays and Thursdays for approximately eight weeks.

When I came into the unit, I looked over the call-out and saw that I'm starting my math class tomorrow from 6-8 p.m.. This class will be held every Wednesday for about eight weeks; I will truly enjoy class and can't wait to join the group.

I've got a couple of hours to read my NYT and I'm starting to share my paper with some of the guys. I've got the Tuesday edition and it's got the science section that's filled with a lot of exciting information and facts, nice pictures, and some commentary on health issues. It's a really good way to stay informed while you're incarcerated.

December 1st-4th, 2010 - Day 97 - 100

It's Saturday and I decided to go to the barber shop and get my hair cut. Luckily, they were not really overcrowded. I went in and had a seat and waited for Mason to come and cut my hair. I figured he really wouldn't have a problem with doing it today so that it's an easier load for tomorrow.

While I was waiting, Rodney came in and we started talking about how the people in Unicor are treating him. This asshole named Frolich talked Rodney into going back to Unicor and he'd get his grade accelerated. However, it did not happen and now he's really waiting to quit or change back to customer service. He needs to tell those people to go to Hell.

Anyway, he wanted to talk to me about his new idea in regards to being an information broker since they've incorporated the new email system. It's a good idea but he needs to think about creating a situation that's win-win and not something that's just about money. He also needs to get away from all of his girlfriends and make sure that they don't control him. Rodney has had to struggle on his own through situations where his girlfriend would make decisions that affect his well-being. All because she doesn't like the way that he wasn't paying her a lot of attention. Think!

December 5th, 2010 - Day 101

It's 11:30 p.m. and the Steelers just beat the Ravens 13-10. I love football.

My friend, Johnson-Bey, gave me a book entitled *Time Machine* and it's very good in regards to science and math. It basically talked about a guy's love of science and what he went through to become a professor. I was validated that reading is the key and studying is its cousin.

I'm planning on going to work tomorrow and working

on Big Papa's book and my GED study books. I'm in two math classes and a business development class. Once these classes are over I'll really begin to work in the ACT workbook and read more of the NYT. I've got to study a lot more and I will as soon as the first week of February passes. College football and pro football will be over and I'll be ready to start studying full force then. I'm starting to block out a lot of what's going on around me and concentrating on the future.

I'm starting to hear that it's really difficult to get a job for ex-felons right now and a lot of the guys are going back to school. I really don't want to look for a job; I'm planning on returning to school as soon as I can.

December 6th-7th, 2010 - Day 102 and 103

I got a letter from one of the guys who was here a while ago. I found out that I really don't have to worry about the ACT test because of my age.

I can't wait until I get to college. I've written the college in Edwardsville, IL but have gotten some of the information from Roland about Carbondale. But I've realized that they are both essentially the same University. I'm still going to study for the ACT test just in case I have to take it to better my situation.

I haven't heard anything from Mom and it's really disappointing that she hasn't written or emailed me in the last couple of months. I hope she's okay; I'll probably call her on Christmas if I have enough money.

I'm starting to write the first chapter of Big Papa's book and I'm really enjoying the process since I'm interested in writing novels and diaries.

I'm also waiting for the laws to come out on May 1st, 2012 because they could allow me to be released even earlier than I had planned. If I'm released early I'm planning on going back to college immediately. I can't wait to start my new life and make sure that residing in prison is a thing of the past.

December 8ᵗʰ-10th, 2010 - Day 104 to 106

I've started reading a book entitled *Cleaning Up*, and the author was incarcerated for 7 1/2 years on a 25-year sentence. I can't wait to see how he got out of doing the rest of his time. The guy's name is Barry and he talks about how he was able to commit corporate fraud and how he would eventually turn away from the dark side and become a disciple of Jesus Christ. This was a very good turn of events in his life and attending Liberty University while incarcerated was an added blessing. It appears he has acquired a couple of master's degrees in theology and some form of counseling.

I really wanted to read his book because it's basically the same type of book that I want to produce once I get my Ph.D. I've read that once you submit to academia, you've sworn to a life of poverty. I'm really not prepared to accept that. While I'm at the university, I want to use the experience as a blueprint to a methodology of rehabilitation. I guess I'm not the first test case.

The new name for my company is RCS Rehabilitation Counseling Services or Training International, Inc.

December 11ᵗʰ, 2010 - Day 107

It's 1:30 p.m. and I'm still reading *Cleaning Up*. Barry has just taught me another lesson. As a felon I may not be able to be licensed to perform some of the services of my company, but all I need to do is train someone else in that knowledge. The business model has to be built around training. How to identify the technique needed to see when someone is in need of rehabilitation counseling.

I just finished talking to one of the guys that has shown

me a way to file another claim in an attempt to get my conviction dismissed for lack of subject matter jurisdiction. It would be really great to be eligible for immediate release due to some overlooked areas of the case from the past. I'm sure my attorney and the AUSA were aware of their errors and chose not to preserve them. When I file this motion, I'm going to send a copy to the inspector general and attorney Eric Holder with a formal request for an investigation. I need to write the court and get some copies of my motions.

December 12th-13th, 2010 - Day 108 and 109

I went to see the book that Big Papa had sent to him by Midnight Express Books. One of the guys brought another way to get back into court in a criminal proceeding to my attention. I really don't want to get started with legal work in court again because I know it's a really drawn-out process.

Every year the symptoms of a cold and flu find their way around, but now it's pneumonia that is being spread around. The guys are really sick and their symptoms are staying with them for four or five months. A lot of the guys are taking a lot of antibiotics to kill the bacteria in their systems.

I'm starting to pick up a lot of work while I'm trying to watch the end of college and pro football. As a matter of fact, I'm writing this diary entry while the Ravens and Texans are playing Monday Night Football.

Big Papa wants me to hurry up so that he can send these people his part III but he will have to wait until I put it together. I might have about 3 chapters for him at he end of this month. I'm starting to put too much on my plate. I just need to focus.

December 14th-19th, 2010 - Day 110 to 115

I decided to stop working on Big Papa's book because of legal claims that I need to file. However, I don't think that I want to file the claim right now because I'd be in a better position once I'm released. Whenever you're behind these barbed-wire fences you lose your standing versus when you're on the street. When I'm released, my plan is to enroll in college as fast as I can so that I can establish residency. I'll still probably have a PO box just in case something happens at school and I'm asked to leave.

It is my intention to carry myself in a respectable manner at all times. I really need to keep taking my medicine because I'm starting to become more aggressive. One of the staff members told me last week that I was aggressive. I don't think that I am, but this is what I'm hearing a lot of.

I don't know if I've got the skill to be a good sociologist but I'm planning on giving it a chance. I do want the complete education in sociology. I'm starting to study a little more to prepare myself for the ACT and freshman classes at the university. I'm not required to take the ACT, but I'm planning on taking it for my records. I am also prepared to take remedial classes if I have to. The money really isn't the issue anymore. I just want to read, write, and study.

December 20th-21st, 2010 - Day 116 and 117

I've come up with an idea for my book in relation to the company: *The 10 Keys to Rehabilitate Yourself.* I can make the keys correlate to the biggest mistakes I've made in my life and state the key to rehabilitation afterwards. I think I'll just call that book *How to Rehabilitate Yourself at 40,* just as a reminder.

While reading the paper I'm starting to see that some of

the republicans are starting to compromise with the president and he's really getting a lot of his policy intentions passed through both houses. It appears that the Department of Justice is really starting to crack down on insider trading. Gandhi said, "Life is not always about trying to speed it up." I love this quote and I'll remember it forever.

I sent in a free subscription offer for China Daily, a newspaper that is relatively new to me but I'm very interested in reading it. It will probably have a better perspective on Asia and give us a better outlook on a lot of the countries on the Asian continent. It's pretty much just a different view on politics and free trade. I don't know if I'll wind up traveling the world a lot, but but I plan on doing a lot of networking and consulting.

I've finally learned my lesson about having debt. You must not have debt and you must use a budget. And don't listen to people who say you can't do something. Try it anyway, then you'll know for sure if it can't be done.

December 22nd-24th, 2010 - Day 118 to 120

It's 9:21 p.m. and I've missed a few days of diary entries. I really need to get back to making my daily entries instead of making them every few days.

I've decided to take the courses at Nations University and get the Master's for Bible-Related Studies. Since I'm incarcerated it doesn't cost me anything, however I'm not sure what the cost will be when I'm released from prison. I remember one of the guys telling me about a place called Northwest Bible College. He told me it was accredited.

I truly believe in karma and I believe that this Bible course was put in my path because of the concentration I've given to going to college. It's not by chance that it's free and it means another seven years of being a student of God. I truly believe that I'm going to enjoy these lessons and I can't wait to start studying.

The staff faxed my paperwork to the university, so I should hear something from them next week sometime. It's really more studying for me so I will watch less television. I don't think I'm going to be a preacher but I will pursue my sociology degree as planned and I think the Bible studies will only help me become stronger in my knowledge of God, the world, humans, and science.

I think I need to pay better attention to who I'm doing business with. No more business deals while I'm incarcerated. I'm starting to see how it feels to have to deal with people who aren't truthful and lack integrity.

December 25th, 2010 - Day 121

Well, it's Christmas and I can't wait until it's over. All we do is sit around and watch movies over and over. The food was okay but it could've been a lot worse. I could've been in Russia, China, or the Middle East. I haven't called anyone for Christmas but they could've easily emailed me. We had a box lunch for dinner and they've had basketball on television all day today. There are no good movies on that we have not already seen.

I'm still reading Ayn Rand's *Atlas Shrugged*. It seems to be very descriptive and pretentious. It's 1000 pages of words that seem to advocate capitalism against socialism. I'm starting to see why the radio host Mark Levin talked like he's God. Ayn Rand was an advocate of capitalism and to Hell with everyone else.

I'm glad I signed up for the Bible classes at Nations University. Now that I've decided to take the courses I really want to get started. I've been keeping this diary for four months now and it should help me learn a lot about myself; maybe it will help me learn something about myself that I'm not really aware of.

December 26th, 2010 - Day 122

It's 10:00 am and it's count time.

I was watching television and Pop Jenkins rolled up in his wheel chair. I started to tell him that he shouldn't be in the wheel chair all the time. Pop was a little upset about my comments because he found out that he's got to go back and repeat his surgery because he didn't follow the doctor's instructions, which was to restrict all movement as much as possible and stay in the wheel chair. Somehow he has caused the surgery to be a waste of time. I hope he gets better.

It's crazy how you'll go to the hospital and get an operation that costs thousands but the aftercare at this medical center is really designed opposite of the surgeon's instructions. Pop's restrictions should've kept him on F-4 in a room with an attendant. Instead, he was sent back to the unit in his wheel chair while the elevator is broken and his room is on the second floor. Every inmate tries to help him by giving him medical advice as if they've been to medical school. Pop asked me who's advice he should follow, an inmate or a doctor. I paused before I told him the doctor because the doctor is not aware that his after care instructions are not being followed. The doctor doesn't know that it takes an act of God to get the medical staff to help you. Maybe this is part of your punishment while in prison.

I wrote down a title of my book called *How to Get Started Rehabilitating Your Life.* I wrote some words to remember, discipline, integrity, contentment, forgiveness, goals, education, greater power, ruler, no drugs, no alcohol, no TV for a little while. I haven't read my Siddha Yoga letters in a while and I'll probably pull those out sometime today. Maybe I should start a Life Rehabilitation Center?

Chapter Five: Dayle D. Hunt

My brother is the adventurer in the family because he loves to travel and meet new people. He graduated from Assumption Catholic High and married his high school sweetheart, Kenya Logan. He and Kenya had three beautiful children, Devin, Dee Dee, and Dorian.

He then enlisted in the military and served in Desert Storm with the Navy and loved serving his country. Over the years he has lead a fruitful life in Las Vegas, NV as an Assistant Store Manager and a good long-distance friend. When I was released from prison, he moved back home Illinois so we could build a family business together.

Dayle decided to move back to Nevada because St. Louis just wasn't his style anymore after living in Las Vegas for so many years. I can't wait to visit him in the summer of 2013.

December 27th, 2010 - Day 123

Billy is my next door neighbor and he's about 65 years of age. He has a lot of ailments including cancer. A few months ago, Billy woke up and he couldn't see out of his right eye. The medical staff ran tests and didn't have a clue; they thought he had a stroke in his sleep. The medical center out at UK thought the same thing after running a battery of tests. So, a few months later, his next door neighbor asked Billy if he wanted to try his eye drops. They didn't know if they would help or hurt... Billy was afraid because they tried not to tell him that they believe he has lost his sight. The eye drops helped him a little in the beginning and eventually the eyedrops - prescription eyedrops - helped his eye clear up.

Today he found out that he's being sent to another medical center in Butner, North Carolina. However, he was sent to the medical center at UK for chemo and radiation treatment without pain medication. How thoughtful of them! Billy is sitting outside my door right now in really bad pain. He said it feels like someone is pushing a knife into his side. Billy said his kidneys and a lot of other stuff inside of him really hurts.

Billy is going to be on a hospital transport to Butner and it will take only 30 minutes for the flight. I wonder if all of this bullshit could not have waited until tomorrow.

There's a couple of one man rooms coming available and it appears the unit counselor is taking her time moving people into these rooms. Sometimes I wonder if race has something to do with it.

December 28th, 2010 - Day 124

I think I'm going to start my business by volunteering my services through a web site. It'll be a sole proprietorship registered with the Government Services Administration or

Small Business Administration. Initially, I'll probably just ask for a letter of recommendation for my services but it has to be an entity other than a church.

The career resources office at this institution has an inmate clerk who's been in prison for almost 30 years. How in the hell does he fit the criteria of an individual that can assist you with your future plans? All he knows is what the staff tells him or what he interprets when he reads. For some reason he's telling the inmates that Distance Education Training Council is not an accredited organization. Even though Peterson's (a private company who publishes the ACT and SAT materials. They also list who is accredited in accordance with the US Department of Education) says that these people are accredited, these guys are being continually told that the colleges will not accept that national accreditation, only regional accreditation. I'm almost certain that no one verified what the career guidance counselor has said. But I don't care because I'm still going to take the classes and learn from them. I plan on using them to learn my career as a rehabilitation counselor/trainer.

December 29th-30th, 2010 - Day 125 and 126

I came back from work at about 2:00 p.m. and one of the guys stopped me. He had surgery on his hand and was scheduled for a follow-up, but the second appointment was never scheduled. Smear said due to him having the cast on his hand longer than was ordered by the surgeon, he had sustained permanent paralysis in his fingers. Now he wants to sue. This kind of stuff comes to my attention all the time.

I'm not interested in a living constitution because you can just amend the constitution if there is such a pressing interpretation. A lot of people use the same document to argue for and against a measure. The document or book is no good when it does not validate their argument. I saw a book on people called apologists and my buddy, Tom, told me that he was going to let me read the book and bring me a Bible he saw. There are very few individuals who I believe are trying to follow the book of God and continue to do so.

December 31st, 2010 - Day 127

Early this morning, as I sat in the sports television room, read my newspaper, and shared the business section with Mr. Blythe. Mr. Blythe went to business school in London and he teaches the business class here at the prison on Tuesday and Thursday. He showed me some of the articles that talked about the exact same thing he teaches in class.

One of the articles was about a university building having a trading floor and the students trading with a $200,000 stock portfolio. I never thought about how easy it is to buy distressed assets in a bankruptcy proceeding. It appears that it is not really hard to start my own private equity firm. I'm starting to think that the private equity firm is the company that I want to establish. I am reserved on taking my time and building a really strong company. It is my firm intention to apply to college and start my company from school. There really isn't any reason for me to resort back to any criminal behavior.

I've been advising my cellmate on securing his retirement account and it seems he really doesn't want to listen to me. I probably need to start keeping my suggestions to myself. Sometimes you have to realize that individuals can only relate to and accept something when they're willing and able to accept the knowledge. You really never know because the individual may not want your advice.

I'm still waiting on confirmation of enrollment from Nations University.

January 1ˢᵗ, 2011 - Day 128

I think I've come up with a new concept for my book series. The main title will be PrisonProof with all the other titles that I've got as subtitles. My trademark is going to be a trash can with the words PrisonProof leaning out of the trash can. The philosophy behind the title is that the justice system in this country, especially on the federal level, is corrupt. Anybody at any time can be put in prison, whether you're innocent or not. My goal is to open the eyes of the public to this activity. All the accomplishments, education, public service, awards, and medals will be thrown in the trash can when you go before that federal judge.

Another idea could be a little man with a hammer breaking up concrete blocks spelling out PRISONPROOF. Maybe one from each end of the word. I want the two men to be black. I want one man in a suit and the other in overalls. I want the letters to start crumbling from within the middle. I want both men to have handcuffs hanging from one wrist. The cracks represent inmates on the inside today. Crack the facade of fairness and rebuild justice through rehabilitating yourself first. I've got to remember my seal or picture in my head for the company logo. Inside, I want a letter P with "rison" and "roof" on top of each other next to this large P.

I need to start practicing patience. The last thing that a well-trained tactician does is rush into a situation or make decisions that haven't been thought out.

January 2ⁿᵈ, 2011 - Day 129

It's 9:58 and I just finished watching *Meet the Press;* it's been a while since I've been able to do so.

I want to start a legal defense/tax trust fund, health care trust, insurance trust, housing trust, education trust, and retirement trust. This could be part of the philosophy behind PrisonProof. It could be one of the tenets to establishing yourself in a way that allows you to function if you're incommunicado. It should keep you out of prison and if you do go to prison, these trusts can help you re-establish yourself. I think this may be a better way to develop PrisonProof.

I wanted to develop a trading floor but I might have to start a business trust for that also. All of these trusts can be established and a court-appointed trustee is attainable as soon as you write the trust agreement and fund the trust. I'll put an apartment building in each trust to continually fund the trust for as long as I live. Once I'm dead I'll require that the funds be released to a charity. These seven trusts may form the base of the PrisonProof philosophy.

Proverbs 22:7, "The borrower is slave to the lender." This is where the idea for a trust came about and that the idea is good for PrisonProof. This technique will be part of the Bible degree book, which will be the first one that I write. This technique will take care of you before and after you're in prison. All of the trusts should have a reserve fund for the interest not used in the trust.

January 3rd, 2011 - Day 130

I need some money but I'm so tired of begging my aunt for money. She used to send me $100 every month, but she has stopped sending it. She has sent money to me for the last 17 years and I find it really hard to ask her for more.

I've sat here today and spent a lot of time debating if I should file another claim in court. Whether or not the claim will be successful is yet to be seen. I think it will be a lot better if I wait until I'm released and off of supervised release. I probably deserve to do the rest of this time. God has made me aware that He is in control of the speed of my release.

We emailed the office of admission at Nations University about my admission application, but as usual it's probably me being impatient and undecided. I really need to study the Bible again so that I may get a better grasp of the wisdom in the Old and New Testaments.

I read a job reference book today that had a lot of good information about speech pathology. It also said that it teaches sign language. I'm really interested in this type of study. I've studied Braille for about four or five years and I've always wanted to look at sign language.

January 4th-11th, 2011 - Day 131 to 138

It's Tuesday and I haven't made an entry over several days. I guess I just didn't feel like it.

A lot of the things being taught in our business class have been found in the business section of the NYT. I found it late last night while reading the paper and I wanted to show our instructor but it was late and I'm sure he was asleep, especially at the age of 77. I really enjoy the business class and I'm really interested in going to business school. I think I'm going to continue on the road to sociology because, when I reach the doctorate, I become the product of success. All I really have to do is put my life in a book at each stage and just monitor my progress.

I've received a response from Nations and the courses have arrived. I'm going to read over the work three or four times before I take the exam for each module.

I've finally got my one-man room and that's perfect because it gives me the chance to study in peace and quiet. I get to read at night until I feel tired. I want to get into the habit of reading for at least five hours a day along with classroom time. I believe that the Bible studies will help me prepare for college.

January 12th, 2011 - Day 139

The New York Times had an article about the coptic Christians in Egypt that are being harassed or killed. I read that these Christians were elderly people. I wonder if they feel the need to die in service to God. Do they feel this will get them closer to God or maybe into Heaven? The Muslim believe that if they kill in the name of Allah that they're martyrs and they'll be with Allah when they die. I'm sure the Christians in these Middle-Eastern countries clearly understand that they're putting their lives in danger. Muslims and Christians have been fighting each other for thousands of years.

I went to my math class today and learned quite a bit about percents and how to calculate them. I'm starting to realize that math is really not that hard. With a little practice and study it's becoming a little easier to accept the fact that I wasn't taught a lot of these things. I just need to do my best and let God take care of the rest.

January 13th, 2011 - Day 140

I'm staring to accept the fact that I may have to keep hand writing my notes because I can't afford typewriter ribbon. Portia hasn't sent me any money but she is keeping the newspaper subscription going. I don't know what to do. I like my job because I've got my own typewriter and desk. No one bothers me and I get a lot of studying done.

I'm studying for the Bible exams and it's a lot of reading but you've got to be able to deconstruct and reconstruct the material in the lessons. The goal that I've set for myself is ten modules a month and I should be done with the Bachelor degree by the end of the year. I might be able to finish the Master's degree before I'm released in 2012. I can't wait to get to start putting my book together and studying toward my Doctorate in sociology.

I've decided not to stay in the state of Illinois because I really need a break from this place. I've worn out my welcome in this state and I need to visit some new terrain. Maybe Seattle, Oregon, Nebraska, or even down south. By the time I'm done with my supervised release, I'll have a good idea of where I want to go.

January 14th, 2011 - Day 141

I just had another idea that I should skip the sole proprietorship and go straight to the corporation and name it PrisonProof. I don't think it will be too much of a transition from a sole proprietorship to establishing a corporation. I think I need some help with the name and marketing of my new idea. When I get to the college I'm sure I'll find a lot of students willing to help me with this plan. I want to start with the book and keep publishing it with DVDs and audio.

PrisonProof is partially about US citizens not being aware how easy it is to be sent to prison. A lot of Americans believe they'll never go to prison, that somehow they're prison proof. I believe Americans should be made aware of the laws of the land in high school so that they understand some of the consequences of their decisions.

Maybe PrisonProof should not only publish my books but the books of ex-felons and other authors out of sociology. Maybe we can set up the jobs for donation from us to them. Maybe publish those diaries from inmates and make the donations to them. This must be done because it is about to get bad in the prison system in regards to jobs. Maybe I could have a nonprofit set up alongside the for-profit. I need to retain control for a while and I need not forget this. Maybe PrisonProof can be the nonprofit and maybe PrisonProof Group can be the private equity firm. Maybe the Hunt Group.

January 15th, 2011 - Day 142

I think I want to do the book as a sole proprietor but I'm not sure just yet. I think I may make the Hunt Institute of Sociology a sole enterprise with my books from PrisonProof. With the proceeds from there I want to develop a private equity firm by buying distressed assets and securities.

I might just form an army of prison advocates for incarcerated inmates which will help them rehabilitate their lives. I need to find some way for them to make money. I'm starting to think that maybe I ought to just let things be the way they are. I can go to rehab centers, drug centers, or churches and speak. I'll probably start speaking for free maybe for a letter of recommendation. This phase of my plan will come into play later. I've got to talk to Mr. Blythe about this.

January 16th, 2011 - Day 143

The copyright laws have helped me come to a final decision in relation to my book and getting started. The legal defense trust fund is a must. I will include a provision that says I can dissolve or take distributions every five years by written notification to the trustee. I also want the power to have the trust provide legal defense to any family member. If it hires the attorney, the defendant makes the decision to strategy and defense. I'm sure I'll come up with other provisions.

I want the trust also to be used as a surety if possible. However, if I decide to leave the country, it will provide distributions at my request. State, federal, or administrative, it should assist me in my claim. It may negotiate and settle claims against me for commercial purposes. I want the trust to provide a security agreement on a UCC_1, indemnifying me up to a sum certain of commercial claims: one million dollars. This is so that I don't have to worry about the contents of the trust.

I think rehabilitating and being a credit broker is the best idea as of yet. Maybe I'll call it PrisonProof Trust or PrisonProof Legal Defense Fund Trust. I can also sell property to the trust. The trustee is required to buy property if the property is offered at 20% below market value after an average of three executed approved appraisals, no down payment, no prepayment penalties, with a recourse clause in regards to a short sale, and if the offer is received in writing.

There must also be a satisfactory home inspection report and insurance and property management contracts in place. The interest rate of the mortgage (if seller-financed) is required to be at 2 points plus prime for 30 years or 5 points plus prime for 15 years. The reserves are to be invested in the S & P stock index at 50%, their bond index at 25%, and the foreign stock at 25%, rebalanced every six months.

Also, I need the trust to stipulate all levels of the criminal defense court process, from the investigative to any reasonable appeal.

January 17th-19th, 2011 - Day 144 to 146

I believe that community service is the linchpin to an inmate's success and to a good career. Giving back to the community is a good way for people to develop their integrity and stay away from criminal behavior.

I can't make up my mind if I want to study sociology along with speech pathology or Spanish. I want to pursue speech pathology. I believe that the sign language that I want some experience with is in the speech pathology program.

I'm studying the courses on getting a master's in religious studies. I'm really enjoying it and I need to accept this course for what it is and use it to my benefit. I should not worry about a doctorate of theology in the future. I'm not interested in starting because I just want to help people that are hurting and need someone to talk to. I'm still working in the GED workbooks and I want to complete those books very soon. I should be concentrating on the religious studies that I want to complete.

PrisonProof is not about a static way of staying out of prison. It's about allowing yourself to believe that you're not or can't be put in prison because of the way you've lived your life or the way you're living your life. Legislators are passing laws that criminalize certain conduct in our society based on public outrage and not with a rational premise. The danger lies in how fast the laws are being passed and executed with dire results and consequences. The prison system is about to explode due to these laws and the economy.

January 20th-22nd, 2011 - Day 147 to 149

I got a letter from a company called Prison Voices and they help individuals put up a bio page on the internet to seek assistance from all over the world.

My aunt sent me some money and I really needed it. I've got to order these books about lawsuits and trusts. I want to write my own trust but I want it to be a legal fund trust. I also need to learn more about lawsuits, how they are filed, and what the parameters for them are in relation to procedural defaults and the like.

I had planned on writing a letter to my case manager asking for a relocation to Kentucky, but I changed my mind. I don't want to cause any waves when it comes to me getting a year of halfway house. I believe that the less I do, the better things will turn out for me. I should stop thinking that I've got all of the answers and let God drive and I'll worry about the level of integrity in which I follow Him.

January 23rd, 2011 - Day 150

I've made up my mind to order the complete idiot's guide to lawsuits, the public domain, the complete living trust kit, and most likely a book on getting money to go to college.

It's 10:00 p.m. and it's count time. The Steelers have won the AFC championship again. The sports commentator said that we were tied with the Dallas Cowboys for the most conference appearances. For the first half of the game, the Jets were really flat and they took a while to really get going. They went down 24 points until right before the half when they got a field goal. I guess this helped them feel somewhat good about themselves. The problem was that time was not on their side. They tried a really good comeback, scoring 19 points in a short period of time. After scoring so many points, we stayed on the defensive and stopped trying to score more points. Big Ben did a lot of scrambling out of the pocket and after the game I couldn't believe how many people had gone for the Jets. The sports commentators couldn't believe how flat the Jets were. However, they played a really good game during the second half and they seemed really disappointed that they started to play late in the game instead of being prepared after they had such a great win against the New England Patriots. Superbowl 45 belongs to the Pittsburgh Steelers.

January 24th-27th, 2011 - Day 151 to 154

Was I arrested or rescued? I'm thinking about renaming my book, the subtitle anyway, as *Arrested or Rescued*.

I think I want my company to deal with distressed properties and assets, a trading floor, and import and export. The counseling thing I'll probably do on the side.

I've completed my first module from Nations University and it didn't seem very hard but I'll take my time to complete the Master of Religious Studies.

I've decided not to go on the web site or do the book order. I just don't have the money. I need to save as much of the money that was sent to me for as long as I can. I have to contact Calvin again and get the address of the university that he was telling me about. I'm interested in theology as well as some other subjects besides the pre-law undergraduate degree I'm pursuing as soon as I'm released. I really need to start working in my GED books and re-typing what I've written so that my book material stays uniform. I'll start typing this afternoon.

I've finally got a really good plan. My book series will be called PrisonProof and the following are the subtitles: 1. *Arrested or Rescued*, 2. *A Puzzling Education in Essays*, 3. *A Diary About Finishing Strong*, 4. *The Bird's Nest*, 5. *The Trust*, 6. *The Company*, 7. *Legal Aid Group*, 8. *Counsulere*, and 9. *U. S. Passport*. My conglomerate will start as a sole proprietorship and evolve into a full-fledged company.

I want all of my lectures to be transcribed and the first appearances should be reimbursed with a letter of recommendation. I'm thinking about making the controlling stock to be divided up according to the following formula. 75% to me, 5% to the ghostwriter, 5% to the security lawyer, 5% to the export/import president, 5% to the distressed assets president, and 5% to the trading floor president.

Chapter Six: Portia Hunt

My aunt, this beautiful woman, has been by my side when times were really hard for me. She gives out tough love and will not take any bullshit from me or anyone else. She is a very powerful woman intellectually and spiritually.

When she introduced me to Siddha Yoga, she helped save my life. During my entire incarceration she was ready and willing to pay for any type of education that I wanted to pursue. She wanted me to learn how to self-educate and seek my formal education when I can.

She is a full-time professor at Temple University and a career business woman. She has been in the lives of me and my siblings since we were born and she has been even more present in our lives since our father passed in 1998. She is another angel that God has put in my life.

January 28th, 2011 - Day 155

I came up with a formula for the book I want to write about education. My education is what I call very puzzled and it has to be put together by someone who's involved to help others understand. I'm glad I've finally made my mind up about how I want to proceed with the books.

When I went to dinner tonight, one of my students named Freddie was eating alone so I decided to sit with him and talk a little bit. Freddie told me that I should try to go back to law school and see if I can do it without having to get a job. He told me that's how the rich people's children helped themselves get really good grades and their parents knew that they'd do a lot better if they could concentrate on their studies.

I've been thinking about taking English as my minor so that I can have excellent writing skills. I honestly believe that I have a real interest in the elements of English grammar. I believe there is magic in words, especially if you can arrange them in a way that really inspires someone to act or suggest your book to a friend. Obviously, since I plan on going back to school, I plan to do a lot of writing.

I got a reply from North West Vista College but they told me that they don't have a degree program for braille. However, their sister school has a program at San Antonio College.

January 29th, 2011 - Day 156

It's 9:00 am and I'm sitting here brainstorming about how I want to start this company. I think I need to start with a duplex or a four-unit building. Whichever one is the cheapest. This should be a very good situation for me and the people that I may have working for me. I realize that there will be individuals who I would want helping me but they may decline to do so. This is also the technique that my aunt Portia had incorporated.

I guess I need to start reading some books on starting a publishing company. I primarily want to publish memoirs, whether spiritual or personal. However, if I'm not able to get enrolled in school, I will find another job and still start my company as soon as possible. I think I'm going to change the structure of the way I set up the different companies that I had planned. I should start each one individually from scratch and figure out a formula for each company. So, the first business plan will be for the publishing company.

January 30th, 2011 - Day 157

I got another idea about a book about going to college and I'm going to name it *The Bird's Nest. The Bird's Nest* will be about my life in college. I want to enroll in college and do every class for my freshman, sophomore, junior, and senior years. I'm not interested in speeding up life.

I just spent the last two hours explaining to this guy why he needs to look into starting a legal defense trust fund. The trust fund could easily be set up with distressed assets, especially with all the foreclosures on the market. I don't think that this guy really wants to protect himself or his family for years to come. This setup would be a boost to personal finance statements in any business venture or especially if you leave the country. The commercial security provision must be insured so that the trust is very well-protected. Some attorneys may tell me that I should do this another way, but it had better be according to my needs.

I don't have the money to start buying the books about trust to start studying, but I've studied enough to know that I need to execute this trust because I don't have anyone to support me or help me if I ever get into trouble again. I also don't have a lot of support for business transactions because

I don't have a history in the business world.

When I'm released in 2012, there will be a lot of potential to make a living especially with the internet and this global market.

January 31ˢᵗ, 2011 - Day 158

It struck a nerve this morning when an inmate said that he was upset because he had been put back on the call-out to go to GED class. He said that he was going to take it up with the warden. I can't wait until I get out to enroll in college because once I'm in I'll never leave again. If I finish one degree, I'll just start working on another one when I get the next opportunity.

I found a workbook on essays and I immediately started to try to write one without working in the workbook first to study the components of an essay. Whenever I take the ACT test at the university I'm sure it'll have a part in which I'll have to write a really good essay. Moreover, I have to write an essay in pursuit of the Master's Degree in Religious Studies. I don't have another lesson to study right now, but I went and emailed Mr. Casteel and told him about the situation. I'm sure I'll have an email response from him sometime tomorrow. It's really hard for me to slow down when I get my mind set to accomplish something.

Mr. Lawrence said he was going to call the financial aid people to find out if I'm eligible for federal aid since I've got drug convictions in my past. However, I was not receiving federal aid when I caught my drug conviction.

February 1ˢᵗ, 2011 - Day 159

I just checked my email and I got a response from Nations University. Apparently, they have not received any of my exams in regards to BRS 16.6. My initial reaction was to get angry and upset about it but I already understand that I don't have control over how my exams are returned to the school. The two people responsible for the mailing are not here this week because they're on vacation. It really feels better if I just accept the fact that I've got to wait around until Mr. Hammond comes back from his vacation. When I get some more money I'm going to email Mr. Casteel and see if he would suggest to Mr. Hammond to fax the tests from now on so that there are no problems.

One of my buddies left the room when I was teaching him about finances and what he needs to do to buy a house. He really needs to start out with distressed properties and work his way into bigger properties. He said he had some investors that want to give him a large sum of money to begin with, but he's got to get more of an education under his belt. He's got to stay in his own field of knowledge or else he'll get taken advantage of.

February 2ⁿᵈ, 2011 - Day 160

The wind was blowing so hard this morning that the staff recalled everyone back to the unit. The wind actually set off the sensors on the fences and scared the staff.

One of the guys that I had talked to about real estate earlier this week received some information on houses that were on sale. The average cost was about $10,000. He seemed really excited about getting the information.

The NYT is reporting that the president of Egypt is considering stepping down sometime in September, but it appears that this is unacceptable. President Obama has sent an envoy to speak to the 80-year-old president to slowly ease him out of power. They don't want another revolutionary war. This same type of revolution was taking place in Iran, but the military began killing its own citizens. I think that the Iranian people should go back to protesting in light of the developments in Cairo.

I had Mr. Shackelford fax lessons to Nations

University because of the email I got from them advising me that they're not receiving my lessons. It feels really good to know that it has been taken care of.

February 3rd, 2011 - Day 161

One of the staff helped me with finding out my grades on my first five exams and I failed one of them. I have to score a minimum of 70% or I have to repeat the exam. I have three opportunities to re-take the exam but that will not be necessary in my case. They also sent me a letter saying that they've accepted my credentials and I've been accepted into their university. There's a form that I've got to fill out and return so I can be formally admitted. They didn't accept my transcript from Ozark Technical Community College but that's okay because it's really good that I start from scratch. I don't believe that the school is regionally or nationally accredited, but they have applied for the national accreditation. The date of my acceptance letter is January 31st, 2011.

This is the second week that they've cancelled the ACE classes due to pure laziness. You can tell that these people don't care about their jobs, at least some of them. But it really doesn't matter because they work for the federal government and they really don't give a shit about inmates.

February 4th-6th, 2011 - Day 162 to 164

We watched a movie called *Robin Hood* and the statement, "Forgotten men are dangerous men," is so true that I want to name one of my books after it. I believe that there are a lot of forgotten men and there will be a lot of forgotten men in the future.

I'm starting to believe that starting a publishing company would be a better job than I thought. I read a book by a lady that talked about how she started her company and how it took time to become successful... I really need to get out of prison and start moving forward with my life.

The essay workbook was a really good idea because I'm learning a lot from it. I think I need to keep working in them and I'll eventually get better with a little practice.

It's 10:30 and the Steelers just lost Superbowl 45 and it sucks. We had too many turnovers and we let our defense collapse. We have got to start drafting for our secondary. I understand the loyalty the Steelers have for their players but we need to start looking for someone to replace our secondary. They're terrible and Troy can't do it all by himself.

February 7th-8th, 2011 - Day 165 and 166

I got an email today from Mr. Casteel and he has informed me that there are several colleges that accept credits from Nations University. I was quite relieved to learn that bit of news. Mr. Casteel is becoming a valuable resource for me. He suggested a couple of colleges that accept Nations credits and the one that I was most interested in was Limpscomb in Nashville, TN. I can acquire my doctorate in theology and a juris doctorate of law as well.

Today I submitted a request for relocation to Nashville, TN so that I may pursue my degree and build on this new education. Mr. Casteel also warned me that the next module that I'm about to test on is the hardest out of all modules and I may have to re-take one or all of these exams. Now that he has warned me, I feel it behooves me to *really* study, break these modules down, and reconstruct them as I move forward. I need to study for their exams the same way I studied for my Nemeth, only this time I'll pass all of the exams. Sometimes I wonder what other courses Nations offers and how much they cost.

I hope my transfer request is approved by the probation

office. I'm going to write him a letter to let him know that I've submitted a request for a relocation of my supervised release. I might even send judge Steihl a copy of my letter. I need everyone to be on the same page. I hope that the request is forwarded as soon as possible.

I've submitted a lot of my work to the judge so that in the future he can have some material to review in regards to any progress I've made. The years go by and some forget who they may have sentenced while others will never forget who they've sentenced.

February 9, 2011 - Day 167

I cleared a lot of my debt today and I always say I'm not going to borrow anything on credit. I'm prepared to put forth a little more effort this time because I don't like the way people treat me when I do business with them.

I talked to the unit manager again today about my relocation and she told me that I really don't have anything to worry about. I'm about to send my probation officer a letter explaining what I've done and that I need his help. I think she's going to be in the cafeteria during lunch. I might just go to her office in R&D and give her a copy of the letter I'm sending to the probation officer and the judge that sentenced me.

Chili Mac was on the menu today for dinner and I'm really tired of eating the same foods day in and day out. However, it could be worse. I could be in China, Russia, Afghanistan, Somalia, and so on.

I've got to set a schedule to study so that I can make really good grades and be accepted into the master's program at Nations University. If I maintain a B average, I'm automatically enrolled in the master's program.

While working in the career center researching other colleges and talking to some of the guys with master and doctorate degrees, I found out that most graduate programs require that you maintain a B average throughout the process or risk being dropped for lack of academic progress. A C average just does not cut it in graduate school. I gather that this is a serious consideration in regards to law school.

February 10, 2011 - Day 168

After about three weeks of delays, I finally went to business class and we had a really good discussion. The investor's deposit is to be offset or secured by insurance or a letter of credit. The assets of the corporation must never be encumbered by debt when there are other ways to present collateral. I also need to remember that I can have as many classes of stock that I want. However, the classes of stock must be designated with a specific purpose.

I also found out that I need to bring my lawsuit for unlawful conviction into the US Federal Court of Claims. One of the guys with a Bachelor in Paralegal Studies told me that all of the states have a federal court of claims. I'm not really sure about that, but I'm sure I'll learn about this in pre-law.

I sent copies of my request for relocation to my probation officer with the hope that he does not have a problem with me re-locating to Nashville, TN.

I got confirmation today that you can receive financial aid with a drug conviction as long as you didn't get the drug conviction while receiving federal aid. One of the guys wants to see my student aid report so that he knows what they look like, I guess.

I think I'm going to stay up late tonight because my New York Times is pretty thick; it should be some really good reading. I can't believe that I'm still working on this journal.

My business teacher wants me to bring him my business plan on Thursday to share with the class. Obviously, my plans aren't ready to be presented to the class just yet, but as I move forward in the process of building them, I will revise them to be more productive. I started a few different business plans but didn't finish them. I need to do some more research at the library, as much as I can at this institution.

February 11, 2011 - Day 169

I realized today that I've got to learn to adapt and change when necessary. Mr. Lawrence really taught me something about considering a college education. I was not as ready as I thought I was and doubted his knowledge and the information that he had for us; I told him that there are a lot of people that would love to talk to him and ask questions and get some real help. I also realized that I need to study a lot more than I have been because it only gets harder from here on in.

Mr. Lawrence has made me re-think my decision about law school and sociology. With my background, I'm sure I can use either degree to help underserved people and the oppressed. I do believe that God has a plan for me and I want to be involved with His plan first. I know God's grace is with me at all times.

I got an email from Mr. Casteel telling me that I was getting ahead of myself and that I needed to be patient. I pretty much knew I was asking too many questions, but I just can't help it. I want to thoroughly investigate everything that I'm involved with. However, I've decided to just lay back and take it easy and study a little harder. I know one thing for sure: these schools are very expensive to attend, especially if you're paying for a meal plan and housing.

We took a look at Limpscomb and it was a very expensive school, especially for out-of-state students. To be eligible for in-state assistance you must have lived the state for at least the last year and paid taxes. The out-of-state tuition is the primary profit center for most colleges because these fees appear to be based on the fact that you're taking a spot originally meant for an in-state student. I think I'm prepared to accept some large fees due to the fact that I really want to get enrolled in college before I'm released from prison. I've researched financial aid and they're only able to do so much. However, I learned it's better to apply to several schools and review your award letter to see which school is offering the best options in regards to your ability to pay the loans off when you leave school.

February 12, 2011 - Day 170

I want to go to the store on Monday and get some candy on credit, but I've had enough of going to the store for other people. I'd rather be broke and have no sweets than deal with that bullshit again. I've tried several times to stop using credit but I've gotten to the point now where I'm just sick and tired of it.

I really don't think that I should go to school unless I can pay for the classes. Starting out at the community college will definitely allow me to use Pell Grants to attend school and I won't have to worry about the cost too much. I'm definitely going to be working because I don't have the money to pay for my living expenses and attend school full time. Plus, trying to start my publishing company will be a real challenge... but I feel I'm up to it.

I don't know if I'm marriage material but I really believe that it's time for me to settle down and get married. I really don't know how good of a father I would be, but I've got a few good ideas. My experience is being a child of an abusive father that was present while I was growing up. I made a lot of bad decisions because I wouldn't listen and I put myself in danger a lot of times because of my stupidity.

These idiots that live on my floor just keep walking back and forth in front of my door. For some reason they believe that the bathroom is their personal residence. One of the guys is on his way home tomorrow or Monday and he's walking around saying his goodbyes. Pitt almost died in this place a couple of times but he'll have a hard time once he's released. He's definitely going to get himself some drugs and alcohol. I think he believes his days are numbered so he wants to have all the fun he can. Pitt worked with me in Unicor in the packing and shipping department. He had no patience and his tolerance level for the staff was not very high.

February 13, 2011 - Day 171

I need to create a schedule for myself in regards to studying because I've got a lot of stuff on my plate. I definitely need to wrap up all of my Adult Continuing Education classes so that I can spend that time reading my newspaper. I want to study my courses at Nations every day. I have to make sure that I maintain a 3.0 average. If I don't maintain this average, I'll have to take the course all over. I'm still waiting to find out my score from the re-take of exam #2. I have to keep reminding myself that I'm not in a hurry and I'm not in a competition with anyone, I just need to strive to get really good grades.

I don't know what is going to come of the young people in Iran but they appear to want to take advantage of this event in Egypt. Their problem is that the military and the police of Iran will kill them if they protest like they did in Cairo. I was surprised to hear on *Meet the Press* that the new house speaker, John Boehner, believes that Obama has done a good job with the crisis in Egypt. There still seems to be a lot of ignorance in this country about whether President Obama is a Muslim or not. It showed me that there are still a lot of uneducated individuals in this country.

President Obama won by 10 million votes last election and he'll probably win by at least a million this time.

I've been looking at the republican party to see who is going to become their presidential candidate. It appears that Mitt Romney is going to be their first choice. I think I heard a report about Mr. Romney bypassing Iowa and moving on to another state, maybe South Carolina. The polling must not be in his favor. The voter laws are being attacked in a lot of the southern states and a lot of guys could really care less about what's happening with the voting rights act.

February 14-15, 2011 - Day 172 & 173

I can't believe that all of these guys that are spending the majority of their time working out actually believe that someone is going to hire them to work out. Since starting to read, write, and study, I've never felt so liberated before in my life. None of the guys are paying attention to what's going on in the Middle East and how they are really blessed living in this country. A lot of them never realized that they don't have to commit crimes to be wealthy; all it takes is a little education. I understand that it's a really easy thing to propose after you've realized your years of folly. But some of these guys can do a lot better if only they would get an education.

The Lexington Herald Newspaper is coming sometime this week or next and I think they really want me to give an interview. I remember when these people were supposed to come years ago and never showed up; I'm having deja vu.

The NYT is reporting that several states are experiencing budget deficits that are requiring them to cut pensions, education, and medical services. However, some of the states are prepared for these types of situations. A lot of those states are in the Midwest, Utah, Nebraska, South Dakota, North Dakota, and so forth. I wish I knew how

Tennessee was doing right now.

I submitted the paperwork for a re-location to Nashville, TN, but I've heard that our case manager is really busy and she's having problems with guys' dates for halfway house residency. She told me that it was going to take a while, but I really don't know how to quantify that statement. I don't want to bother her because then she'll start feeling pressured and not want to help me. Her caseload does appear to be rather large.

February 16, 2011 - Day 174

I've been thinking about how I'm approaching the future and I may make a few changes. I think I should contact a self-publishing company and have them publish my series under the title PrisonProof. I really need to focus on school and getting a job as a paralegal. However, if I'm not able to do that then I'll have to resort to a legal aid office. I really don't know how difficult it will be in regards to finding work as a paralegal or legal assistant.

My next move will be to finish my Master's in Religious Studies at my own pace. I'll probably use my summers to work on this degree until I'm done working on both of my degrees. I probably shouldn't start working on my company until I'm done with school. Oh yeah, I almost forgot about the claim I want to bring against the government for unjust conviction. If I win this claim, the monetary damages that could be sought in a Federal Claims Court should be enough to help me with law school.

I really want to make sure that I' m not in a hurry to finish the courses. Everybody is planning to take courses with the intent of finishing so that they can get into the job market. I'm really not interested in the job market. I just want to take my time to read, write, and study.

I plan on studying for the next 30 or 40 years. I want to enjoy life in a different way... maybe one day I could be a professor or a lecturer. I don't understand what there is to do if you retire and sit at home. You're simply going to spend money, which is okay, but that will deteriorate into laziness. I believe that writing books is the foundation to having a solid start, if you can do it. I believe that the 10 books that I've mapped out for myself will benefit me greatly in the future. After my law degree, maybe I'll enroll in business school. I should have the money to be able to. I might not really need to because of what I know and will learn in pursuit of the law degree.

I'm in the Career Resource Center now and there are very few guys who pay this place any attention or even visit.

February 17, 2011 - Day 175

I just got my certificate from the Socio-Economic and Business Development class and it was definitely a good use of my time. The ACE coordinator came to our class to respond to a complaint form some of the guys about how the certificates were made up. She appeared to be saying that she was deceived by what the class has evolved into and that the class is cancelled until further notice. Ms. Thompson was at fault because she should have cancelled the class as soon as the people teaching the class went against what they wrote on their curriculum.

She informed the class that the certificates that are given in the classes don't mean anything and are not accepted on the street by anyone as a credible document. She said the way for you to receive credibility is to go to college. I felt that her statements were an insult to the men that could not afford to attend college, and if they had any hope in regards to trying to learn or better themselves... well, she just made them feel that they're wasting their time.

What I really should've done was stay out of it and let

it run its course. Ms. Thompson made some real accusations in regards to books needed for the class, which were ordered and not used. I believe that they both were wrong because once they did not follow the plan, she should've shut them down. Also, they should've stuck to what they told her that they were going to do. It appeared to me that Ms. Thompson was very flexible in her approach to the situation, but as always, there are two sides to every story.

I swear I don't want to be an employee but I must in the beginning stages of being released. The whole situation with the business class was really bad and the things that were said were totally unnecessary.

Some of the guys and I did some mock job interviews today and I performed poorly. I guess it's because I've been incarcerated for more than 15 years.

February 18, 2011 - Day 176

I'm helping with the re-entry program being developed by the Supervisor of Education who is leaving this year to retire. I don't have any clue who is going to be the new supervisor and I really don't care.

I've not heard anything from my case manager on the relocation, but I've heard more complaints from other inmates about her lack of competency or efficiency.

I can't believe how these idiots here love playing with the police. This institution is non-violent, but it's really not a good place to begin doing your time. I don't want to encourage violence on anyone, but sometimes things need to be explained in a certain way. I spent a lot of my life behind bars and under some kind of pressure. It really hasn't been stressful because I don't have any children or expenses to worry about.

My aunt has told me in her last few letters that she is sick sometimes. I hope she's doing a lot better.

I'm really enjoying reading my newspaper every night.

I've been thinking about getting married and I'm reserved to the fact that I want her to be enlisted in the military. I'm sure there's some dating site that has some of these women on there looking for Mr. Right. I don't know if I'm Mr. Right, but I'll try if the right woman presents herself. I want a military woman because she's used to structure in her life. This might be my type of woman.

February 19, 2011 - Day 177

How can one addiction help counter another addiction? I know that this will really be a controversial name for a book.

I've been re-evaluating my options about the legal classes and I remember something that Mr. Jefferson taught me about the government having records about everything that I do. However, I think that I'm really going to enjoy taking sociology. I love social studies and I'll probably add some political science classes as well. I would make legal studies my minor. The road for me to get a doctorate in theology is already laid out for me.

Having a career as a writer doesn't sound that bad. I'm really interested in real estate but I just don't want to deal with a lot of people. I really want to stay focused on my studies and find a job. The prospects for paralegals are great and I'm going to have an inside line to some law firms in Nashville, TN. I think the re-entry coordinator is going to help me get a job in TN if I'm released there. Moreover, it really doesn't matter because if I have to go back to Illinois, I'll probably return to Edwardsville.

I don't think I want to study for the ACT. I know I don't have all of my general education studies done yet and I want to go back to school to learn them. It really doesn't matter to me that I have to start over because I'm going to enjoy this time I spend in school.

One of the guys got a letter from a high school sweetheart and she wanted to hook up and start a relationship again. She told Marty that she had a bachelor in science and that she wanted start a night club. Marty needs to stay really far away from this woman.

February 20, 2011 - Day 178

I studied the Hebrew Scriptures today in one of my courses at Nations University. I realized while I was reviewing the modules ahead that this course covers the entire Old Testament. I've read the entire Old Testament but I didn't try to memorize every fact. Our next test consists of multiple choice questions asking for facts. A lot of re-reading the first five books called the Torah should help me become more familiar with the course.

Today one of the guys asked me how to clean a hundred thousand dollars. This guy wanted me to teach him money laundering techniques. I should have just said no I don't know. I thought about really showing him for free hair cuts for the remainder of my stay at this institution. They'll be back to ask me again and we'll see what happens. I've got to remember that they could be confidential informants.

I've learned that men in my position that want to move forward in this country must be willing to return to school and learn a new trade. I think I should go for the AS in paralegal studies and start working as a paralegal. If I'm rejected by the probation office in regards to my request to TN, then I should proceed to Illinois and make the best of it. I want to follow God's lead on this thing but it's hard for me to just let go of my control.

I went down to the chapel to get a book on the Old Testament and I found a really good one. It had the geography of the entire Biblical episode, the Old and New Testaments, as they were developed over the years.

I've started working on my resume and it's a real pain in the ass. But I've got to do it to get a job, or at least try to put one together. I don't think it's going to matter what format it is in but the substance of the work and training programs should highlight the resume... at least I think that's the way it should be.

February 21, 2011 - Day 179

Today was the day that the talent show for Black History Month was happening and some of the guys wanted to make sure I was there. Cowboy was scheduled to put on a show. He was scheduled to do the speech of Martin Luther King and a comedy skit for Black History Month. The concert was really good and I'm glad that I went. I can't wait to see Cowboy so that I can tell him how good a job he did. I really enjoyed myself and I usually don't attend big functions.

I was with some guys down the hall that were working on drafting a complaint against a trial attorney that may have given this guy some really bad advice. I asked them what jurisdiction they are proceeding under and they read me the Biven's case. I do not believe that they can proceed under that case, but the court will let them know. They're submitting the document in writing in an attempt to encourage the court to appoint a CJA attorney. I don't know the language or the statute to sue a lawyer for malpractice in a federal court. However, since they're working for the federal government, I should be able to sue under federal jurisdiction. I could file a claim right now but I want to wait until I'm released so that I may put my claim together in the best possible way. I'll probably need some help but that's just fine.

Today, I realized that I just need to slow down and try to enjoy the courses from Nations University. I'm so hyper that sometimes I can't believe how fast I'm moving, especially if I'm cleaning or just working with my hands. Sometimes I miss working in the kitchen, running around like my hair's on fire. The cleaning and scrubbing takes your mind off of the streets or any beef that you may have with your family on the outside.

February 22, 2011 - Day 180

The entire Middle East is on fire and President Obama has his hands full. The president of Libya is trying to kill every one of his citizens, according to CNN and the New York Times.

The republican governors are trying everything that they can to deconstruct the public sector unions. There are so many battles brewing around the country, especially in the states that are taking legislation like Wisconsin and New Jersey.

Afghanistan and Pakistan are going to continue to be a problem, even for the next president. I hope President Obama is elected to a second term; however, I don't believe that he'll win by 10 million votes again. Maybe one million, but he will win again!

I continue to believe that middle-aged men around 40 have no other choice but to return to college and re-leverage their marketability in regards to employment.

Some people from the Lexington Herald Newspaper came to interview the braille class and some guys felt that they were treated like idiots. I refused to be a part of the circus, but I still believe that this program is being run recklessly and inefficiently. The braille coordinator is incompetent at best and really doesn't care about braille.

I talked to my case manager today and it took us about an hour to get on the same page about my relocation for supervised release. Mr. Lawrence said that he would help me with the transition to Tennessee and that he would pay my case manager a visit. Some of my plans I want to keep to myself. She said she's going to see if they were interested in allowing me to relocate based on educational purposes. If they decline, I won't argue and I'll just relocate in Illinois. I just have to decide which school I want to go to. I'll have to keep a close watch on this.

February 23, 2011 - Day 181

Today, a couple of youngsters were about to fight, and as usual, some idiots broke up the fight. I believe that they should've let them fight and learn from their mistakes. I believe that coddling the boys trying to be men is one of the reasons that we're having so many young men becoming confused about their manhood. I don't want to promote fighting, but we must be allowed to fail and to learn from failure, and fighting is a failure to communicate. I don't believe fighting or turning into a savage is what makes you a man. However, I don't want to suppress the learning experiences that they need to go through.

The way some of these guys carry themselves is really ridiculous. I may seem harsh, but that comes from years of being in prison, drug rehab, and jail. I really don't want to see them fight, but sometimes you have to. I do believe that walking away from a dispute is the best example. This is a hard thing to do for young men. But someone who gets in the middle of the wrong fight usually gets stabbed, anyway. When these fools get themselves stabbed or cut a few times, they usually stop being the hero.

The prison system is losing its rules of the road and there's going to be a lot of blood and violence in the future, even if they've got 10 or 20 years remaining on their sentence. Every man learns at his own pace. Some men need to learn the hard way to humble themselves.

Violence is never the answer; however King David was not a humble man while killing thousands of people. The Bible says that God condoned slavery but all of the blacks' churches believed what the Bible says. Some of the treatment slaves received was not authorized by the Bible, but shit happens when you're under the authority of another person. I guess what I'm trying to say is that violence and slavery went hand in hand throughout history, especially Biblical history.

February 24, 2011 - Day 182

I got a new idea from one of my guys to help me with my studying. I'm going to publish a book called *PrisonProof: The Diet Kitchen*, but I need to start taking notes right now. Marshal suggested it as a jailhouse diet plan based on the food these guys eat and the regimen that they go through. I don't know if I'll be able to put together an entire book based on what these weight lifters eat and their exercise regimens. It'll be hard because I normally don't pay the weight lifting pit too much attention. However, the weightlifters are not the only ones watching their weight and health for that matter.

This place is supposed to be a medical center but sometimes it is a co-dependency of eating whatever is in front of you. The commissary is absolutely horrific when it comes to being a diabetic or having some other chronic condition. The dieticians at the facility do check your commissary receipt and weight once a month to determine if you're working the program to actually lose weight. I haven't seen anyone come in skinny and leave out really fat. I've seen some leave with more stress and anxiety than they had coming into the institution, though.

I need to pay more attention to what I purchase from the commissary and how I exercise (or don't exercise) anymore. I know running up and down three flights of stairs is some really good exercise, especially when you're doing it all day long, day after day and month after month. And then you wake up one day and find you've been doing this for about eight years and counting. But you realize that there is always some older man here who is sicker that's getting it done one day at a time. It can be done and it's true that God doesn't give you more than you can handle and he's always pushing you to fail and learn.

February 25, 2011 - Day 183

Today was not productive enough for me. I should've gotten a lot more accomplished but I washed clothes and watched a little television.

The president of Libya is killing his people because they protested without violence about the condition in which they live in their home country. Mr. Quaddafi took control of the country about 40 years ago and he ran the place as if it was his personal business. However, all dictators do something similar to oppress the population and control them. I really don't understand why these oil-rich countries treat their citizens like dogs. These countries make billions of dollars and it would not cost them much to share it with their people. Why don't they start with oil revenue sharing? Give the people $10,000 or $5,000 a month as a stipend to let them share in the wealth of the county, like Saudi Arabia. The Middle Eastern countries don't really want any form of democracy because it opens the door to them losing control over vital assets of their country. I'm surprised the military has not made the president resign and leave the country. This man has lost his bearings and he has done so on national television. I believe that this is going to cause oil prices – along with other commodity prices – to rise substantially in the near future.

There are about 1800 men incarcerated on this compound and you might find 250 that have any clue about the situation in Egypt, or any news at all for that matter. The new re-entry coordinator is really trying to find jobs for some of the guys that are working for him. He helps whoever he can if they truly want his help. Some days, Mr. Johnson doesn't have the time to work individually with guys but he tries to assist the best he can or is allowed.

February 26-27, 2011 - Day 184 & 185

The movie committee in the recreation department here at the institution has some real issues when it comes to selecting cartoons for 1800 incarcerated men. Tim and I walked back into the unit from the barber shop and Tim called the guys sitting in front of the TV, "pedophile playground." He said he knew he had to watch cartoons with his little girl but he doesn't feel he should watch them with grown men.

I personally don't think we should be watching cartoons but some of these guys are still in their pre-adult stage and find it kind of hard to evolve into a mature adult. The first thing you'll find out about being incarcerated is that just because you're old enough to be an adult doesn't mean you're mentally prepared to conduct yourself in a mature manner.

I'm starting to hear a lot about the crack law becoming retroactive at the end of the year. This is very encouraging because I really don't want to remain in prison until November 5, 2012. I believe that my incarceration from this point forward won't help deter others from committing a crime.

It's time for Obama to start strategizing about his future campaign and who his competition will most likely be. I watched *State of the Union* this morning and Senator John McCain and Senator Joe Liebermann were being interviewed from Cairo, Egypt. As usual, they went right after the Obama administration for not being more proactive in regards to the rebels, the opposition to Kaddafi, and his mercenaries and assassins. The opposition has taken the city of Tripoli and they'll probably run Colonel Kaddafi out of the country.

I believe that these harsh economic times are just what the doctor ordered. These are the types of occurrences that allow for systems, processes, procedures, and offices to be shaken up and rearranged for better or worse. However, you still wind up with some change and the effectiveness of the change is in the eye of the beholder.

The president's election in 2012 is going to be a wonderful political experience for me because I'll be out of prison for the election. It was really depressing to be in prison when President Obama won the first primary in Iowa; however, I'll be present for several of the next elections.

Chapter Seven: Leroy Washington

This man served his country by enlisting in the military. When he came home, he worked for Union Electric Company for three decades and retired in Southern Illinois. His lovely wife, Debbie, has been by his side for many years. Even though he is retired he has stayed active in golf and part-time jobs.

My uncle never treated me different because of my problems and supported me the best he could. He has always wanted his nieces and nephews to grow up and learn to stand on their own merits. He wanted us to never walk around with our hands out because we were afraid of work or content with what we had. He is a shining example of an accomplished black man and the last of a dying breed.

February 28, 2011 - Day 186

Yesterday, one of the guys was telling me about what the government had tried to do to force him to cooperate with them. Mr. Jones said the government tried to give him a folder with another person's information so that he could testify against a person he had never met before. The federal government conviction rate is the byproduct of a corrupt prosecution office that uses Americans' ignorance against them. IF you were to explain these things to the regular guy on the street, they would call you a liar or write you off as a conspiracy theorist.

The NFL lockout is approaching and I don't think that they will come to an agreement. I believe the league wants them to go to 18 games but the players are saying hell no. It appears the owners have a four billion dollar fund just in case there is a lockout. The Players Association wants the court to issue an injunction to freeze the owner's access to the fund. If these guys do not save some of their money, they will be ill-prepared to live comfortably in their retirement years and beyond. I think the Players Association should start a pension fund for these guys so that they can be financially secure once they've retired.

My ambition is starting to be anxiety because my hands are tied in regards to what I can do while I'm incarcerated. I have to remember that I shouldn't be trying to speed up life.

I had 100 bags of tea and I can't wait to get back to my coffee, even though the price of coffee is going up because of the bad weather in Columbia. The Folgers in this commissary was at $5.00, and now it's over $6.00 and change.

Today, the probation office told me that I had to have a job and establish residency in Nashville, TN before I can relocate there.

My top dog, Ray Ray, embarrassed one of the COs.

Ray Ray was a little reckless when it came to talking business in public. You never know who's listening or what they will do with the information.

March 1, 2011 - Day 187

I had a conversation with a gentleman that was a patient at the Cleveland Clinic and he swears by its service. We wound up talking about how the judge had a conversation with the regional director about being able to take care of his health problems. In the judge's chamber, they assured the judge that the Bureau of Prisons would take care of the inmates' health care. When Mark reached the federal prison system, the regional director said screw the judge. To summarize, they will not give him his medicine, then they lost the battery pack to his pace maker, and were about to lock his butt up standing up for himself. His wife made repeated calls with good results and the staff really hated it.

I talked to the admissions counselor at SIU-C and all of my questions were answered to my satisfaction. I stayed on the phone and asked her all types of questions. However, I talked to two different advisors. I felt really assured that they would review my life and give me due consideration in regards to my admission request. This is a good day for me, especially when there are few to begin with. Just being on the phone with the university is encouraging on its own and the fact that they would assist me is even more so.

Sometimes I would tell some of the other guys about these conversations just to encourage them that their life is not over and to push forward. This has backfired on me because a lot of these guys don't believe that they can succeed at anything. Some people can't handle being successful and some are afraid of it. So some men choose to stay subpar due to their inability to embrace success and build on it. Some men don't want to try and fail because their family may have told them that this is exactly what their life is all about: failure. Standing up for yourself is another example of handling success in regards to prison. You get used to being denied or oppressed when you've been wronged or told you're wrong when you know that your right.

March 2, 2011 - Day 188

I just left the commissary and I bought a book of stamps for $8.80. The stamps are really becoming expensive. However, I used the entire book except for one stamp. I want SIU-E to understand just how important their evaluation is to me and that I take their consideration of me very seriously.

Since today is commissary, everyone is running around paying off their debts and gambling bets. Store day isn't like any other day of the week. It's one of the only opportunities you get to taste the outside a little bit.

Aunt Portia sent me a $50 money order and I think this will be the first time that she hasn't sent me $100. It doesn't matter what it is; I need it. I need to remember that it is God's grace that allows this to happen because the money came at a perfect time. I need $30 to submit with my admission application to Southern Illinois University Edwardsville. The money order making the money available immediately was not an accident or chance. It seems that every time I'm given a test of some sort and I proceed with integrity, the end result comes out in my favor. Moreover, I'm starting to realize that the consequences of my choices, bad or good, are aggregated in favor of helping someone else or hurting myself. I need to focus on always making my interactions with people a win-win situation.

Some of the guys that I work with in the education department are helping with resumes because they can't find anyone willing to help with some experience in resume building. However, some of the guys' techniques are unorganized and they really don't care what type of product that they give back to these guys. It's a volunteer program aimed at helping near-release guys with resumes and interviewing skills. I seriously doubt the guys plan on using these resumes and think that maybe they're just wasting my time. So, I always inform them that these resumes could be the beginning of an official biography to have all of their pertinent information in one location.

I believe a lot of the population that is 40 years of age or younger really don't have a clue that not planning for 30 years down the road *today* will cost them when that 30 year mark starts to approach. All the guys have to do is sit down and try to figure out what they want to have or be able to do in 30 years. Make a plan and get with it. Everybody just wants to play cards, lift weights, and watch television until it's time for them to go to bed or count time. I have done the exact same thing in my last two incarcerations and I saw how incapacitated I was in regards to education and work experience.

Today I sent my admissions package for Southern Illinois University Carbondale. I got a chance to talk to an admissions counselor and I think I sent all of the relevant information that's needed for me to get a favorable evaluation in regards to admission acceptance. I can count on one hand the individuals here who want to go to college and get married once they're released. I'm making the conscious choice to get married and settle down and stop the cycle of going in and out of prison. I don't know if a wife and children will help me slow down bit, but it will certainly be a change from my last 25 years.

This guy named Dave doesn't understand that he's doing a revocation of a Power of Attorney the wrong way. Dave's relying on what some guy is telling him because he's white and he assumes the white guy knows what he's talking about. I've been trying to explain to Dave the difference between a circuit court clerk and a county recorder. However, I have not had great success because he now has a very short window of time to act.

The Republican Party is going to do everything they can to make sure that President Obama is hen-pecked at any new accomplishments for the next two years. Even though the Democrats control the Senate and the appropriation bills come out of the House Ways and Means Committee, it's the appropriation bills that matter. I believe that a lot of our congressmen have gotten away with crimes, be it a misdemeanor or felony, maybe even some high crimes of treason? Power is very strong and will corrupt an individual who's not used to it or has been hypnotized by it.

March 4, 2011 - Day 190

Mr. Lawrence, the re-entry coordinator, went on the web today to try and find me a lawyer that specializes in social security disability claims. The Federal Medical Center in Lexington, KY does have social workers but I just don't think they're willing to help as much as everyone thinks. I really think that Mr. Lawrence is getting tired of the staff not appreciating what he does for re-entry, even though he could retire if he wanted to. After Mr. Lawrence and I talked a lot he mentioned that he may just retire even sooner. The majority of the staff here believe that if you go out of your way to help an inmate then you're somehow a lesser person than the rest of the staff. Or the staff believes that you should not be working at the institution.

Sometime this year I think the teacher's union was asked to make a decision in regards to higher healthcare premiums and higher contributions to their retirement funds. The teacher's union had a proposition on the table to take a five percent cut or lose 400 teachers. The union members voted to lose 400 teachers. I guess the union members showed their true colors when it came down to self-interest. Or maybe they knew they needed to purge a lot of underperforming individual teachers and this deal was one way to get started in that process.

I just came from downstairs in the unit watching the NAACP awards and the presentation that they did for the surgeon general that President Obama picked was really good. She has done a lot of good work for the poor and underprivileged. This is probably the only award show that I will watch and I really do enjoy the awards categories and individuals.

One of the things I really feel bad about is that I continue to see is the rape of women in Sudan and the Congo. I read another article that talked about how young boys are raped and they're never reported because of the potential of it being so humiliating. I don't understand how one rape could be more humiliating than another, but we need to understand. The Tibetan monks in their many protests have suffered the horrors of being violated repeatedly.

One of the guys that I've been locked up with for a long time has returned for violating his supervised release for the second time. He wants me to help him file a motion to quash two bench warrants for misdemeanor charges, but the Intestate Agreement on Detainer's Act doesn't compel law enforcement in other jurisdictions to act on these types of charges.

March 5, 2011 - Day 191

I had a guy come and talk to me about some comment that he had read on CNN. Because of some changes in the crack law, all states were required to reduce the sentence of all offenders remaining incarcerated because of the excessive sentences received. I never got the chance to see the quote, but I believe that he was correct about what he saw.

I've decided to file my social security disability claim myself. My kidney disease, possible mental defects due to excessive incarcerations, alcoholism, and drug addiction will be my grounds for the claim. I don't think that I'll be able to find employment because of these problems. However, it doesn't stop me from going to college. I also should get a referral to a vocational rehabilitation department. I'm thinking about filing my claim in writing myself initially, and when they send me the forms, I will ask one of the social workers to assist me with the application. I want to send my own written statement because I want them to know what I feel should be submitted. However, if it can be made better that what I've prepared, then I'm all for it. I'll probably wait until I file my claim before I try to secure an attorney. I think it may be a little hard to get an attorney to take my case this early. I guess being in prison may be a little problem, too.

I haven't heard anything from my brother in a long time. I guess he's still in Nevada, partying and chasing women. I really don't know what's going on with my cousins and aunts that I grew up with, either. But I'm a firm believer that out of sight is out of mind.

I think I will re-start my paralegal endeavors and make a little money. It's starting to get a little tight and my job is great, I just don't make more than $10 a month. I really don't like Unicor or being around a lot of people, so I take jobs where I've got a desk and some quiet time.

The institution had a medical emergency in the law library today. The law clerk collapsed while gripping his chest. Once the medical staff confirms that his blood pressure, oxygen, EKG, and temperature are all normal, they will not call the paramedics. I didn't know this and I've been incarcerated in the feds for more than 15 years.

I got two emails from FAMM and they're saying that the sentencing commission has started its process to make the temporary amendments created at the end of 2010 permanent. For the Sentencing Commission's amendments to become permanent, they have to go through the normal process that sentencing amendments go through. The process takes about a year to go through and includes a 60-day commenting period for the public and the rest of the time is reserved for congress to intervene. If congress chooses not to pick up the amendment and bring it to the floor for a vote or a change, then the amendment becomes law on November 1st.

I watched *Meet the Press* this morning and the congresswoman from Minnesota, Michele Bachmann, is really serious when she says that the Obama administration is a gangster government. I'm starting to learn that there are so many subtle ways to call a black man a nigger. I believe that this woman, who has a law degree, is really dangerous to herself and constituents. Mrs. Bachman's language will cause individuals to act out and I hope they hold her responsible for inciting a riot or mayhem. Mrs. Bachman is clearly causing the president to be put in harm's way.

I still haven't heard if the attorney general, Eric Holder, is going after Roger Ailes for conspiring to obstruct a federal investigation. The New York Times has reported on this extensively and I think the facts are pretty clear in regards to the law. Mr. Ailes instructed his subordinate not to cooperate with a federal government investigation, specifically failing to answer questions through omission of facts.

I haven't studied my course work from Nations in about a week, so I'll probably start getting back to reading and studying the Bible. Even though I study four to five days a week, I need to read, write, and study as much as possible to condition myself to concentrate for a long period of time on specific tasks.

I believe the African American men who do not have a formal education will have a rough time in the future. I want to go back to college because I want to learn, and learning must be a continuing part of life. I want to be a skilled writer to tell institutionalized persons that their life is not over and show them how not to make the same mistakes I made. I think a lot of individuals in drug rehabs and in society are on a path that's not sustainable, especially in these times.

March 7, 2011 - Day 193

I just finished talking to one of the guys that I've been incarcerated with for about 15 years. This is Owens' second time violating his supervised release; however, he doesn't have any more supervised release left to finish once he's released this time.

Owens told me about how he established a boarding house and some other endeavors that didn't reach fruition because he was not mature enough when it came to business. I think he's a good dude and he wants to turn over a new leaf and stop selling drugs. However, Owens had to make some moves to make ends meet on a few occasions. It always requires some risks but the severity of the risks depends on the drugs that are involved and this is how he looked at doing what he did.

It was about 6:00 p.m. and we were having this conversation in his 10-man cell, so his cellmates started to come in from work and recreation. We moved to my room and started talking about starting a non-profit. We also talked about some juvenile departments of corrections that allowed him to come in and speak to some of the youngsters. I don't know exactly what he told them, but Owens said he just told them how it was on the street after an extended part of your life is spent hustling. Owens said that they got something out of his story and I guess that's something positive for him to build on if he chooses to do so.

I want to be a little better prepared to talk not only to them but also to the adults in charge of them. It also appears that Owens needs to slow down and reevaluate what's going on in front of him. When we were housed in the Federal Medical Center in Springfield, MO in 2000, he was wild and loved to fight. But as we grew older, I quickly grew out of this bullshit and Owens still loves the power. I don't know if he's ready to settle down, but for some reason, he's contemplating marriage with the lady he met during this last release. Owens wants to have a little boy but he's not sure about having another child with his current girlfriend. The young lady did get her tubes tied without his knowledge; however, he initially wanted her to get an abortion. Go figure.

March 8, 2011 - Day 194

I prepared a package to be sent to Southern Illinois University Carbondale. I executed the check so that the ladies up front knew that the check was supposed to be included with the package. Today at mail call I got the certified mail receipt dated March 7, 2011. However, the money that was to be included in the package was still on my account. Now I've got to call the admissions office and alert them to the fact that my package may not have included the $30 because an error occurred on the part of

167

the business office at this institution.

I need the rest of the evening to work on my temper because when stupid shit like this happens it really pisses me off. I need to calm down and try understanding that somehow this is God's will. I understand it wasn't her fault, but it's really hard not to be pissed off about something so simple.

I called Binder and Binder and asked them about me forwarding my records several months ahead of schedule and they told me to wait 90 days until I was ready to be released and file the claim. The nice lady said I should contact them once I'm out. For some reason she was pitching me as if I might want another firm to do the claim.

I know my ambitions have rough edges, but this is the way I am and I'm most likely not going to change.

It's hard dealing with government employees due to them not suffering consequences for failing to complete tasks on time. This doesn't apply to all government employees, but in the Bureau of Prisons it's really prevalent. I just need to let go and let God do his work. It's really easy to say and very hard to accomplish. I really shouldn't worry because I have plenty of time to enroll and make sure that the money reaches the admissions office.

March 9, 2011 - Day 195

The staff in the business office really screwed up my application package by not sending the money order with it. A lady named Ms. Carter told me that I'm not getting my money back even though it was not my fault. However, when I went to lunch during what's called "mainline" (this is where all of the staff has to take shifts standing in the cafeteria to answer inmates' questions; it's a general open house for the inmates to talk to staff they don't have access to). I went to a man named Mr. Kinsel and he took my information and told me that he would look into the problem.

Earlier this morning, my counselor tried to help me, but I don't think he really understood what was going on. I called the admissions office and they told me not to worry about the application fee because it can be sent in at a later date. The admissions counselor told me to either get a waiver or send in the $30 as soon as I could. I'm going to call them and find out how I get my application fee waived.

March 10, 2011 - Day 196

No matter what you're buying at the commissary, it's a really good idea to keep all of your receipts. Not only do they provide you with a plausible alibi, they also provide you with a clue to help remember certain times, dates, special events, etc.

I had program review today and they feel that they really did something for me by saying that they're going to give me six months of halfway house. As soon as this new law or amendment is passed, the rest of my time will disappear along with all of my supervised release. I am prepared to start my lawsuit against the federal government about this unjust conviction in the eyes of the law. I know that they think I've forgotten, but I've got a rude awakening for them.

I got an email from Mr. Casteel and he said that he has sent the exams for BRS 1 again. So that means that Mr. Hammond has made a mistake and put the exams in his recycle bin, *again*. Mr. Casteel wants me to let him know if there's a problem with our proctor receiving our exams. I really hope that this is not interfering with our status. Mr. Hammond did give me some work to finish, but it's still not completed as of yet. I talked to him about my grade 2 and he said that he was going to check and see how many more grade 2s the department may have available. I talked to Ms. Eads and she wants me to keep this quiet. She didn't want a line of guys coming to her office inquiring about getting pay raises because they already stalk her about the bonuses that they've never gotten. I'll see what's really going on in my next paycheck. I'm sure that as soon as I walk into the job site tomorrow, Mr. Hammond will be standing at the front entrance to tell me he received the exams.

I have a very bad feeling that the 2012 presidential election is going to get very violent. There are a lot of people that are incarcerated and I believe that our prison systems will become a place of refuge for the elderly, sick, and ignorant. Not only will the federal prisons become very violent, they're going to turn into full-blown nursing homes. These prison jobs will be fought for tooth and nail because they're jobs for people who are unemployable at best or choose not to build a career of some sort.

March 11, 2011 - Day 197

It's 9:04 p.m. and I'm still drinking Folgers and will be up going to the bathroom all night long.

One of the guys who have been talking to me about his case for a few months just left my room. He finally sat down and explained to me exactly what is going on in his case and why he may need my help. It took me about an hour to get a grip on his situation and I believe that he will have one hell of a Motion to Correct, Vacate, Set Aside a Sentence pursuant to Title 28, United States Code Section 2255.

It appears his sentencing lawyer never objected to the government's grounds for a four-point enhancement that they admittedly couldn't prevail on. However, the defense attorney (according to the government's brief) failed to raise any objections to the government's request to apply the enhancement. I've a pretty good idea how his motion should've been done, but he may be better off if he gets some professional help. I have an impression he's got the money to ask for my help and I could use the money. I still think it's important that he gets some quality help since this issue is all he has between him and 17 years.

The professional help will charge him about $1,500 just to review the case and then they'll probably charge about $3,500 to $5,000 to do the motion and maybe his appeal.

I had a tough day at work trying to do two or three assignments at once. However, I believe that I'm good enough to get the job done.

I talked to the admission counselor today about my admission application fee waiver and she directed me to the school's web site where I can download the forms. The requirements are really easy to meet and I should have the form filled out and ready to go first thing Monday morning. I'm sure one of the staff members in education will help me get this done so that I will be able to enroll as soon as possible.

My main man, Mr. Shackelford, really helped me and a lot of other men get their lives together. He's helped people get certifications, pass exams, and get registered with the necessary agencies out in the real world. I don't know why we call it the real world as if the prison system in this country isn't part of the real world. All you've got to do is commit a crime and you'll see just how real it is.

March 12, 2011 - Day 198

At 11:30, I went to the chapel to watch some DVDs on Exodus because I'll be taking my next set of exams from Nations University sometime next week. I think watching the video will reinforce what I've already learned and help me start the process of training myself to remember.

Yesterday there was an earthquake and a Tsunami that hit Japan. The news said that their nuclear reactors are in danger and it really should be an all hands on deck type of situation. I'm pretty sure the Obama administration has extended a hand to the people of Japan. I believe that it is in the best interest of the international community to assist Japan. However (as usual), the president has one fire after another to deal with and there doesn't seem to be any sign of letting up any time soon. I believe that he is a lot better under pressure, but he's starting to collect a lot of gray hair.

I forgot to tell Mr. Lawrence that we can't all work together because he can't be around us for at least a year or two once we're released into the community. If prison staff comes into contact with and inmate, the bureau policy says that they must prepare a memorandum explaining the encounter.

I need to re-read my literature in religious studies a few more times so that I'm more familiar with some of the geographical sites and the stories surrounding them. I should also get a stronger grip on the people in these first five books of the Old Testament.

I'm starting to learn a little more patience and tolerance. My many years of Siddha Yoga have really helped ground me. I really need to meditate a lot more, especially when I'm walking to work and to class. Some of the guys want me to start some type of re-entry boarding house or program to house-released inmates. I'll probably wind up doing something like that in the future but I've got to build my future first so that when I start helping these guys I will be able to sustain my efforts for many years. One of my goals is to buckle down and study really hard until I'm about 50 or 55. I might be able to become a professor of sociology by the time I reach the age of 55.

March 13, 2011 - Day 199

I studied my lessons from Nations all this afternoon. I had to read Genesis for the second time and I couldn't believe all of the information that I had missed over the years of reading the Bible. I'm starting to remember how to learn, that re-reading material at least three to five times does help with memorizing the material and getting a better understanding. It feels like when you read something for the first time your eyes glaze over certain portions. However, when you read the material the second time, it is as if there were portions you totally overlooked.

I've got to constantly remind myself that I'm taking this course because I enjoy the material and I need to spend this time contemplating God, right vs. wrong, past vs. future, and my ability to help and not get angry. I've got to always remember that I'm one drink or one joint away from drug rehab or another prison term. Ever since I found out about my kidneys I've been really reluctant to even think about getting high or drinking again. I definitely do not want people around me that are using or have other addictions. I may try and stop them or counsel them in regards to the consequences but they'll ultimately have to make the decisions to stop themselves. I think I'll name another one of my books by using "Breaking Points" as a subtitle.

I really believe that I am going to enjoy taking sociology at the university. Moreover, I may not stay at SIU Carbondale and I may move to Minnesota or Washington or somewhere Northwest. I'm really against staying in Illinois, period. I understand that change has to be within you and that's where a real change starts.

I believe that after next week I'll be able to wrap up my efforts in regards to SIU-C and really start focusing on my Bachelor of Arts in Religious Studies. I completed my resume using some software set up in the computer class, but I need an official biography instead of a resume.

I forgot that daylight savings time has taken effect so I missed *Meet the Press*. I may be able to listen to it sometime late tonight on 590 AM radio. I forgot what time it comes on but I do remember hearing it late on Sunday on the radio before.

I went to mail call and I got packages from SIU Carbondale and SIU Edwardsville. SIU-E sent me a course outline for speech pathology and I really don't think that I'm cut out for that skill. Some of the pictures in the brochures were reassuring about the campus size. At this point in my life I just want to stay on campus and take everything really slow. I don't mind staying in college for four or five years acquiring my undergraduate degree.

The idea of making a living, retirement, and a family is really not in my purview. I want to spend my retirement in school. I don't want to go to beaches in Florida or Belize to retire. I would love to visit but the academia world is where I'm headed. I'm really interested in being a professor of sociology and I've got a really decent shot at it. Obviously, I'll continue Religious Studies and obtain my doctorate in theology.

I wasn't able to get a lot of work done on my lunch break but I need to break away from my partners who want to talk about nothing and gossip and complain about their environment. I got really sick and tired of listening to these guys talk about not going back to school, not supporting the mother of their children, not giving up drugs and alcohol, not challenging themselves to change, not willing to contemplate anything of substance, and not willing to engage in regards to political conversations. It appears that, in this unit, if you watch the news you've committed a grievous act, and *how dare you* turn this TV off BET.

I don't know how long it will be before I'm sent an admission letter but I really hope that they accept me and at least give me a chance to be a supportive part of the community. I can just imagine the looks on their faces when they receive applications from an inmate in federal prison.

March 15, 2011 - Day 201

I talked to one of the guys that self-published and he basically started his own publishing company. He mentioned Authorhouse and particularly didn't want to deal with them because of the fees that they charged. I was shocked when he told me that he had an initial run of 10,000 books. He said that it amounted to about $1.00 a book. All of his expenses put together its initial investment was about $12,000. I believe that once you set up your company and start selling books, you should start contacting the major bookstores to sign contracts to sell your products.

I think I should start the company in college and be well-established when I graduate and move on to graduate classes. There should be plenty of students to help me start the company if they can share in the proceeds. I forgot to ask him how many of his books he has sold and how he is getting the word out about his book. He said that after he started to get momentum, he was contacted by an agent and signed a contract to be represented from that point on. I believe that I can find all of this at the university.

I want to publish this diary first to introduce my thinking and ideas about my books and the company that I am going to start. It's difficult for me to tell my life in a book, so I've decided to use a few books.

March 16, 2011 - Day 202

Over time, through the collection of my series, a definitive guide will result in an experiment that began with a destitute, incarcerated, uneducated 40-year-old African American man. Sometimes, starting with nothing is really okay. No credit? Ok! No Debt? Ok! No Money? Ok! No

Job? Ok! So when do I start, who can I get to help me? The young men in and out of prison? Plus the new economy is going to put even more of a burden on men trying to be fathers or businessmen.

Some of the men think that it's too hard to change, to learn, to listen, to challenge themselves. Contentment is a good quality but not when it comes to taking care of yourself, your family, community service, and being a mentor to the younger community as a whole. Why? How far is a man prepared to go to get through to someone? What if it's a life or death situation?

Today, I was offered another job as an inmate companion participant. I guess it's something like hospice work. I want to keep my job in education because I'm able to study and attend GED classes and brush up on my general education skills. I am really weak in mathematics. The university told me that I was not required to take the ACT; however, if I'm able to score high enough, I could become eligible for some scholarship monies. "I may not become a successful author, but I am a success at trying with endeavors forever."

I talked to the tutor, Mr. Kelly, and he wants a new job, but he loves the freedom he has with working in education. I want to take the ICP job but I really need to be in the GED classes. It's hard for me to swallow my pride and sit in class while peers wonder why you're sitting in GED classes. I learned to overlook these guys because they don't see the future in my plan. The staff thinks I'm this liberal intellectual but I'm a mediocre student of politics and law. Everybody always watches me and wonders what I'm up to.

I really shouldn't go see the counselor, Mr. Smeeks, but I don't want to lose his confidence in my skills to do a job. Right now I make about $10 a month, and with Smeeks, I will make about $50. I'm going to try and hold both jobs, but I will not let go of the education spot.

This diary has become the symbol of my efforts at trying to do something to better my life.

Sometimes I wonder why people think that I've got a lot of money stashed somewhere. If it wasn't for my family this incarceration would've been really bad.

March 17, 2011 - Day 203

"A black sheep's path to redemption is one day at a time."

"We have legitimate right to the land of Israel," said Moshe Goldsmith, 47, the Mayor of Itamar. "The Bible is our deed."

I don't have any money on my account and I really don't have that much coming in. I owe $15 to my buddy and then I'm clean out of debt again. Humphrey wants me to find a calculator for him from education and he'll pay for it. I want to sell him mine to cancel all of my debts.

One of my buddies just gave me a book on algebra and I'm not at that point just yet where I can give it my full attention. I need to build a foundation first. That's why I want to spend the rest of the year studying in the GED classes, basically getting a refresher in all of the subjects.

I took the first exam in BRS 1 and I think I did really well. It didn't take me very long to finish the exam and I pretty much knew all of the answers except one or two. I still should receive at least an A on the exam. However, I do realize how I need to study to be able to pass the next four exams.

I talked to one of the black female guards about real estate and she's taking my advice and doing quite well with some rentals. She could do a lot better, but she has other priorities. She bought some of those trailers down in Louisiana that the Federal Emergency Management Agency tried to give the Katrina victims. I don't know if she knew that the drywall in those trailers were from a Chinese manufacturer and were deemed hazardous by the EPA and other government agencies.

March 18, 2011 - Day 204

I watched President Obama's speech today on C-Span and it appears we're about to not only destroy Iraq and Afghanistan, but Libya also. It appears the international community knows that Kaddafi and his family are not going to just walk away and give up power. Even more surprising was the fact that the United Arab Emirate, Qatar, and one more Arab nation are about to partner with western nations to impose international law and sanctions on another Arab nation. This appears to be another case of President Obama executing his duties with a steady hand while in control of the country's foreign policy.

While all the congresspeople are debating what and how much to cut out of the fiscal budget, President Obama's hands are tied in regards to what extent he can supply humanitarian aid. However, there are a lot of private organizations that do a lot of the heavy lifting. I have to make sure that I contribute to these organizations as soon as I'm financially able to do so.

I really miss reading the Foreign Affairs periodical because I loved reading the essays and the in-depth research and logic the writers brought to every subject, especially foreign policy. When I write my book using essays, it'll probably be one of my greatest personal accomplishments.

I haven't gotten any emails or letters from anyone in my family for a while. My Aunt Portia and my mother may send me a card every now and then but they're too busy with their own lives and I understand this. Sometimes I wonder if I'm supposed to be a messenger of God? What is my message? Am I supposed to be an advocate for prisoners? Their families? The handicapped or the blind?

The poor?

Sometimes I believe that we as Americans really don't understand in this day and age, what it physically and mentally means to suffer... to drink infested water, to defecate in water trenches in front of our hut or where we sleep. I know I don't have a clue. To be brutally raped repeatedly every day, all day, like the women in some of the African countries. Or maybe the human trafficking happening in Europe and China. A lot of the men in these institutions from other countries believe that if a man is an American and he's poor, it is because he has chosen to be in that state. I won't say that I agree, but I surely understand this point now that I've got several years of reading under my belt.

For some reason, the group on wall street doesn't want to draw any attention to their daily inside trading until the entire stock market is put into jeopardy. However, the executives and the investment bankers never get put into prison. But it's just like President Obama said, "What they were doing wasn't illegal, however, it was immoral." Immorality is not a crime in this country, not yet anyway.

March 19, 2011 - Day 205

It's 1:51 p.m. on a beautiful Saturday afternoon and I'm reading, writing, and studying, as usual. I've decided that I wanted an education in history along with sociology, law, creative writing, and theology. I'm going to purchase all of the back issues of Foreign Affairs all the way back to 1922 and start reading. That should cover a good portion of history.

I'm going to make *Empty-Handed but not Empty-Headed* a series, but what kind of series is still up for discussion. I really need to get out of prison and into the university. I feel that I need to be a part of something simple that involves me and not a lot of employees.

I'm starting to hear about guys that want some legal work done and it just so happens that I'm back in the market for some work. My pay will not be increased but I do have ways of helping my situation just by coming out of my so-called retirement. I had been saying for years that I was done but I've got expenses and I'm tired of writing my aunt and begging for money.

I'm going to have to think of another series to start besides *Empty-Handed*.... If I were to get a series under this title after I get my master's then I'll definitely be publishing another book series and it'll probably be a children's series. I need to think of a series involving a convict while he has been released or while he was in prison. However, my life is a story, a real story with twists and turns and excitement. It just needs to be told in a really creative way to engage the reader. I'll come up with a purely fictional story after a couple of years at the university.

My health is okay but I haven't seen a specialist in about one year and that's not good. My time spent doing my yoga has all but disappeared. Sometimes when I move too fast or start bending and twisting like I'm eight years of age, I start to really feel the stiffness. I'll work it all out when I'm released. I just need this time to put my thoughts, plans, and ideas through some long contemplation.

Sometimes I wonder what my high school friends from St. Phillips Catholic High School in East Saint Louis, IL are up to. Chris, Herb, Terry, Shaun, Tiffany, Elisha, Monique, Stephanie, Trina, Ezzard, and a lot more.... It was the greatest time in my life. However, going to an all-black Baptist church and/or an all-white Catholic Mass was quite a bit to handle. Our parents made me and my sister, Angel, and brother, Dayle, go just to get us out of the house.

We just finished watching 60 Minutes and they covered two stories: the earthquake in Japan and the word, "nigger," in the Thomas Finn book. Some publishers thought it would be better to remove the word for the convenience of those who wish to use the text to teach without that word and use the word slave instead. I'm not interested in changing history to make my son or daughter feel better. Everyone who is an American needs to know the full history of this country, especially in its education system.

A while back, one of my buddies told me that the single letter used before the different series of state inmate numbers in Illinois over many years spelled out, "black man." Every decade, the Department of Corrections issued inmate prison identification numbers that started with a letter. If you look back and separate all of the letters, you will see that it spells out, "black man."

Whenever Japan has the capacity to restore itself, they will not have any natural resources that they'll be able to export. However, if any digestible product is able to be exported to America, I believe the first customer to receive any of these tainted goods will be the US prison system.

Earlier today, I overheard a conversation about a convict versus an inmate. When I first started doing time, some really old guys explained the difference as follows. They told me that a convict was the person that choose 12 ½. This number represents 11 jurors, 1 judge, and ½ a chance. A convict was someone that got convicted by a jury. Whenever a person pleads guilty, they are not convicted in the full definition as opposed to someone who was convicted by trial.

It's taken me a long time to realize the difference between men in regards to their perspectives. One of the major, primary things that need to be learned about any man is whether he sees life as a cup half full or half empty.

There is no such thing as a snitch. Any and everyone will spill their guts to the authorities if they push hard enough. I had plenty of opportunities to cooperate and get a reduced sentence before and while I was incarcerated.   I never cooperated because it was the way I was raised and didn't want to be known for that decision. However, there were many nights when I wish I would've cooperated because I wanted to get out of prison. But whenever I was put up to the microphone, I just couldn't do it due to my hatred for the prosecutor.

I'm starting to see that if I write my entries instead of typing them, I'm willing and able to expand on some of my ideas.

March 21, 2011 - Day 207

One of my old ideas was to start an institution to teach young people about the state laws in which they reside and the federal laws regarding crime. We all really need to be more aware of the laws of our society and that each of us needs to have legal defense funds developed to shield ourselves throughtout our lives. This should be another step in the process of realizing we're not prison proof.

The trust should be set up for life and the proceeds should only be used to defend yourself against criminal charges and maybe some civil charges as well. Somehow I've got to make the trust a private copyrighted document. Moreover, this means that the name PrisonProof has to be written in the language to trigger some action tied to the Hunt Institute of Sociology or PrisonProof. There needs to be a code written somewhere in the trust agreement that says or does something to cover these areas.

The trust could also stand as a surety for a large fine instead of imprisonment. I haven't quite figured this plan out but I'll keep contemplating it until I get it together. My best bet is to start Hunt Publishing Company and write my book.

After I'm done with college, I really want to run for political office. At that time I should just throw my hat into the fire and see how well I can actually do. I'm really starting to study politics and history and my stint in college. The time spent in college will help me build a platform and run for the Senate or the House.

I really need to create jobs for incarcerated men and women so that they can pay for the damage that they may have caused and be able to have something to return to.

March 22, 2011 - Day 208

I watched my co-worker finally get around to cleaning out his desk and shelves which were littered with the Weekly Standard, American Free Press, Human Events, Washington Times, Washington Post, and Wall Street Journal, The Nation, and many other conservative periodicals. Buckley has brow beat me with these publications for the last few years. I've had to endure many articles which I blatantly disagreed with but I wanted to remain respectful and debate it if I didn't agree with his stance on the issue at hand. Sometimes I think he misconstrued columns and quotes to support his position in an attempt to recruit me to become a republican. It took him a while but he finally admitted that this was always his underlying intention when he would discuss politics with me.

I've not heard anything from SIU-Carbondale but I'm going to go ahead and start preparing to get admission at SIU-Edwardsville. The process is basically the same except now I'm more prepared to put a package together. The most important part of the admission process is getting accepted and taking care of the housing contract deposit. I'm definitely going to the university so I don't have a problem with committing to it. We'll probably call the admissions office on Thursday or Friday just to see if they've received the admission package. I constantly want to think about this process and focus on the particulars over and over to remind myself to follow through on the small stuff. Get it done!

March 23, 2011 - Day 209

I just finished one of the GED workbooks and I believe it was language writing. I read some of the material while completing an exercise and I have come to the conclusion that being a child psychologist may be a better answer for me. Maybe I'm losing my freakin' mind. I had some literature that covered a demanding child and I believe that the technique mentioned should be used on some adults that I've met over the years.

I had to leave work early today to catch my case manager and review my criminal record in the Pre-Sentence Investigative Report. I need to make out an affidavit about my prior criminal history. The crime prevention units at the universities want records of your past criminal history, especially if it is violence.

Somehow our unit has moved up on the meal rotation. The meal rotation is done based on the grade given to the unit during the weekly unit inspection. I guess the staff member that did the inspection gave use a good report based on our new, friendly unit manager, Mrs. Hall. I see on staff alley that Mrs. Hall moved her office down towards the end where she had more access to inmates. I firmly believe that she is a very smart woman and will make a great unit manager.

I talked to Mr. Lawerence about applying to a second school and he said that it's not necessary. He said, however, that it's different when you're talking about graduate school.

March 24, 2011 - Day 210

Yesterday, I got my envelope back that I used to send out certified mail, which included my admission package for SIU-Carbondale. The package was cut up and all of the contents were lost. It did have some of my personal information on the documents, though. Obviously I was pissed off, but getting mad will hinder me from moving forward. It took me a few hours to regroup and remember some of the progress I had made in regards to the university. So I put together another package, but much smaller and very effective. I will be very cautious about certified mail and baggy envelopes.

I've got this burning desire to study English because I've found that it is such a solid skill and a craft that needs to be acquired. However, that's *a lot* of reading.

Last week I was stuck on a math lesson in the GED books dealing with measurements and I felt bad and put the math book away. I was having some problems with the math questions and just got frustrated. Today I decided to read it over and over until I understand what I'm reading and I worked through the lesson. I learned a lot about just staring at the problem and not giving up. It's really something special when you learn on your own.

March 25, 2011 - Day 211

It's 12:48 am and I'm still reading my NYT on my way to bed and saw a name in the paper that was familiar to me, Barry Minkow. I read his book a few months ago and know he's in the paper on his way back to prison for conspiracy to commit securities fraud. It looks like it took a while but his love for money got ahold of him again. When he returns to prison, the thing he'll grab is the Bible and the first place he'll go is the chapel with the rest of the child molesters and rapists or people who were sent here for housing child pornography. There are some good men who are Christians that go to the chapel, but they are few.

I can't believe that I just read about this guy in the NYT. I can't wait until tomorrow to talk to my ex-cellmate because he still has Mr. Minkow's book in his locker. I don't know if he even read the book yet. Kelly is going to flip out when I show him the article.

March 26, 2011 - Day 212

I just finished reading my current lesson from the Siddha Yoga Foundation and it asked us to write down some of the things that we are grateful for.

I'm grateful that I was allowed to go to an outside specialist to check my kidney disease and monitor it. I'm grateful for all the times I went to sick call in the last 16 years and received some type of assistance. I'm grateful to be able to go to the pill line and receive medication that helps prevent the failure of my kidneys. I'm grateful for the lab technicians that took the time to take my urine and blood samples thousands of times. I'm grateful I've been given Hep A and B vaccinations, flu vaccinations, and other vaccinations because of my chronic kidney disease. I'm glad I was given medication for my acid reflux. I'm grateful that I've been given foot cream for my athlete's foot. I'm grateful that I've had my teeth cleaned every six months for 16 years. I'm grateful to have had my wisdom teeth pulled. I'm grateful I had a kidney biopsy. I'm grateful that the psychologist will see me whenever I'm in need. And most of all, I'm grateful because I didn't have to pay for it. I'm grateful to my Aunt Portia, my mother, my uncle, and my sister for their support. I'm grateful that my mind, body, and soul are still holding on. I'm grateful I'm 40 years of age with grey hair in my beard. I'm grateful I still have all of my teeth. I'm grateful that I haven't contracted any fatal STDs.

I'm grateful to receive the New York Times. I'm grateful to have spent, unfortunately, half of my life in prison, but am able to learn from the experience. I'm grateful to be able to read and write. I'm grateful for the opportunity to go to college. I'm grateful I don't have to sleep with a knife and my boots on every night. I'm grateful to be in a one-man cell. I'm grateful to be getting out next year. I'm grateful I didn't have children that I may have abandoned or neglected.

March 27, 2011 - Day 213

It's 7:12 p.m. and Kentucky just beat North Carolina to move on to the final four. I really enjoyed watching the game and I found myself cheering for Kentucky. Usually inmates want to see the school lose that represents the state they're housed in. A few people wanted the Tar Heels to win but it wasn't as many as the UK fans.

I finally got a chance to study my courses at Nations University and read a little of the Bible. However, I need to read a lot more this week so that I can move on and continue with the rest of the module.

The unit counselor, Mr. Jennings, went on the SIU-C website to pull down an application for housing and I'll type in the information tomorrow and get Shackelford to fax the papers to the university. I'm sure Shack will not have a problem with this.

I got a chance to listen to *Meet The Press* on the radio on 590 AM at 4:00 p.m. because I missed it when it came on at 9:00 am. Secretary of State Hillary Clinton and the Secretary of Defense stated that the case that took place in Libya was a necessary action. However, Ted Coppel made a good point as a commentator: What about all the other countries where people are being killed and immigrating to other countries in the millions? Sudan, Congo, and other countries in Africa are in the middle of an all-out war.

I truly believe that the president really has his plate overloaded but he's handling it very well as far as I can tell. I do not believe that he should have gotten involved in the problem with Libya because all of the other nations should've been able to deal with Quadaffi.

March 28, 2011 - Day 214

Life's problems are bullets. This will be the main premise of my book. And that no one is prison proof.

I have to remember to apply for scholarships every year once I get to college. I'm also going to make sure that I'm budgeting my time as Dave Ramsey teaches. I went to my managing debt class this morning and watched a really good DVD on Dave Ramsey. I do believe that I'll be a really good student.

I'm sitting here at work with water and sewer pipes over my head. While watching the GED DVDs I realized that I need to add more details to my writing, but that deficiency is why I decided that my first book will be a diary.

I read in the Wall Street Journal about web sites that allow lawyers to bid on work from prospective clients. There aren't many websites set up for this, but I just may enlist them to help me with my Federal Rules of Civil Procedure Rule 60(b) motion and lawsuit.

This idiot down the hall owes me five dollars from two months ago and it's time he paid up. My loan sharking days have passed and gone but sometimes I feel that I've extended my kindness and someone perceives that as weakness. After a while I will strive to change their perspective.

March 29, 2011 - Day 215

Maybe my publishing company will specialize in diaries. I'll have them sign in on a specific date and maybe on the copyrighted paper that I provide. Maybe I'd give a donation every 90 days of $100 or more. It'll have to be hand-written. It should be typed but some people are not going to be able to get access to a typewriter. I want all of America's felons to start writing because I believe that words and reflection will cause a small change in a lot of men; it caused a real change in *my* life. I have more energy for creating ideas and contemplating past bad choices.

I'll probably only accept diaries from individuals that are institutionalized. I should call it PrisonProof Publishing. However, I may create a PrisonProof Legal Defense Trust Fund to hold the accounts until these people are released, then release the money to them and get an address to send future payments. Moreover, if they go back to prison, we will revert back to the original setup and they'll receive just less than the required amount of money as donations while they're incarcerated and when released the funds will be released again.

Next I need to make sure that my company is not easily accessible to the public. Maybe I should have a security guard or key pad entrance to the offices. I also wonder about claims of resitution and fines. I may authorize a pay schedule, but I'll have to think about this one. We may even send the check to the institution on the day of their release.

Maybe the legal defense fund will be for employees only. I think my deal may be more attractive because there is no initial investment from the authors. This is for women and men who are poor and really hurting for some type of assistance. The only capital an institutionalized person has is their words and paper. I should have one-year plans, three-year plans, five-year plans, and 10-year plans. After 10 years they'll receive the donation until they're released.

All of the subtitles will be named after the person submitting the manuscript. When an individual writes for more than a year, we'll just start naming them fourth and fifth editions. Maybe I'll hold their money in escrow at the company; I haven't decided just yet.

I'll probably be the trustee or the beneficiary of the Defense Trust Fund. It's their way of having their mark in the world, something other than a conviction, and it allows them to have money to pay for the adverse affects of their crimes on society. Maybe some could go toward the cost of their incarceration? What about the indivdiuals with life sentences? What about violent individuals who've committed horrible acts? No one must be excluded! The one thing that all inmates fret about is being excluded from some reason.

It's 10:15 p.m. and Kelly and I have changed the company name to PrisonProof Enterprises and created an internship for incarcerated parents and their children. I'm going to make Kelly a co-founder and give him a seat on the board of directors.

March 30, 2011 - Day 216

This is going to be my life's work. I'm going to visit every prison in the US to lecture about my program and I'm going to take my time and build this compay so that it can last forever after my death. It will become my legacy; this is my vision.

When I'm really into my religious studies, sometimes I wonder, why has this been hidden from me for so many years? It wasn't hidden from me... it was in a book. Sometimes I wonder what the intent of moving from a scroll to a cover was.

It's 7:39 p.m. and it's time to read. I took the unit three review test today in language arts and writing in my GED workbook and scored an 86%. I didn't do so well on the lesson itself, scoring a 65%. I got a 100% on the practice for lesson 14 and an 88% on the mini-test.

My grades did not start out this good. Some of the earlier lessons were terrible. I need to start making entries about my progress with these workbooks. I should've started keeping track of this stuff from the beginning. I just need to remember that it's a learning process. I wonder if this is a qualatitive or quantitative analysis that I'm producing here.

I was just at the microwave talking to a guy who has retired from two jobs, put all of his children through college, and at a late age decided to start snorting cocaine. We didn't get into detail about his case since he received 12 months and one day. It kind of speaks for itself. However, he wanted to talk about the wine he used to make at home. I keep teasing him about what part of Cali he's from. I told him my favorite wine was Mad Dog 20/20. I said that I might have a glass of wine with my dinner, but I know that's a really bad idea. The last thing I need in this stage of my life is liquid courage. Cheap and legal liquid courage. The majority of this county wouldn't believe that the most deadly substance in society now is processed sugar.

Chapter Eight: Kelly Johnson-Duncan

This lady has been a good friend and supporter since the day I was released from prison. She has sat up many nights listening to horror stories about the distant past lives I've lived. She has three beautiful children and grandchildren in her life that keep her busy. On many mornings and nights she was awakened out of her sleep to take me to work or retrieve me from getting lost trying to find a job location. Her friendship is really important to me and she has a really big heart.

I really appreciate you and your support for all the loans and time spent working on my re-entry to the community.

It's 7:54 p.m. and I just got back from talking to one of the guys on the alley named Frame. I asked Frame how long he's been down and he told me 30 years. He got maxed out on life in the state at 20 years old for illegally selling firearms. Mr. Frame was released to the halfway house, and while at the halfway house, he robbed banks to support himself. Frame was at the halfway house for five days before he caught this federal charge for which he's currently incarcerated. Frame gets out this year and I asked him whether he'd had enough and he said, "I'm not working at no motherfucking McDonalds." The first thing he's going to do upon being released is rob a bank. Frame's health is really bad so his mental state is not very good and it'll really start to decline once he is released to society. I hope to God that he doesn't run into the people that told on him or aided in his federal prosecution.

I got SIU-C course catalogs and I was really impressed with what they had to offer me in my situation. They've got a program called Capstone that would allow me to bring in my accomplishments and have them evaluated for college credit. I didn't make copies of my certificates or diplomas because I wanted the request to be professional.

I worked on lesson 16 today in the Math GED and got a 50%, 100%, 50%, and a 67%... just terrible. I'm all over the place and all the mistakes are stupid, careless errors, just going too fast.

April 1, 2011 - Day 218

It's 9:18 p.m. and Mr. Kelly just brought me my science GED workbook after grading leson 15. I got a 100%, 33%, and a 43% on the mini-test. I don't know if I want to write this information down, but I wanted other people who believe that they aren't smart to have the courage to write about themselves. It's embarrassing and uncomfortable since I've been reading the New York Times for the last 2 1/2 hours. I need to read a couple more hours but I want to save some for tomorrow morning.

Mr. Lawrence faxed my certificates to the university and I really need to settle down and wait for a response from them. I tried to go ahead in the lessons in WIN today and Mr. Lawrence and I got into a big debate about it. However, I conceded the argument and relented to wait and complete the sections in the way the company suggested that they be completed.

I need to study harder on the GED workbooks because I really need to maintain a B average while I'm in school. I prefer to hold an A in all of my classes since I will not have time to party and just waste time. If I want to get grants and scholarships to pay for my education then I need to make exceptional grades.

April 2, 2011 - Day 219

"Only he who carries the load knows how much it weighs." - Arab Proverb

It's Saturday at 1:25 p.m. and we did not have the ususal 10-minute move at 1:00 p.m.. 10 minutes to the hour, they usually announce the move and unlock all the doors and inmates are allowed to be in other areas of the institution.

I've found that the Trulincs computer system for the law library has a lot of prepared template forms available to be copied and used to file in the courts. There aren't that many people in the library today, but some of the guys are in here trying to get some relief in regards to a sentence reduction, or at least a review of their claims. The computer system is a little complicated, so some of the guys have had some real problems with research and basic navigation.

I'm looking at a lot of old books in suspense, thriller,

romance, fiction, and non-fiction genres. John Grisham, Sidney Sheldon, David State, and memoirs on Stalin, Hitler, Reagan, and Clinton, just to name a few.

Also, the system is now set up for us to email the staff. I'm sure a lot of inmates are going to get themselves in trouble with that system. This will probably allow us to contact our doctors and get prescriptions changed and so forth. If any staff members receive email from me it will be written in legal jargon and not personal in nature at all. You can never be too careful.

Even though I had to stay in here for an additional hour, it has been well-used by making this journal entry. I've got to calm down and slow down because my hypetension is starting to get the best of me. I came over here to research filing a motion for sentence reduction based on post-conviction rehabilitation under 5K 2.19, but I'm not allowed to present this claim unless I've been remanded for resentencing.

April 3, 2011 - Day 220

Yesterday, I read some text out of the SIU-C course guide to Kelly and I realized that it did not say what I thought it said. I realized that reading something out loud is more effective in memorization and studying. As I'm reading the Book Of Samuel right now, I can tell the difference. I also need to change my schedule so that I can get more of my courses completed at Nations. I'm going to study the Bible courses at night and read the newspaper at work. I believe I can make better progress with the course work this way. I'm also going to send an email to Mr. Casteel and find out more about the accreditiation process.

We watched *60 Minutes* and I couldn't believe the fraud that mortgage services had become involved in with the major banks. There are people who were supposed to be notary public agents and knowingly notarized documents that they knew were not being signed by that actual person. However, the servicers didn't care because they were being paid. I really can't believe that no one is going to go to jail over this fraud. Think about the thousands of ignorant people that got put out of their homes because of this fraud over the last ten years or more. CNN showed people sitting outside in line at a colossuem for two dayds waiting to get in to have a meeting with a bank representative to modify their mortgage. I can't believe these people just didn't walk away and rent some place until they're able to get themselves together financially.

When I went to dinner I talked to one of the guys who had successfully completed the drug program and went to the halfway house. After having discussions about it, I've come to the conclusion that I still may not go to the halfway house. I probably will not be able to go to school, so I really have no interest in dealing with these people.

April 4, 2011 - Day 221

I got my Language Arts reading GED books back from Kelly and I did absolutely terrible, again. I got a 50% and a 55% on the mini-test for lesson 18. That was terrible! Damn! I also learned that when someone says you're being impractical or unrealistic, it means that you lack common sense. I've heard this before but I didn't put the two together.

John Casteel emailed me back and confirmed what I knew already: they're trying to get a national accreditation from the Distance Education Training Council designation by the US Department of Education.

I found out today that I have chronic hypertension and that's not good because I just don't slow down. I can do well in school but I'll probably crash and burn in other environments. I think I'll be okay once I reach college.

The NCAA championship game is on tonight; it's

Butler and Uconn. We've got count in 20 minutes so I'll just wait and go down after count. My friend, Flip, across the hall is from the Philippines and he's already asleep from working the early shift. Flip has to go in the diet kitchen at 4 am to cook breakfast for the inmates on special diets given to them by the institution diet technician. I'll have to wake him up in a few minutes for count. I ran out of coffee and I really need a fix. The tea is keeping me from having headaches due to withdrawals from caffeine. My handwriting is really bad and getting worse. Sometimes I wonder, am I a couple sandwiches short of a pinic?

April 5, 2011 - Day 222

Mr. Kelly just returned my GED Social Studies workbook and I did absolutely terrible again with a 72%, 50%, and a chapter 17 mini-test score of 58%. However, I figured out my problem. I'm not taking the time to read the questions. I went back and reviewed the answers and I should've easily gotten those correct. If I paid a little more attention to the questions, I would've made better choices. Sometimes I just need to re-read the question and the summary.

My Christian buddy, Tim, finally gave me a book I've been wanting to read called *Beyond Opinon* by Ravi Zacharias. Ravi appears to be a Christian theologian and I can't wait to start reading this material. It also says that he's the world's leading Christian apologist.

One book that I read and loved was *Measure of a Man* by Sidney Poitier and that's how I found out about all of the newspapers he reads every day. I can confirm that reading the paper every day will broaden your mind and ability to locate and consume information. Sidney worked his butt off to get where he is in the acting world today and surely he deserves it.

April 6, 2011 - Day 223

I just finished studying the Bible for about three hours and I did good on my Language Arts Writing GED workbook for chapter 15. I got a 100%, 100%, 100%, and a 67% on the mini-test. That's crazy! I finished the last chapters but Kelly didn't grade them; I think he was a little tired today.

I got a letter from SIU today and it was thin. I thought it was a simple denial for admission. However, they were just asking for more official documents in regards to my prior and current convictions. I might go ahead and give my cop-out to counselor Jennings and have him just fax information to the college. I probably should call and let them know that my PSI and the judgement of commitment are the only documents that I have. I just need to remember that I'm not going to enroll this year so I probably should slow down and be aware that this is the only piece of information holding up my admission request.

April 7, 2011 - Day 224

I worked hard in my Mathematics GED workbook for lesson 17 and I got a 75%, 24%, 81%, 78%, and a 78% on the cumulative review. Algebra is up next and I don't have a clue.

The youngsters in here are walking around with their pants falling off of them and showing their underwear. If they were in state prison that would've been taken as an invitation to their body. My father would kill me if my pants didn't have a belt, let alone hanging off of my body.

I was very blessed today to get copies of all of the necessary documents to send back to the college. It appeared in their response that the only documents I needed were the ones dealing with my prior convictions. Counselor Jennings and I put together a good package and he walked it down to the mail room himself. I'll never forget this man for putting forth this effort for me because it's not a regular occurrence.

Sometimes I think about giving up on PrisonProof because I constantly encounter guys who don't deserve a second chance because the plans they've built say they don't want one. Nobody thinks about what it means to be a great man, a good contributer, or just really good at anything.

I just ate a steak and cheese sandwhich in the cafeteria and it was really good. The potatoes were cooked all the way through for a change. As usual, I ate my food really fast and left the cafeteria to start reading.

I got a chance to watch the news at 4:30 p.m. today and Senator Harry Reid and Boehner are about to shut down the federal government. I heard on inmate.com that the staff here at the prison were told they cannot use sick days or vacation days and they had to show up for work. I get the feeling there will be some very upset people here in the morning. I humbly believe that the republican party has been hijacked by the tea party and the republicans will regret their sweet little victory in the near future.

April 8, 2011 - Day 225

I just realized today that I should pursue the Masters of Law LLM at SIU-C just so that I don't need to hire counsel when I launch PrisonProof. I could still hire attorneys, but I wouldn't have to worry about an individual running a con on me. I've thought about the dual degree of sociology and law; I'll keep that on the back burner.

I asked the supervisor of Education to let me see my admission status on the computer but he couldn't get it done. I'll just wait until they send me the results through the mail. It's a good thing the mail doesn't stop running on Saturdays.

I forgot to write about the new class F shares, or founder shares, that were created to stop venture capitalists form gaining control through equity manipulation. It's done through option contracts and they dilute our equity somehow. I'll learn more about this later when I get to college. I read about it in the NYT I got yesterday. I think this new idea was created by the founder of Napster.

The movie tonight is TRON and I'm glad it's not a cartoon. I'm really interested in the news tonight because I want to see if they've shut down the government.

I've just finished studying Samuel I and II and I can see how a lot of the rituals and customs of this country originated from the Old Testement.

The institution is serving beef stir fry for dinner and we're last on the meal rotation, as usual, which means we'll go and eat at about 6:30 p.m.. I'm thinking about watching the movie, but I might just skip that and study for my religious studies exam.

I did poorly in the science GED workbook today with a 33%, 75%, and a 55% in the chapter 16 mini-test. Even though these grades are not good, I shouldn't allow them to discourage me in regards to going to college.

There's a guy here by the name of Kom and somehow he's getting the exams sent in to him and taking them while he has his study guide with him. He said Casteel knew about it, but I don't think he knows what's really going on here.

April 9, 2011 - Day 226

I remember reading a saying from a man who wrote *How to Read a Book*. He said that sometimes people can't tell the difference between reading a lot and being well-read. I want to be well-read and I believe you've got to be able to deconstruct and reconstruct the information to be considered well-read. Reconstuct your own ideas about what you read. The only way to do that is by writing about what you've read.

I read the introduction to *Beyond Opinion* last weekend and I finally remember some of it. I plan to read one chapter each weekend and write a little about what I read in relation to my life. After reading chapter one, it appears that Mr. Zacharias was making the proposition that when an individual argues against something they inevitably argue against themselves. So, in the first chapter, he began slowly with examples of philosophers and laymen purging their belief system on society without regard for the consequences. What were the conseqences? They overlooked the bias, prejudice, and pre-concevied perceptions of their own ojectivety.

This reminds me of a time when I was in a Federal Medical Center in Springfield, MO. I met a man who was a Montana Freeman. These guys felt that the federal government should be re-organized due to the fraud of creating fictitious entities to mirror a strong financial stability at our own personal peril.

However, this argument was based on the same laws that supposedly deprived them of freedom or control over the fictitious entity. For example, the Uniform Commerical Code talked about sight drafts, but the way they used the instruments caused unforeseen consequences in the operation of the bank and the customers. It's simply a dog chasing its tail. Moreover, the one thing that they said gave them the right—not the power—was the Bible and Jesus Christ.

I've just realized that this diary is my business plan, my official biography, my resume, my notebook, road to riches, my confession, my witness, my testimony, and maybe a philosophy.

I've got to figure out a way to break the diary into chapters or sections so that the reader can breathe and have a sense of accomplishment as they go. I'll probably divide them with summaries in hindsight at 30 day intervals, a snapshot at the past form the future.

April 10, 2011 - Day 227

Today I started my workout so that I can be in better shape when I'm released. I had always planned to start with push-ups, so I'm going to start with 50 push-ups by 10:00 am every day for the rest of this month. Then I'm going to increase the monthly amount by 50 until I'm released or reach one thousand push-ups a day. Living in this one-man cell really helps with this routine. I'm old school and I want to keep my business to myself.

I didn't get a lot of sleep last night and I probably won't get a lot tonight, either. As I get closer to going home, I'll probably start losing more sleep. The Sentencing Commission has decided to hold the hearing on retroactivity on June 1, 2011. I believe that they wanted to see the outcome of the budget fight in Washington, DC. The negotiating went right up to the last hour and I believe that this was done intentionally. It's just a hunch but I'm sure I'm not that far off the mark.

I met a Jamacian today named Pablo and he's successfully suing the Federal Government for medical reasons in a medical tort under the 1983 bivens. There are some defendants being sued individually, but there're being represented by the federal government. Something that I found interesting is that he was told that because the federal government put a pacemaker in his chest, they're responsible for the maintenance and orderly function of the device. If he was sent back to Jamacia his medical needs not being met would be certain death for him. I don't know how much truth is to this, but it seems credible at face value.

April 11, 2011 - Day 228

I just found out that I don't like fiction. In lesson 19 in my Language Arts Reading I got a 40%, 14%, 50%, and a 50% on the Unit 2 cumulative review. I absolutely do not like reading fiction but Mr. Kelly told me that I better get used to it if I'm headed back to college. In addition, I'm not under any real pressure to do well except the burdens that I impose on myself. However, this is the time that I should be pushing through my courses at Nations because I would love to start at SIU with 60 credits transferred when I arrive. At the present moment they've got 11 transfer credits.

I'm planning on staying up late tonight so that I can re-read Joshua, Judges, Samuel I and II, and Kings I and II. I probably will not be able to read all of it by 12:15 tomorrow, but I'm going to give it one hell of a try. It's beginning to be very clear that Nations wanted to go through the Bible in the first 30 credits. After the next modules we'll be done with the Bible and begin to test on the material that they provide us. I'm trying to get to the general education material so that I can start working on the basics.

April 12, 2011 - Day 229

Mr. Kelly and I took the second exam for BRS and it was a brain buster. I should've studied more. Mr. Kelly told me about another correspondence course for Bible study and that it progressed one book of the Bible at a time along with a work book. This new course requires a lot more reading and the lessons are structured a little differently to challenge your thinking. I'm going to send the lessons and use the course as support of study for my courses at Nations.

In 2009 the president signed into law that low-income individuals only had to pay 15% of their yearly income for

25 years or 10 years if they had a job in public service toward their education. This is a large motivator when it comes to me deciding to return to school. And as I'm watching politics and reading a lot of political periodicals, I'm starting to realize that it's really hard to overturn a law once it's passed. This is one law that I hope never gets overturned.

Around 2:00 am last night, I heard a loud yelling like someone was being raped. Then I got up and looked out into the hallway and everybody was standing in their doorways, looking at the bathroom and just listening.

I decided to investigate the situation. I walked into the bathroom and took a quick glance under the stall door and didn't see any feet. I thought to myself, *holy shit this guy is getting raped in the shower.* So I went around the corner and looked in the shower and it was empty. Then I was really confused! So I turned around and looked over the wall of the stall and Korn's chest was on his knees and he was having stomach pains while making himself throw up by sticking his finger down his throat. I had to ask him if he wanted me to go get the help because he could've been having withdrawals from snorting heroin. He might not have wanted the police to intervene and he was going to clean everything up. However, he told me to go and get them. So they arrived and they thought that he was drunk off of some hooch because they've been finding it all over the unit in the last few weeks.

April 13, 2011 - Day 230

I've started missing my paper on Mondays and Tuesdays and I think my aunt has limited the subscription to Monday through Friday. However, it is still very much appreciated by me and the guys that read it day in and day out.

It's been a while since I've gambled on anything, but

this is really good news because it's not on my mind. I'm no longer interested in just throwing money away.

It's really hard sitting here and not being able to verify anything you've put in motion outside of the institution. I believe that the sentencing commission is going to change their sentencing guidelines to make them retroactive and I'd get an immediate release with nowhere to live. I'll probably go to the motel for a few days or maybe even a month or two.

I'm interested in opening a mailbox at the UPS Store as soon as I get out. I see that I'm going to need an email account and a phone so that people can contact me when I initially get out. I know Mama, my aunt, and my uncle may want to call me to see what I'm doing.

I've been thinking about the future, I mean 25-35 years down the road, and I'm going to publish several books to supplement my income. Waiting on the federal government is a non-starter. The public can vote anyone into office and change the laws for entitlement programs and make it hard for people depending on state-sponsored retirement. Even the state pension funds are not really a good safety net. You need to depend on your own ability to create an asset that produces income and has the capacity to do so for a long time.

Well, I finished Unit 4 in Language Arts Writing and in Lesson 15, I got a 100%, 100%, 100%, and 67%. In lesson 16, I got an 88% and 55%, and in lesson 17, I got a 100%, 100%, 88%, and the unit test was a 67%. The post test was a 72% and the simulated a 70%.

April 14, 2011 - Day 231

I'm eating a honey bun and drinking tea for dinner. The honey bun is about 560 calories and very healthy food for a youngster like myself. The meatloaf that was being served in the kitchen is absolutely horrible. I'll leave the tea on my window sill just in case I've got to get up and get a drink. This way I can stretch my legs every now and then.

I was wrong about my subscription because I got Saturday's paper today, which is Thursday. I guess I should be thankful that I even get the paper.

So I completed lesson 18 in the Math GED workbook and got a 95%, 71%, 34%, 64%, and a 60%. These scores were not great. This was the beginning of the Algebra section, Unit 3, and it was tough to say the least. The last time I looked at an algebra problem was in 1993 and I wasn't the sharpest pencil in the bunch. The next unit section is geometry and it's really a challenge at 41, but I still need to learn that it's okay if I don't know the answer. It will take a little time and some work but it can be done. A lot of repetition of working problems will eventually get me across the finish line.

April 15, 2011 - Day 232

I did my work in my science GED workbook for lesson 17 and got a 50%, 67%, and 77% on the mini-test.

I may need to take the full four years of college instead of the Capstone option and receive a bachelor's in two years. I'm almost certain that I will do better than a C average once I get settled in. I called the college today. The admission lady that I talked to said she had just been hired. She helped me as much as she could, but I wanted someone more experienced. I have to remember that everyone has to start somewhere. She answered my questions to the best of her knowledge and transferred me to the people who could help me most. I learned that they will send loan documents for my signature with my acceptance and award letter. I could not have been more happy because I am committed to going to college. The admission counselor told me that since I'm a felon my application goes through a more thorough review and takes a couple more weeks to be evaluated.

One of my braille students told me about this book he had about law school and I couldn't wait to get my hands on it. I started reading it about an hour ago and I finished it tonight—it's only 210 pages. I haven't read anything out of the ordinary except getting accepted to law school might be a little tricky.

April 16-17, 2011 - Day 233 & 234

I've read the second chapter of *Beyond Opinion,* and the author tries to discredit other philosophies in the same tone and language in which other philosophers try to discredit Christianity. The crux of his position is that the religion, meaning the word c-h-r-i-s-t-i-a-n-i-t-y, is not radical, but the perception of the individual is radical once it is believed and acted upon.

I guess he's saying that the word Christianity, Islam, Atheists, Muslims, are not human beings. They're simple alphabets that have been aggregated together to be given meaning and ascribe a certain response.

When I was born, I was not conscious of the word, "baby," or any word for that matter. So how is it that I learned words and their messages? Obviously, through another human being's perception. Moreover, I did not realize that the linchpin to separation of church and state stood on the simple axiom of not having a specific Christian denomination as the controlling authority of the state government or office.

I watched television and heard these words thrown around by the media anchors, conservative religious leaders, educators, and others, but no one goes to the core of the idea. What if we threw away all books, scrolls, or written words? Then what? Then we could only progress by discovery. Maybe through necessity we would force ourselves to move forward or backwards to another place of realization in regards to what cannot be smelled, touched, tasted, seen, or heard. Can you get an answer without asking a question?

This is the only way to keep out contamination in whatever presents itself, whenever it presents itself, and in whatever form. And why it presents itself. Some do say that wars start with religion; if not then why do Americans say may God be with a soldier? God is present in every aspect of the American culture. Even not believing in God invokes God. What if you're a practicing Christian, but just in case when you pray you address God *and* Allah? So if I'm having a religious discussion with this individual, then what are we actually discussing? It appears someone is switching hats just for the sake of having a position.

It kind of reminds me of a federal judge and the federal sentencing guidelines. You're damned if you do and damned if you don't. But what was the real reason behind your decision, and have you already made up your mind to overturn yourself one appeal, knowing what you just decided is against what you believe in or knowing the defendant may or may not believe the same?

Now take this entry and shred it. What have I said? What do you have in your hand to read? Absolutely nothing. Because that's exactly what I just spent 50 words saying: absolutely nothing!

April 18, 2011 - Day 235

I just finished a session in my Managing Your Debt class and it was about the misunderstanding about giving. Another part of it had to do with serving.

Well, I finished lesson 20 in Language Arts Reading and did quite badly. I got a 33%, 42%, and a 56% on the mini-test for the chapter. I started to question my decision to record these scores because some of them are based on 10 or less questions, sometimes as little as three. They're not all test scores but they reflect a struggle I'm having with studying at the age of 41. I'm going through these exercises quickly to refresh my energy and exercise my brain in anticipation of the rigors of college classrooms. When I'm taking my courses at Nations University or any other college, as long as I keep at least a B average then I'm happy. However, I will strive to get an A average.

The federal debt ceiling and the 2013 final budget is really going to make the campaign in 2012 interesting. A lot of the politicans running for office have done and said things under the radar. Well, it is about time for some of that garbage to hit primetime.

When I read book on law school I ran across something that I never paid attention to. The author often mentioned flash cards and that it was the normal way to get through college. She said that the flash card method was absolutely useless in law school. Subsequently, I've decided to get my master's in legal studies and leave the juris doctorate to the ultra-smart guys and gals.

April 19, 2011 - Day 236

I met a young man today who had scored a 520 on his pre-test for the GED, however he said he was taking the horticultural class so that he could learn to grow marijuana to sell. He's been in federal prison for 10 months, black, 27 years of age, and this is his first incarceration. In addition, he has beaten several state murder charges. I preached to him for two hours about education, college, money, and the fact that I was going back to college at the age of 41.

It's 12:30 and right in the middle of lunch we were told the institution is having a total recall. This means that all inmates in all areas of the institution must report back to their housing unit. Kelly thought that it was because of a funeral or a retirement party for the staff. I quickly informed him that they don't schedule these things in the middle of lunch for 1700 inmates. However, if the director of the Bureau of Prisons has shown up by surprise, then that might just cause this type of response.

I'm starting to realize that no matter where I go, there's going to be someone there who will help me. Whether it is in prison, drug rehab, jail, college, home, business, employment, or friendship.

I talked with a young man today who is publishing his own book because he couldn't find an agent, and now he has found a movie producer who wants to turn his novel into a movie.

The guards just finished a bed book count. A bed book looks like an oversized restaurant menu that's double-sided with clear sleeves. Those sleeves hold large index cards with our photos and other information. We have to stand up with our photo ID in hand and tell the guard our registration numbers.

I also read in the NYT about the author of *Three Cups of Tea* and how his story or memoir is being discredited because of factual inaccuracies. This is another reason I'm doing this diary: to document the creation of PrisonProof. This book is a plea, a request for any type of assistance to help develop my idea.

In lesson 19 in the Social Studies GED workbook I got a 50%, 64%, and a 87% on the mini-test for the lesson. In lesson 20, I got a 72%, 75%, and a 77% on the mini-test. In the unit 5 cumulative review I got a 94%, and on the post test I got a 76%.

Everyone that has cash stashed away in their mattresses is buying gold like crazy. If they change the currency, the big losses will hit people with paper currency.

April 20, 2011 - Day 237

Last night I had a conversation with a 65-year-old African American named George who sees life as a cup half empty. Everything that you put on the table as an idea is not going to work according to him, except selling more drugs. He claims he needs to do this because he's afraid of living life as a poor person. It is my belief that this man will spend the rest of his life in prison, besides the last 45 years he's already spent behind bars. He is an example of what I do not want to become: a career criminal and incarcerated philosopher. I don't believe that he should be allowed around young men because he's not constructive in his views because he's older. His perception is shorter than that of a 20-year-old. He would advise from a perspective that may not be realistic.

PrisonProof is not about shielding you from going to prison if you commit crimes. It is a philosophy about shielding you from the thought process that allows you to make bad choices and decisions based solely on erroneous assumptions, misinformation, desperation, or intolerance, which inevitably will lead you to some form of incarceration in prisons or incarceration in the federal welfare system.

I just finished reading the science section of the NYT and there was an article entitled, "Empty Years Along, a Longevity Study Still has Ground to Cover," by Howard S. Friedman, Ph.D and Leslie R. Martin, Ph.D. They believe that one of the factors of longevity of life, according to the article by Katherine Bouton, is education or the pursuit of education. Surely, if I had $29.95 I would buy the book, however, I can only wish to purchase it in the future.

Also, yesterday on CNN, I watched as McDonald's offered 50,000 jobs and the line for an application was so long I couldn't believe it. The piece also said that the line had a majority of people with bachelor degrees. And these guys locked up in here say they will not work at McDonalds. We will see.

I read an article in the National Conservative Weekly entitled, "Liberalism: The New Crack," and also read a quote by Rep. Allen (R. Fla): "For too long, the choice has been to give a handout instead of a hand up. Liberal politicians continue the same old tired politics of dependence on big government." I respectfully disagree.

If I don't want to prosper, If I don't want to read, write, and study, if I choose to use alcohol, any type of handout or hand up is the same as being incarcerated in my mind. If I take a stick and smash a watermelon, it doesn't change the fact that it's a watermelon. However, depending on your knowledge or perception, the seeds that lay on the ground hold the true value of the watermelon, so what have you actually destroyed? Ignorance? The same way you are shown how to walk to the public assistance office, I can show you how bad thought processes can walk you into prison. I've just decided to change the name of the book to The PrisonProof Project.

April 21, 2011 - Day 238

I talked to a young man today that told me that he wanted to go back to college, but he's got four children to take care of. It's really hard to try and encourage a young, black, 25-year-old gangster that's been selling drugs ever since he was 10 years old to go straight. I know he hasn't got the capacity to deal with his peer pressure because he still glamorizes his past and the influence he has over his younger peers. Moreover, these are the young peers that have witnessed him commit murders and get away with it. However, what can the PrisonProof Project do to help him in his situation? So far I've come up with a family unit and an internship of some kind.

When I finish my legal studies and start the path towards sociology I'll start to gain better insight on developing some policies that are geared towards rehabilitation instead of incarceration. Once the parent is incarcerated, their children are also in prison, no matter where they're located.

I just finished watching the TV show The Mentalist and it appears that the women take on more masculine roles and the mentalist has taken on a more feminine and pacifist-type character. They respect him for his intelligence, but his lack of common sense automatically projects him into the friend category for the women detectives on the show.

April 22, 2012 - Day 239

I should have a subscription to several newspapers so that I can cut articles out and contemplate their veracity.

John Casteel at Nations emailed me and basically said that I have to stay on the course of study that the school has designed for me.

I can't decide if I want the project to be a sole proprietorship, LLC, or some form of a charitable trust with an education exemption from the IRS.

I was supposed to have worked in my science GED workbook but I procrastinated because of the resume class I volunteered to help with, which was cancelled so I wasted a good amount of time today. However, life is not about how fast you go.

The closer I get to being released, the more frustrated I'm starting to be with the small things – stupid comments and things like that.

If they reduce my sentence and terminate my supervised release, then I may just stay in Kentucky and go to school. I really don't want to go back to Illinois. We're all waiting for June 1, 2011 to hear about the Sentencing Commission's hearings and decisions about the retroactivity of the Fair Sentencing Act.

It is 11:30 p.m. and I just finished watching the movie "Country Strong" for about the third or fourth time. So I went to my room but made a pit stop in the bathroom at this urinal. I saw something moving in the trash and I decided to look closer. The antennae on this cockroach were as long as my pinky finger. I looked even closer and it was a really huge roach. I wanted to go downstairs and grab one of those black widows or brown recluses and just set it nearby.

I woke up one morning a while ago and found that I had rolled over on a centipede and squished it. I've got to remember to keep the bed away from the wall. The mice run up and down the hallway all night, too, trying to find a locker or trash can with open food.

April 23, 2011 - Day 240

I just finished reading chapter three of *Beyond Opinion* and it primarily dealt with the youth and their assumed ignorance of the intellectual part of Christianity. Some of the reasoning he uses sounds close to Taoism, but the youth are not the only ones that can't intellectually defend or define their beliefs. Adults at the age of 40 still have trouble coming to a conclusion about their faith or belief in God, myself included. Parents haven't failed to teach their children because they may not have been in a position to learn as teenagers about Christianity. You definitely will not find intellectual understanding by reading only the Bible.

The author himself was privileged to proceed to instituttions of higher learning to come to his position in this book. So if parents teach their children what they've learned from college, then aren't they indoctrinating them to use the same logic and reason they were taught? Is progress tainted in any way? Was your female professor's sister-in-law raped by a Muslim? Was your tenure denied because you are a Buddhist? Why are the majority of college men liberal? Should they be more conservative? Should there be equal representation? Does everything have its equal? If someone asked me right now what my religion is, I would have to say I lean more toward eastern philosophy and I really couldn't explain it.

If someone asked you, "Would you take a million dollars or a lethal injection?" which one would you accept? Your first choice is irrelevant, but the first thought that comes to mind is how you have been conditioned to perceive things as important. Most may choose the million dollars, but what if you found out later in life that the lethal injection was the only way to Heaven? That you couldn't commit suicide, be murdered, or have an accidental death to get into Heaven. Now what?

April 24th, 2011 - Day 241

I really didn't want to do an entry tonight because I was feeling a little depressed. Depressed about not hearing from the college, whether they were going to accept me or not. Depressed that Nations will not let me take five courses at a time so that I can start getting used to college life. Depressed that I don't know what's going to happen with the crack law and the fact that if it doesn't become retroactive I might not be able to enroll in a regionally accredited school until 2013. Depressed that I've gotten to the algebra section of my GED workbook and I'm stuck and don't want to ask for help. It's easy to get rid of this depression with a little hooch or weed but I'm really not interested in getting high anymore. I dread not being able to function or think straight.

When I used to drink I would say and do anything. I would sleep with married women, even some of the women of my so-called friends. Sometimes I got so drunk I'd tell them and they'd try to beat the hell out of me. It turned out to be a little tougher than they thought.

I guess I need to start reading Isaak so I can get ready to take exam three of this course and just complete it. I just have to remember that I'm not in a hurry. I've got to stop thinking that I've got to act to make things turn out the way

I think they should and let God drive. The day you don't want anything is the day you've got everything you need.

April 25th, 2011 - Day 242

I've just read an article in the NYT about the uneducated Evangelic Preacher who's a Nigerian and teaching Christians in Ukraine. He told them that they have to be strategists like Steve Jobs at Apple. "Apple takes a model and keeps expanding on it." That's exactly what I'm going to do with the PrisonProof Project, create a model and keep expanding on it.

In my Language Arts Reading lesson 21, an exercise with four questions, I got two right so I wound up with a 50%. In another exercise, I had five questions and got three right for a 60%, and on the mini-test I had nine questions and got four right for a 44%. I really don't like writing this stuff but I want all the guys and gals incarcerated that have given up on education to know that they're not alone when it comes to being an uneducated adult. There's a good chance that I may not be college material, and believe me, these scores are not a great ego-booster. At the sake of embarrassing myself I'm willing to move forward and be an example and a social experiment to change at a late age. The men in our country need to realize that a lot of the labor jobs are not coming back.

I just read a column in which it noted that the private derivatives market is valued at $466 trillion. The issue of national debt is a joke.

April 26th, 2011 - Day 243

My neighbor, Mr. Smith, just got a solicitation from some law group that's claiming that Title 18 *(note: could also be IV)*, 21, and 26 are not lawful under the U. S. Constitution. The name of the firm is Legal Advocacy

Workgroup in Austin, TX. They're charging $500 to join the brief and be in a position to receive the benefits of the decision by the courts.

I worked on my Science section in the GED workbook and got a 33%, 86%, and 75% on the lesson 18 mini-test. This is not that discouraging but it still needs to be improved. I went and found some different GED books, but they belong to Mrs. Campbell and she didn't want me to have them because she only had five. However, there weren't any people lining up to use those books. I think we need some type of ACT test that you can take before you leave prison. It's just too hard to try and set it up through ACT and the Federal Bureau of Prisons.

These new guards don't want to hand out the mail upon request; these idiots want to wait until they finish playing poker on the internet or doing their email soap opera. I'm surprised they didn't have a can of Skoal in their back pockets.

We had the second level of the resume class and it went pretty smoothly. Tomorrow morning I'll get started on re-drafting the resumes so they can get more copies to send out.

April 27th, 2011 - Day 244

I volunteered my services to assist the re-entry guys with resumes and general preparedness for the mock job fair. This class was really ready to get going with their resumes and that helped me rebuild the default template to accomodate the skills resume.

I'm glad President Obama released his long form birth certificate so the nonsense would just go away. However, he knows that it wasn't the real reason people support the berther bullshit. I firmly believe it to be an avenue to discriminate based on his race.

The people had a lockdown census count and they

caught about 30 people out of bounds. Out of bounds means you were somewhere in the institution where you were not supposed to be. They all received incident reports and a lot of them are going to lose good time benefits.

April 28th, 2011 - Day 245

I just finished watching the NFL draft for the first round and my team, the Steelers, picked a defensive end out of Ohio State. I can't believe I waited three and a half hours to see one pick.

While I was in the lunch line today I had a guy ask me if I was from Southern Illinois. I told him I was from East St. Louis. He told me that he was from Mount Vernon and he was 31 years old. He said he was back on a violation because he was at his girlfriend's house and the police kicked the door in. The police found three ounces of marijuana but the girlfriend said it belonged to her. He said the cops told her, "Hell no, we're putting it on him."

Nine times out of 10, the weed did not belong to her and they made sure he was responsible because it's easier to lean on an ex-convict. Whether he's guilty or not is irrelevant because he's black, an ex-felon, and poor. Once you become an ex-felon, it's not hard to plant drugs on you or intimidate you to do or say things under duress. I hear a lot of people say that ignorance is bliss, well I have seen a lot of ignorant people and they are not very blissful. I understand the wisdom behind the saying but a lot of us don't grasp the other side.

I'm feeling a lot better than the last two days since I've been able to get some extra sleep.

I've found that when you're in a depressed state, one of the ways to deal with that is to get some good, long hours of sleep. I used to feel this way every day when I was originally incarcerated, but after 16 years it comes and goes once a year or not at all.

I was pissed off because Red, the new guy, didn't finish getting the reserves printed and given to Shawn. My friend, Mr. Kelly, didn't get his finished either, but he printed his on some expensive certificate paper that Ms. Leslie forgot she left in the printer by mistake. Kelly used about 30 sheets of it and she was very upset. I don't think that she's ever going to get over this one.

I did a mock job interview and the person giving me the interview handed me a pen and asked me to sell him the ink pen. After I got through trying to sell him the pen, he said he wanted a pencil. I didn't know what he wanted, so how could I sell him anything? I don't want to participate in this process anymore. These idiots are acting like they're doing us a favor.

The tornadoes in Oklahoma and some other southern states were really bad and a lot of people died. One of the guys here that works in UNICOR lost his wife and three children in the storm. Supposedly they ran across the street to get better shelter and the storm totally removed the home that they ran to.

I've got to calm down and realize that I'm not helping myself by getting angry. For some reason I get better results from people when I stand on them. Sometimes a little pressure needs to be applied so that they can move ahead. Mr. Kelly told me about an old saying that he was told: "Pressure will either make a diamond or bust a pipe."

Chapter Nine: Elizabeth Granger

My aunt gave out justice evenly with the switches off of the trees in my grandmother's back yard. She married my uncle Eddie Earl and they had several children: Sherry, Cassandra, Eddie, Kenny, Gwen, and Debbie.

My uncle died while I was incarcerated but my Aunt Elizabeth, a.k.a Baby Sister, lives in Southern Illinois in retirement from working at Ford. She travels regularly with her sisters and brothers to Mississippi to visit distant relatives.

It didn't matter who your mother was, if you acted out you got dealt with. She would beat you with a smile on her face. I have come to appreciate why she did the things she did when we all got out of line.

April 30th, 2011 - Day 247

I've been skipping out on doing my math and essay GED workbooks because the other work assignments drain all of my energy. I need to get that back on track.

There was an artice in the Friday NYT titled, "Criminal Past Makes a Job Search Even Harder." It discussed evidence of discrimination in regards to your background even though you may have rehabilitated yourself or your crimes are minor offenses.

Incarcerated individuals have got to stop hoping to find a job and become determined to be idealistic entrepreneurs. I want to help them start their process while they're incarcerated with an internship program. Even if my idea created a small amount of progress, the foundation will have been laid for improvement by me or someone else with a better idea. We shouldn't have to rely on established law and non-existent rights under Title VII of the Civil Rights Act of 1964. I'm not aware of what rights we have under the EEOC, but they should still be consulted.

We just had count and our counselor, Ms. Hall, just said we need to get rid of all the free-standing fans because the safety department could show up and take them. She suggested that we figure out what we want to do or take the chance of losing the fans. I tried to explain this to the guys on the floor but all they want to do is argue.

May 1st, 2011 - Day 248

I just finished reading chapter four of *Beyond Opinion* and it gave a good summarization of Islam. I can't believe how ignorant I am about this. I never knew that Islam is not just a religion, it's a whole way of life in the Muslim community.

The author warns that if you choose to study Islam you should use a 4:1 ratio in regards to Christianity: for every hour you study Islam, you need to spend four hours on Christianity. I've always heard about the Quran and not the Qur'an and I've never heard about the Sunni. The author gives a lot of inference in the commentary that there's a lot of manipulation in events and times. This chapter alone will help me better understand what I'm reading in the NYT in regards to Middle Eastern Foreign Policy and our policies in regard to Muslims in this country and abroad.

I went to the chapel and found the Catholic Priest to get myself a big print Bible, which will make my studies at Nations a lot easier. I need to start reading Isaiah and getting prepared for exam three of the current course.

My plan to do push-ups every day is working and I've got to start doing 100 a day starting today. Sometimes I get lazy and don't do them, but for the last few weeks I've been really consistent. I need to get to the scale to see just how much weight or fat I'm losing.

We've got less than 30 days to hear something from the sentencing commission about the retroactivity of the crack cocaine amendment.

March 2nd, 2011 - Day 249

The Class Act is being reviewed by the Secretary of Health and Human Services. The article says that she is making changes within the regulations to implement the law. The long-term insurance plan will not be subsidied by the federal government but by private monies. The article says further that we should stay tuned to see what changes are being made.

I completed lesson 22 in my Language Arts Reading and got a 75%, 60%, and a 50% on the mini-test, which was horrible. The scores have the potential to make me a pessimist but I will move forward no matter what.

We got word last night that Osama Bin Laden was killed and the body recovered by the US Military. A

Muslim and a Jew came downstairs to tell everybody that they had heard on the radio that Osama had been killed. None of the guys wanted to turn their televisions to the news because their shows had about 10 minutes remaining. I intervened and told them to wait until the shows finish. They will talk about that news for days. At 11:00 p.m. the guys watching the shows got up and put the news on. I couldn't put my finger on how I felt, but I was more interested in what everyone else felt. It appeared that no one was willing to show any type of emotion. Everybody walked around and started to whisper about their thoughts, and as time went on, all the brothers got very vocal about their position. The thoughts were mutual: we thought that President Obama wouldn't get the credit for orchestrating the capture of Osama.

I was at the microwave and a young black kid of about 28 was holding up the wall while drinking coffee, I hope. Some of the tattoos on his face I thought he got before he arrived here. I walked up and said to him, "You've gotten more tattoos on your face since you've been here." He replied, "I've gotten all of them since being here," and handed me his ID card. He was right. I yelled, "Are you crazy! Why did you do this?" He said, "I'm in to the end." I had no idea what that meant. I asked, "What does the P stand for on the side of your face, the Pittsburgh Pirates?" He said, "No, it stands for PIRU!" I said, "Oh, you're a Blood?" He said, "Until I die!" Suddenly I realized I was talking to a youngster that had killed before and would kill me, no problem! I decided to lower my voice and not question him anymore. He laughed at me as I walked away, shaking my head in disbelief.

May 3rd, 2011 - Day 250

I'm my own case study! This book is the notes for said case study. I just realized that.

Well, in lesson 19 in my Science GED workbook I got a 67%, 86%, 75%, and a 55% on the mini-test for the lesson. I thought I would've done better on this mini-test, but I've got a lot of room for improvement. The post-test on this workbook is coming up shortly, so I hope I'm able to do better.

I had three call-outs today. One was for my yearly EKG, the second was to see Dr. Massero, and the third was my yearly lung exam. One of the medical staff shaves patches in the hair on your chest to stick the pads on that connect you to the machine. It takes about 10 minutes to complete the process.

I went to the Catholic Bible study and watched a lecture by a professor named Mrs. Spirits. The lecture covered I Kings and II Kings. At the end of her lecture, an outside visitor asked questions about what was just reviewed. I really enjoyed myself because I knew a lot of the answers. When I first arrived, there was an attendance sheet to sign in. It asked for my religion and I hesitated because I didn't know what to write.

I've been studying Siddha Yoga for over 12 years, but I wasn't educated enough to defend my belief. So I stood there while the line behind me waited and I wrote Bud for Buddhism. It's what is in the computer because I thought at the time it was the closest thing to Siddha Yoga. I don't know if Siddha Yoga is even considered a religion. I can't memorize the teachings, but as you read and contemplate them they become part of your life, and through grace you can witness God intervening in your life. The closer you get to God, the more He will test your faith, your integrity, your forgiveness, and your sacrifice.

The last few times my aunt sent me money, she didn't write me like she usually does. I guess after 16 years it just wears you down. I clearly understand; I guess I'd be tired, too.

May 4th, 2011 - Day 251

In the China Daily it is reported that the Chinese government is starting to crack down on intellectual properties being stolen by their citizens. I need to look into intellectual property and trademark laws before I'm released.

I got my science workbook back today with a 66%, 33%, 72%, and a 77% on the mini-test for lesson 20, and a 57% on the Part 3 Cumulative Review. Terrible! I guess I'll take the post-test tomorrow and see what I get.

When I awoke this morning, my shoulder was hurting really bad and the day before the doctor told me it's called getting older than 40. I laughed and laughed.

I still haven't heard anything from SIU-C, but I expected it to take a while for them to get around to me.

My friend, Flip, told me the Chinese are building schools in America called Confucius Institutes. They say that once the dragon is awakened, the world will be amazed.

It really doesn't matter what President Obama does; he'll never receive credit for his efforts and decision-making techniques. When he is re-elected in 2012, there are really going to be some partisan attacks on him and his family.

For some reason we didn't have to go to work because they were having a meeting with all of the correctional officers. This new warden has been getting things done and I think some of the male employees really don't like that fact.

May 5th, 2011 - Day 252

Last night at mail call, the case manager decided to pass out the mail along with her true disdain for inmates. She started to call out the mail, and if the inmate wasn't present, she would just throw their mail on the floor in a pile. However, as the pile got larger, she began to stand on the mail with total disregard for us. I couldn't take it anymore and I walked up to her and told her what she was doing was wrong. She then took her foot off the guy's letter and kicked it over to the rest of the pile. A real patriot, as the people would say.

Today I read an article about safes and why a lot of Americans are putting safes in their homes instead of jewelry boxes. This all depends on what you need to put in the safe, the value, and the level of insurance you have on the contents.

I got the post-test in the Science GED workbook graded and I got a 62%. I think I need to return to junior college and work my way forward. As I just told Kelly, I don't want to just pass a test and I'm tired of people telling me I'm smart. I'm not that goddamn smart! I dropped out of school after the 8th or 9th grade. I may have some skills that an ordinary inmate may not have, but I'm still missing some of the basics.

Everybody wants me to hurry up and study and learn so I can move forward, get my degree, and get a good job. I want to go slow and take my time. In the last few months that I've been working in the GED workbooks, I've realized that they're for individuals who want to prepare to take a test and just pass. I'm not interested in that. I want to go to a classroom and have someone explain things to me one step at a time, and I don't care how long it takes or how much it costs.

Some of this has to do with me not wanting to beg someone to help me with Algebra and study. These guys will say that they will help you, but eventually you'll start to get on their nerves. I'm in lesson 19 in math, lesson 23 in language arts reading, and lesson five in essays, all of the others are whatever. I've decided to stop here because this is not what I want. I think, listening to so many opinions, I got myself off the course that I really wanted to take: getting that information from SIU-C. This course catalog and all of the different things I could apply for got me off my original course.

I just had a revelation. I'm in search of something I already have. I'm enrolled in a university for a Bachelor Degree. I've been saying I wish I knew about their program years ago, but God is always right on time. So I need to finish the free degrees offered by this accredited university.

May 6th-7th, 2011 - Day 253 and 254

I forgot to do my journal entry last night so it'll get added to today's. I turned my radio to 590AM and heard Dave Ramsey say that he looks for property in areas where the cap rate is at least 8%, but he prefers 12%. In addition, he always makes an offer that is at 70% of the market rate of the property. I really need to start listening to his show a lot more. After a few years in I thought I had heard it all. That's not the case.

I've decided to add another aspect to the internship. A lot of us have state charges and parole that hangs over our heads and we don't have any assistance. When I caught this case and was sentenced to 282 months, I had at least 6-10 outstanding warrants. I was in Fayette County Jail, and after I stopped crying about my sentence, I sat down with a pen and paper to write a motion to get the warrants taken away because of my new sentence. There were a couple of law books lying around so I looked in them and copied the format for a motion, got copies, and submitted them to court. I got an order from the court a couple months later saying all charges have been dismissed.

I just finished watching the new Sex in the City and it was really good. I think the marriage counselor was very effective. I don't think I'll need a marriage counselor after I get married.

I think my wife and I will be able to work out any situation that we face. I can guarantee that my marriage will work because I'll never hit her and I'll never be unfaithful. Just because a woman is attractive and wants to have sex and knowing you could get away with it is no reason to be unfaithful. Just because they call us dogs doesn't mean we have to act like dogs.

Sometimes guys act like it is a sin to be honest. I've sat back for 20 years and watched the aftereffects of divorce, the single life, and space cadet status. I've got to have a commitment and I'm ready to be home every night before the sunset when I'm not running my business or with my family.

May 8ᵗʰ, 2011 - Day 255

I've thought a lot about what I would do if and when it came time for me to hire employees. Dave told his listeners that when you work for yourself with no employees, you're an employer who owns his own job. You become an employer when your company makes money when you're not there to contribute to make it earn a profit. I needed to know this definition.

Today in *Beyond Opinion* I read Chapter Five: Challenges from Eastern Religions and it appears to me that the author wants you to rely on what is read in sacred text books, not what you've experienced. I get the impression that he has had some experience with eastern philosophies. In his attempt to accept those fallen in enlightenment for what they are, his logic is surrendered as subpar, nonexistent in an unwantedness of engagement.

The day you don't want for anything is the day you have all that you need. So whatever is left after that is the truth; it doesn't need further explanation because it stands on its own. I believe God can be found at that point if you surrender to your higher power.

If there is truly only one God, then the only place we have to go is to Him in the end. Our beginning is our end; they're not separate.

The author mentioned Taoism on page 98 and nothing more about the discipline. Why? I love Bruce Lee's philosophy, "The way of no way."

May 9th, 2011 - Day 256

Mr. Logan pulled 30 inmates that had participated or are participating in a current re-entry class. I stood at the end of the hall, held the door, and directed people to the correct classroom. Everybody wanted to go back to whatever it was they had been doing. They all complained about being on call-out for something which they had no idea about.

The call-out was for a mock job fair with 16 or 17 volunteers from nonprofit organizations willing to come into the prison, subject themselves to scrutiny, and keep a positive attitude towards helping us. I started to get really pissed off because these guys don't understand what's in store for them once they're released.

I finished watching a VHS video about three hours long on King David. This will surely help me when I take exam five in the module I'm working on. My next three-hour video will be on King Solomon. I have Catholic Bible Study tomorrow at 1:00 p.m. and read over my Siddha Yoga studies during lunch.

I'm still struggling with my spending habits. I've got to stop getting stuff from the store room. I clear my debt with him every month and get more stuff when I feel like eating it. Grown people devise a plan and follow it, children do what feels good. It seems I've got some growing up to do.

I need to start working on this one day at a time and maybe one hour at a time. It's one thing to have knowledge of something and it's another to put it into action or heed its warning. I guess this is the definition of wisdom. I wish I had the wisdom of King Solomon.

May 10th, 2011 - Day 257

I just finished watching the movie *Notorious B. I. G.* for the first time and it was heartbreaking. It brought back memories of long ago. I loved Tupac's music and Biggie's music, too. They thrived with their music and died because of their music. It was all a big misunderstanding. The thing was that Tupac and Big were too young to realize the effect that their music had over a lot of people. They had money-hungry advisors who only preached getting that dollar bill.

I watched Mrs. Spirits lecture again today and she caught my attention with a statement that sometimes God is not looking for a good or right result, sometimes he's looking for the best one. This is how I've got to start writing the ideas, thoughts, responses, planning, and strategy to my life and the project.

I told some guys today that homosexuality is a bigger sin than murder. Was this a good statement? Was it a righteous statement? Was it the best statement to make? Was the statement made because I was tired of people thinking I might be gay? Did I think it was a greater sin?

It was a poor way to express a belief that there are some lines I just will not cross. And caring what other people say or think is hard to overlook or disregard, but someday you've got to stop acting on what feels good and stand on your values. I do not support same sex marriage... Marriage should only be between a man and a woman. I think civil unions are the way to go. I am not prepared to accept that homosexuality is not a choice, that you're born that way.

We've got the mock job fair tomorrow and it should be really productive. I had a youngster come up to me today and ask me about taking college courses. He just passed his GED and he wants to know how a degree would benefit him. He hung on my every word; somehow tomorrow I'll make sure he signed up at Nations University because I gave him all the information.

At dinner I had another youngster ask me for some advice. He told me that he couldn't get himself into studying the way he needs to in order to pass the GED. I told him about the GED workbooks that I worked on and that the schedule that I had set up would be good for him to get back into the groove of studying. One day at a time and one hour at a time. He needs to be encouraged every day until he starts to move on his own.

These guys want to be successful, it's just the fear of failure that is so insurmountable. The fear has to be overcome and then ideas, thoughts, and dreams have to be rebuilt one day at a time. They have to be taught to be resolute at dealing with obstacles, lessons, setbacks, unexpected success, and unexpected trauma. When you're upset, sit down; if you're still upset later, lie down.

I read about some insurance companies that have successfully lobbied some states into allowing entities called captives to be established in the states. Normally these entities were only created offshore because their accounting techniques disguised the true financial structure of the company. The insurance companies have to keep a constant level of reserves in relation to the amount of policies that they issue. However, the captive is created to hold a large amount of the policies of the parent company and then the captive is re-designated as a single policy holder of the parent. Of course all of the records of the captive and the process in question are confidential. Why? Because the enterprises give money into the state treasury. So the consumer laws that have been in place to protect them have been effectively circumvented and the beginning of another financial collapse has its origin.

I would like to buy a short in the market for 15 years and the value of the contract needs to be $100 million. This next financial collapse is going to happen, so how do you strategically place yourself with this information? Excessive liquidity! Cash and lots of it! What we just went through in the financial collapse has been re-engineered to happen again to make the future generation of the elite stay uber-rich.

It's 11:38 p.m. and somebody is smoking cigarettes. The guards will be here in about 30 minutes and they'll smell the smoke. Then they'll be back to search because cigarettes aren't allowed in federal buildings or property. But that doesn't stop *them* from smoking right out in plain sight. It's okay for them to break the law, who is going to arrest them? No one! Who is going to report it? No one! Who's going to report that they use the United States Postal Service mail bins and bags for storage of everything except mail? Who's going to report that federal employees have the mail bags and bins at home, being used for storage? No one!

May 11th, 2011 - Day 258

All of the interviews went very well today. Everyone who interviewed me said that they would hire me. My last interview was with a lady from the VA and she thought my resume was good. She told me that I should apply for a job at the VA as soon as I get released. Another gentleman gave me his email and he wanted me to keep him informed about my progress. I think he wants me to come work for his nonprofit.

I just found out that Mr. Moon was having chest pains and was rushed to the hospital. He's about 65 years of age and he drives himself very hard with working out twice a day, studying two languages, guitar, eight hours of reading, and a job. He's going to kill himself if he doesn't slow down.

The lady from the VA told me to submit my certifications with my resume because of all the paper mills being created. Paper mills issue fake degrees in six weeks or less. By submitting backup documentation, the hiring process is easier for the employer and potential employees.

May 12ᵗʰ, 2011 - Day 259

A rent ratio is the sale price of a house divided by the cost of renting an equivalent house. When the ratio is below 15, most people should lean toward buying.

I read in the Times about two women and two social workers who were being indicted because of the death of a young child. The state agency also had a private contract with a private company for services. I might put something like this in my project. Some sort of social service mechanism. However, what I don't want are the social services that are here because the individuals will compromise confidentiality for the sake of keeping their job. But they're saying that it's operational security that dictates their level of client/inmate confidentiality, which I believe is horse shit.

The other day we had the job fair, and now that I reflect on my interviews, I interrupted them while they were talking to me. I need to learn to listen better, be more patient.

I almost went and got some food from the store man but I didn't. I don't have an eating disorder, but I do have a real, actual sweet tooth. I still weigh about 226 pounds. My acid reflux will not go away even though I keep taking this medicine.

I just got out of the shower and was in my room drying off and putting on more clothes. As I finished, I peeked down the hall and saw Mr. Smith helping another inmate stand up and walk to his room. For some reason he got really dizzy and almost collapsed as I was watching them. I took off toward them and offered to help but I wondered how this guy was supposedly going to find the people who helped get him arrested, kill them, and go on a bank robbery spree while he's barely able to stand in 70-degree heat. I told him I'd go and get the guard but it's really useless because he wouldn't do anything unless it's an emergency.

May 13th, 2011 - Day 260

Today I had to turn into a politician because I needed to see my FBI rap sheet and the NCIC federal and state report. I was shocked to find out that the reports lacked certain information and duplicated other information. It was clear to me that these systems are ripe with errors and could cost someone a really good job.

I've decided to request that the business office starts to designate all deposits into my account to my pre-release balance as of June 1st, 2011 until I reach about $500.00. It shouldn't take me more than about six months to accumulate the amount that I need. I found out during my unit pre-release that I need to have clothes sent in and a bag, if needed.

Sometimes it's really hard to overlook someone's incompetency or unprofessionalism. Moreover, you've got to realize that a lot of employees (and that includes federal employees) in the Federal Bureau of Prisons are in desperate need of administrative training. They receive security training, which is useless because if there's any killing going on they're going to turn right around and run back the way they came. If this woman weighs 120 pounds soaking wet with bricks in her pockets, what is she going to do with a 250-pound inmate who first shoved a plexiglass knife into a guy's chest and broke the handle off to make sure the sharp end stays in him?

Initially I'd thought that China Daily had stopped the free subscription, however I continue to receive the paper with much gratitude. I saw a solicitation for a job offer in China but the solicitation request was a little different. The Chinese entitled their solicitation Request for Expression of Interest. I think I'll use the same language in my project.

I talked to a young man late last night and he was incarcerated for drug distribution for a major drug cartel. He told me about a nonprofit he started to help ex-felons and the elderly and some abandoned children. I learned that the nonprofit was easy to establish and advanced degrees opened doors for funding and credibility. While listening to him it appeared that he had accomplished quite a lot with his family's assistance. Now his wife permanently maintains the operation and the integrity of the organization, along with the board of directors.

I just had an idea. I want to still do the commentary before every 30 days in the diary, however I'm going to have a ghostwriter do the commentary in regards to the substance of what I've written, the enthusiasm I feel about what I've written, and the extent of my effort behind the project.

So basically I'll do 12 tape recorded interviews and I'll probably hire the ghostwriter on an hourly basis. Plus the individual will probably need me to interpret some of my handwriting.

It's 7:44 p.m. and I just finished chapter six in *Beyond Opinion* and loved it. This is the reason I'm going to enjoy the religious studies. If I had a choice between atheism, theism, or pantheism, I would choose theism without question. I have studied pantheism for over 12 years and it is quite appealing because I do like Taoism. However, I outright reject atheism as a whole.

May 15th - 16th, 2011 - Day 262 and 263

I worked on my book of essays yesterday so I watched a lot of TV instead of studying.

I got my certificate from a debt management class and the last DVD we watched was Suze Orman, "The Laws of Money and the Lessons of Life." Some of her ideas I did not agree with, especially the credit card debt. I learned something about how to operate within retirement accounts, though.

She presented five laws to follow and I believe that Dave Ramsey's principles encompass what she has offered only with more substance and a better outcome. Mrs. Orman did not encourage these people to do something to generate income besides being an employee. She told the truth, though. (1) Look at what you have and not what you had. (2) Do what's right for you, not your money. (3) Invest in the known, not the unknown. (4) We left class before I got this one but I bet that it's, "Always ask questions."

I was reading and studying the book of Zachariah and I knew that God had communications with his Angels and Satan! Every time I pick up the Bible and study, I find it to be more intriguing than anything else.

May 17th, 2011 - Day 264

I learned a great deal today at the Catholic Bible Study session. Some of the facts dealing with the Kings of Israel and Judah were a little confusing. I've spent more than eight hours studying the Old Testament today.

Sometimes I need to remember that the federal employees at prison don't appreciate you taking the initiative to help them do a job. Oh, well!

My case manager, Ms. Hoskins, called me to her office to have me sign my supervised release agreement paperwork. This means that this paperwork is being done a year in advance. This is a good thing, even though I believe that the law will change or the amendment will appear on June 1st.

Knowing that this endeavor, the PrisonProof project, will take a minimum of 20 to 30 years makes it a really good, long-term goal that I look forward to. The missing link to my long-term goals can be found in Proverbs 31:10-31:

"Who can find a virtuous woman? For her price is far above rubies. The heart of her husband doth safely trust in her, so that he shall have no need of spoil. She will do him good and not evil all the days of her life. She seeketh wool, and flax, and worketh willingly with her hands. She is like the merchants' ships; she bringeth her food from afar. She riseth also while it is yet night, and giveth meat to her household, and a portion to her maidens. She considereth a field, and buyeth it: with the fruit of her hands she planteth a vineyard. She girdeth her loins with strength, and strengtheneth her arms. She perceiveth that her merchandise is good: her candle goeth not out by night. She layeth her hands to the spindle, and her hands hold the distaff. She stretcheth out her hand to the poor; yea, she reacheth forth her hands to the needy. She is not afraid of the snow for her household: for all her household are clothed with scarlet. She maketh herself coverings of tapestry; her clothing is silk and purple. Her husband is known in the gates, when he sitteth among the elders of the land. She maketh fine linen, and selleth it; and delivereth girdles unto the merchant. Strength and honour are her clothing; and she shall rejoice in time to come. She openeth her mouth with wisdom; and in her tongue is the law of kindness. She looketh well to the ways of her household, and eateth not the bread of idleness. Her children arise up, and call her blessed; her husband also, and he praiseth her. Many daughters have done virtuously, but thou excellest them all. Favour is deceitful, and beauty is vain: but a woman that feareth the Lord, she shall be praised. Give her of the fruit of her hands; and let her own works praise her in the gates." (King James Version.)

May 18th, 2011 - Day 265

The idea I had about the pre-release balance designation is not feasible because this installation has not set up the mechanism to use the designation for the inmate population. I've looked into this credit union which only requires $5 to open an account, but the membership has too many restrictions. So I've decided I really need to buckle down and save so I'm only allowing myself a spending limit of $5 dollars a week until I'm released. I should be released with $500 in cash and a check mailed to a forwarding address that I will provide.

I ordered some supplies today for the Education Department and saw a company called AbilityOne – a major employer of handicapped individuals – and they're registered as a contractor with the GSA.

I tried to call SIU-C to get a status report on the admission application, but Mr. Lawrence wanted me to wait until tomorrow because he was filling out his retirement paperwork. The re-entry program is not going to stay together for very long after his departure.

I met some guys today that just got in from the Federal Medical Center in Butner, NC and they couldn't believe all of the education programs offered at this institution. They said that all of their programs were being closed for some reason. I asked him about the college classes that are required because of the law in NC and he said the waiting list is really crazy.

May 19ᵗʰ, 2011 - Day 266

Last night, I had a gentleman come and ask me for assistance with his expulsion from the Residential Drug Abuse Program. It appears that he was having a political discussion in his GED class and one of the students didn't appreciate his views. So the offended individual informed a friend of his in the RDAP program, who happens to be mentally disabled. The mentally disabled person made specific racial slurs about Mr. Moore, and subsequently, they were both expelled at the last minute before graduation. It went something like that.

I talked to an older gentleman from Indiana who had also put up a Facebook page and he said that about 40 people had contacted him and that he was amazed at the people who sought to reach out.

I called the admissions counselor at SIU-C and they informed me that they had received my public safety documents but the counselor has not made a decision in regards to my case. The counselor explained that, since my admission would not happen until Spring of 2012, they had other current applications to consider first.

I went downstairs to get my NYT and it wasn't in the mail. This seems to happen when someone gets lazy and doesn't want to sort the rest of the papers.

I saw a book in the library entitled *Effective Immediately* and I tried to get it so that I could read it but they said it was being sent to the multicultural library. So now I've got to go to the multicultural library and find that book.

May 20th - 21ˢᵗ - Day 267 and 268

I want to make sure that it's known that my company will be inmate-friendly. I want to hire exclusively ex-felons and I'll probably be doing the hiring in the beginning.

It seems June 1st is not that far away and I'm hoping that the sentencing commission will make the 18-1 amendment retroactive so that I can have an immediate release.

I've had a couple of the guys approach me about doing their 2255 petition to the court and just help them better understand what's going on in their cases in the appeal process.

I don't believe that President Obama and Prime Minister of Israel, Mr. Netanyahu, will see eye to eye on the Mideast peace deal with the Palestine authority. Israel will never trust Hamas. Even if they wanted to and entered a deal, there are elements in both governments that would do anything they could to see the peace deal collapse. I noticed that Israel is on the border of the Mediterranean Sea. They should be more worried about a tsunami washing them out of existence.

One of the guys named AJ died this morning. They found him sound asleep at the 10:00 am count. This is a normal occurrence at this place.

May 22nd, 2011 - Day 269

We just finished watching *Meet the Press* and the republican, Paul Ryan, is advocating this voucher program for everyone 34 and under. But one additional concern of mine is, 26 years from now, a mentally disabled person at 70 has to negotiate with a private insurance company and just breaks down on the phone and starts crying. This is the exact point where my mother apparently was until she told me what was going on and I intervened. She is not mentally disabled, but at her age, senior citizens do have a diminished capacity to interact with other people, especially in a hostile environment.

One of the guys was explaining to me during the commercials that he got 32 years for bank robbery. He said he got caught because an individual told the police about the crimes. He started to explain to me that the 924(c) possessing, brandishing, or discharging of a firearm is the commission of a felony act. I was already aware of this but I was happy he was able to explain his charge to me. He got convicted under the Hobbs Act, committing a crime while affecting interstate commerce. After he told me some facts about his case, I started to realize that there were some subject matter jurisdiction questions that needed to be addressed. Count time just concluded so I'm going to go back downstairs and find him. I need to take him outside and explain to him some of the tenets of subject matter jurisdiction.

It's 11:46 am and I just finished watching President Obama at AIPAC giving a live speech. While listening to his speech, I realized that he has masterfully set up the media to misconstrue his words so that he can come back and expand on the literal meaning and context while at the same time controlling the news and radio cycles for over a week or so. President Obama seems to me to have become more tactical and mechanical in his message, policy changes, and language over the years.

I went to the mess hall to eat lunch and I ate very quickly so that I could hear some of the analysis of his speech, and when I returned, I was denied the opportunity because the TV was changed to the speed racing highlights on the speed channel.

This lack of interest in changing government has to be a tenet of the PrisonProof Project. Maybe every intern in the program must run for some level of local or state government if they can. Maybe they should be required to participate in an individual's candidacy and witness the wheels of government.

I need to set up my web page to sell my books, answer questions, and provide advice that trains people to handle a problem or situation they've presented for a low price. On the social media pages I should have a link to my master web site for people to become "peer trainers" by purchasing a book or a Q & A session by appointment. The Q & A session does not have to be the next week if people just want to submit other questions, to which I could just respond in writing at any time. This is a great idea to avoid dealing with the self-publishing companies or starting a publishing company. I could just start this internal company. I'll probably ask $2.99 a session to ask questions and $19.99 or more to read the book.

I don't want to respond to anyone on their social media until they've become "peer trainers" because our conversation could venture into legal or financial advice and I'm not licensed to practice those trades. However, I am lawfully allowed to train individuals on what I've learned and experienced or because of a degree that I hold that's been accredited by the US Department of Education. Maybe I should set the sessions in regards to what's written in my books and my life. Once you've purchased one or the other your email is your password.

Maybe the Q & A option should be an annual amount that includes all three books and the Q & A option for $49.99. Just the Q & A option should be $24.99 annually. I think I've just decided to put up all three books at once.

A couple of hours ago I had a friend not afraid to stop me and say, "You can speak to me sometime!" I told him that I was sorry because I'm in my own little world in my head. I have the ability to block out what is going on around me, especially when I'm not in a dangerous environment.

I read the Bible today and found a passage that caught my attention. It was Nehemiah 2:13 and it spoke of a thing called a "Prayer Well." I've only heard of such things in Chinese movies. Studying the Bible being a part of academia brings certain aspects of its history and text into a better level of comprehension.

I've decided to do a weekly column on my web site and I think I'm going to make my books available to my readers on my web site first. However, if the sales are really good then I'll look at paper publishing and eBooks. I might have it to where I can send you a hard copy of the book by ordering on my web site. I'm going to post the weekly column every Monday or Friday. The article should be about my progress and setbacks and what's ahead with the project. It should also address feedback, whether constructive or not, especially since I'm going to be on every social media site on the internet. All sales go to paying my education and the project.

May 24th-25th, 2011 - Day 272 and 273

I think one of the components in the RDAP program should include a law review class. These women with their psychology and drug treatment certifications are not receptive as far as the men are concerned. To the inmates it's a game and they're wondering what women can relate to in regards to a black man growing up in the ghetto. Personally I believe that men should be running these programs so that there's a better level of responsiveness.

I was sitting in my office yesterday and in the horticulture class across the hall, all of the students were asleep. I saw a real waste of time right in front of me.

One component of the drug program should be that these guys could leave the country once they're off of supervised release. I think that people should be allowed to ask questions about the law. Once these guys realize there are serious consequences behind continuing their conduct, then they may realize that continuing bad behavior or choices is not good if they want to live a better life outside of prison. Maybe I should stay away from prison and just visit juvenile centers and drug centers.

We had to prepare for graduation today. The education department in this institution holds a graduation ceremony for GED, ESL, Apprenticeship, Vocational Training, Computer Application, and other categories. Only the GED graduates wear the cap and gown with the tassle that they're allowed to keep.

May 26th, 2011 - Day 274

I went to the yearly graduation and we got a real shock. The guest speaker was an ex-felon who was currently employed at the University of Kentucky. I forgot his name, but he got his Ph.D. in research and communication and he shared his story of redemption with us. He talked about how he was disappointed about the Pell Grant being terminated and the good it did for him.

One of the guys I counsel sometimes asked me if I wanted to read a book entitled *The New Jim Crow* by Michelle Alexander. I can't wait to get started with that book.

My friend had to have his hand re-broken so that it can properly heal with some aftercare. He shouldn't have to have his hand or his finger broken again because there was no follow-up on his medical care.

I saw on the news yesterday that an aide to Sarah Palin has written a book that talks all about her real spirituality. While being interviewed, this aide said that she does not carry a Bible, she doesn't pray regularly or before meals, and never before and after an event.

May 27th, 2011 - Day 275

In Alexander vs. Sandoval, decided in 2001, the Supreme Court made all ex-felons effectively disabled due to the ruling that there is not a private right to action under Title VI of the Civil Rights Act.

"Conduit leasing" is a new term for me and its history really needs to be studied. I'm thinking of starting a franchise with PrisonProof so that I can provide jobs and housing for ex-felons.

I also realize that if I'm successful in helping mass amounts of ex-felons, they would probably try to find a way to re-incarcerate me.

One of the goals of PrisonProof during (or after) the process of acquiring my L.L.M (international law degree) is to visit every prison, state and federal, to teach the group the truth about their conditions. Hopefully I'll have enough strength to do all of the drug treatment centers.

I took three exams last week in my Nations studies and failed exam three. I've been in a bad mood all day. When I was on the street I would start drinking when I felt down because of a failure of some sort. Today I just have to stop and look at it, see it for what it is, and let go. Start studying for the retake.

Ms. Haskins, my case manager, was standing at the front door a while ago and she stopped me to tell me that my halfway house packet left the institution to be processed for halfway house in May of 2012.

I just read a statement by Martin Luther King: "Nothing in all the world is more dangerous than sincere ignorance and conscientious stupidity."

May 28th, 2011 - Day 276

I read in the newspaper that the US Supreme Court has upheld the Arizona law that will specialize in employers who hire illegal immigrants. This is a really big deal. The US Supreme Court just guaranteed Obama's reelection in 2012 because this ruling will effectively drive down the unemployment rate to under 5%, easily.

If I believe the justice system is the new racial caste system, how do you deconstruct the system? The 2.5 million incarcerated people in America must be sacrificed and redirected to the juvenile detention centers and the drug treatment centers.

We need to be vigilant when a young person contracts their first conviction and work to erase it from their record. We also need to be vigilant about informing the young of their restoration of civil rights in the state laws. A lot of the bias in *The New Jim Crow* could be avoided if convicts knew about the law in regards to rights in the constitution. Can you plea bargain to retain certain rights? Can a statute be re-written to include the statement, "unless otherwise agreed with the Attorney General of the state?" Mr. Moon believes no man will have a strong chance at success after being in prison unless he does his due diligence, which is read, write, and study.

It took me less than 24 hours to finish reading *The New Jim Crow.* It was an excellent book.

I just finished chapter seven in *Beyond Opinion*, "Conversational Apologies," and it was very interesting. It finally confirmed for me that I'm not really a Buddhist and I may have an unclear understanding about faith and what it means to *have* faith. I had always pushed back on the word "faith" because it's the unknown. However, I do unmistakably believe that God exists, physically and spiritually. I've always had faith that God exists. I don't have enough education and experience in defending any faith, but I can defend the existence of God very well. I can give several examples of his grace in my life and I continued to sin anyway.

May 29th - 30th, 2011 - Day 277 and 278

I didn't get a lot of work done, so I finished reading John Grisham's *The Associate* and it was really good; however, I didn't like the ending.

Today is Memorial Day and we had fried chicken, dinner rolls, corn on the cob, and fried onion rings. Everything was cooked until it was so tough you couldn't chew the food. They were obviously understaffed because today was the first time on a holiday that we didn't have to scan our ID cards. The rumor was that one of the staff members got written up and the rest of the food supervisors didn't like it. I guess the AW, a black lady, chose to write him up for evaluation. Apparently the food administrator gave him an instruction and he refused to follow the order.

I talked to my friend, Hakim, today and he told me he's on his way to the camp. I explained to him that he may not like going to the camp. He said he's tired of being around these "zero-ass niggas." All of the hustlers in here have been transferred or are in the process of being transferred. He was right, but I felt that way in 2003 when I first arrived here. Nobody was really on education and these guys don't realize that going back to college is really the only answer.

Chapter Ten: Rollie Allen

My aunt was the family doctor and she always had an answer to any medical question. She is a registered nurse practitioner and has worked in the medical field for decades. If for some reason she could not answer that question in relation to your medical problem, she could point you in the right direction.

She married my uncle Clarence and they had three beautiful children, Michelle, Keith, and Terrell. She and her family still reside in Southern Illinois and accompany the families on extended trips to Mississippi and Kansas City, MO.

I loved seeing her smiling face when I was released.

May 31st, 2011 - Day 279

I got Saturday, Monday, and Tuesday's NYT and four China Daily USA. The next couple of days are going to be tough.

My buddy, Frank, has been down for about 30 years and he's an old school mob guy. He wants me to let him know when they report something in the NYT about the mob families in NY. Every time he reads the newspaper, he gets mad as hell. Sometimes it takes him hours to read one article just because it's too upsetting.

Today, Frank and I were going through the chow line and Frank told this youngster to put extra rice on his tray. The youngster told Frank it would cost two stamps. Frank said okay, put it on there. The tray made it to the slot for Frank to grab it and the youngster asked where his two stamps were. Frank said, "Whenever you get some free time just come by and pick 'em up." Everybody in the chow line fell out laughing because the youngster doesn't know who Frank is, but all the guys who've been down 10, 15, or 20 years know. So, I yelled at Frank: "'Ey Frank, you gettin' soft, man, the youngster wants his two stamps." Frank started laughing. "I got his two stamps, tell 'im to come and get 'em."

Tomorrow is the big day for the sentencing commission to hold public comments on whether or not the new crack law amendment will be retroactive or not. We didn't get 1-1 but 18-1 is just the beginning.

Every corner I turn, guys are stopping me, asking me what I think will happen tomorrow. I must display as much confidence as I can muster and be strong for a lot of men in these institutions.

Today I was at work when two of the psychology interns came walking briskly down the hall looking for someone. I thought they were looking for Mr. Logan because that's who they're usually down here to visit. I asked them if they were looking for him and the very large girl said yes and the other skinny one said no.

Evidently they were looking for an inmate who's deemed to have been reckless, eyeballing them. This is the most ridiculous accusation that is allowed in prison. You lock a man away for 30 years and then keep sending women in his face thinking that he should maintain his composure because you told him to. I'm still trying to figure out how you bring a 23-year-old white girl into a prison and then give her a Ph.D. in psychology. What possible background could you have to deal with anything outside of what you remember from all the tests you took?

Every staff member in correction should be made to submit to random drug tests and annual pysch evaluations. These people in a daily environment verbally abuse, physically abuse, mentally abuse, lie, steal, make false statements on office documents, allow kickbacks, use government resources for personal use, abuse their authority, sell drugs, and compromise themselves and other staff and the security of the institution. And they all cover for each other because 80% of them are either related or have lived and hung out together since they were children.

Just because sociology and psychology is offered doesn't mean that certain people should be allowed to practice it. The psych staff at this place doesn't give a rat's ass about anyone else but themselves.

I talked to Mrs. Campbell today and she told me that once she retires from the federal prison system, she's going to work at the state pen. I gave her one warning: "You need to try and get a job at a pre-school and stay away from the pen." This is why some women are so gullible; they have no sense or perception of danger.

June 2nd, 2011 - Day 281

One way for me to provide a massive amount of housing is by using a huge mobile home park. The only problem is that the trailers start to go down in value the second that they're purchased. This may not be a good idea but I'll look at it when I get to the stage of being employed or self-employed. I always have to remember that I need to keep my job until my self-employment brings an annual income equal to or greater than my job's earned income.

Today, the NYT had an article about the hearing that was held at the sentencing commission. The Attorney General, Eric Holden, came to testify that he and the administration support the 18-1 to become retroactive. I was hoping that this would happen. I believe I may change my plan and attend SIU-Edwardsville and major in sociology. I talked to the lady named Susan at SIU-C and she couldn't tell me if I got approved for the Capstone option program.

I'm starting to realize that, to have great success at your project, it will require great sacrifice.

My buddy told me about a young lady who started a virtual secretary business and she was incarcerated for at least 10 years. He said she's having a hard time staying above board but she's doing better than previous years. I think the business name was Lullylee or something like that.

It's going to be very hard for Obama to get the unemployment rate back to 5% but I believe he's got a plan to take a really good swing at making it happen.

June 3rd, 2011 - Day 282

I just realized that the education reforms that are needed in the prison system need to be executed in such a way that the guys have as little dependency on the staff as possible. A lot of us have taken exams from Nations at the beginning of this week. It is now Friday and our exams have still not been sent to Nations. The process to send the exams takes about five minutes, but the staff are lost in their email soap opera. Some of the staff actually *do* do work, but for the most part waste, laziness, and personal use of government property is rampant.

The main problem is that the world is changing very fast and these guys are going to find it much harder to adapt upon release as well as more into the future. Some sort of educational system has to be developed where these guys can have direct contact with educational institutions.

I believe that my internship program for the PrisonProof Project should have a writing course for essays. I need to find a way to supply the guys with research material. In the internship, certain subscriptions should also be provided. I need to make a mortgage corporation and probably a business management and consulting firm.

I watched a seminar today by Mr. Dolf de Roos on Real Estate Investor's College, which was on DVD. It was alright, a lot of the stuff I already knew. We have a lot of education and experience in the real estate markets, especially in other countries.

I put myself in a really stupid, unnecessary situation today because I asked a favor. The day that you don't want for anything is the day you'll have everything you need.

June 4th, 2011 - Day 283

I believe that I really need to start the publishing company and the trust company so that I can publish diaries and memoirs of ex-felons through the internship and have a good amount of their proceeds put into a trust for them upon their release. I should make sure that I include a provision for a court-appointed trustee to be allowed at their request. I need to keep control of the copyright, but the royalties can be split 50-50 or whatever is expectable.

Writing a diary or a memoir doesn't require a college education. An individual's best effort and a good ghostwriter can make all the difference. Writing fiction is an intimidating endeavor for an uneducated person. Even for ex-felons that can't read and write, they can dictate their life story to the best of their ability to another inmate or family member and submit their work. Maybe I should do this for prisoners all over the world. And no one can be turned away because we'll work with you until we can get a finished product. If, however, the individual becomes problematic and the selection of material becomes unworkable, then I just relieve them for a period of time and re-engage them later on.

I anticipate a lot of people going against me and trying to stop my project. I'll be very well-prepared to make them pay a steep price for their recklessness.

Mr. Moon told me that back in the days when the economy was really bad, people made good money with story commodities. Stuff like make-up, cigarettes, liquor, and things like that. I don't know how far I want to go with this advice, but I'll remember it.

I have not called home in a while and I know my mother wants to hear from me. I'll call her tomorrow. I've got to study for exam 5 at Nations which covers Psalms, Proverbs, Ecclesiastics, Job, Lamentations, etc.

June 5th, 2011 - Day 284

Some of the things I want the trust in the internship to cover are all of the budget items listed in *The Total Money*

Makeover by Dave Ramsey. My concern is, could the trust take the position on financial responsibility that the individual isn't adopting? Will that create an administrative nightmare? I may need an army of African-American sociologists to help me reach my goals. One other mechanism that needs to be added to the trust are a live item of compensation for court orders, child support, victim compensation, court fees, attorney fees, and so forth.

I just finished watching *State of the Union* and I was surprised to see that the unemployment rate was 7.8% when President Obama took office and now it's 9.1%. I do believe that President Obama can get it below 7.8% before the election date in 2012.

Candy Crowly interviewed Ron Paul, who's running for president for a third time, and I believe he's going to make the conversation around the presidential election quite different. I wonder what type of message the administration would receive if all Americans stopped using debt?

Earlier, when I went to get my laundry from the laundry room, I could smell the alcohol coming out of the pores of a group of guys. They don't understand that the alcohol is coming out of their system. I knew these guys were going to get drunk when I saw them earlier breaking into a hatch in the ceiling to retrieve a five-gallon bucket of hooch.

If these types of people are going to continue to be a drag on society and welfare recipients, then I'd rather have a program that gives them the opportunity to create an income-producing asset with no up-front capital when they're in an environment complimentary of producing this opportunity.

To accept the word of those who urge you not to believe in faith is merely to take their word on faith instead! This is a summary of a chapter in *Beyond Opinion*. It recognizes Taoism again for some reason. However, I am becoming more comfortable with calling myself a Christian.

June 6th, 2011 - Day 285

The one thing that is available to inmates in regards to college courses is Bible studies because they generally don't cost anything. They may not be recognized because their accreditation is not regional but national.

I want to find a ghostwriter and offer $5,000 a book with a minimum of 400-600 pages per book for three books to be paid in four increments as the completion of the book moves forward. I'm going to have to set my company up first. I would really prefer that this was a graduate student because a credited professional is going to charge me more money than I can afford. I need to think about covering research time plus expenses. I have to make sure that a confidentiality agreement and a no-compete clause is included.

I could set up a website and ask for gifts or donations and explain what the goal of the site is. I probably should put my goal at $100,000 to start my research project and continue my education. I need to talk about my three manuscripts, what I plan on doing with them, and list the dates of release. All donations of $20.00 or more will receive a free autographed copy of every book published in regards to this project.

As of today, I've scheduled 10 manuscripts over the course of 10 years which will articulate a plausible PrisonProof strategy to combat the increasing prison recividism rate.

Once a donation is received, I'm going to email a confirmation within 48 hours with a PrisonProof code. When a new book is released, fill out a purchase order, select no charge as method of payment, and enter your code. Once you select a book using your code, you can no longer get a free copy of that specific book; all others will remain available to you.

June 7ᵗʰ, 2011 - Day 286

I've looked at the nonprofit and charitable trust, but they don't give me the control I need and I'm not educated on those entities. However, I'm very well-versed on the DBA sole proprietorship.

I talked to Mr. Blythe, who is 80 years of age, and I asked him how he feels about the people who run these institutions. His answer was very informative and it changed my perspective a little bit.

My buddy, Ray-Ray, was having a problem collecting some of his money from one of the Mexicans named Castro. He asked me to have a word with him and see if he'd finish paying the debt. I talked to Castro, retrieved the money, and thanked him for his cooperation.

I went to the Catholic Bible Study and learned a lot about King John and all the nonsense behind his decision and the demise of his family.

It's 11:24 and I just went to the sports TV room to see the Dallas and Miami score and noticed that every trash can (20 gallons) that I passed was full with about three feet of trash on top falling all around the trash can.

Earlier today, I was outside in the courtyard watching MSNBC and I felt something crawling on my arm. It was a baby spider and he was running real fast, but as I looked past my arm I could see a couple of roaches as big as my pinky fingers.

Here's an example of how sharp some inmates are. They'll smuggle the radio through the metal detector, in front of the guards. Basically, they will hold the radio in their hand and swing it through the detector so they won't set it off. So later, the guards will reset the machine so sensitive that my pen won't pass through! Idiots!

June 8ᵗʰ, 2011 - Day 287

I think I might have and idea for homes for which I can issue a license to ex-inmates so they have a place to live for a few years. I assume everything would have to stay in my name: the utility, water, trash... maybe the name of the company. And I would charge more per day when you don't leave on schedule.

I got paid today - $33.00 - and I made it from my last payday without debt. I put $2.00 in email minutes and $5.00 at the store. I've decided never to go into debt and just spend $5.00 a week until I'm released from prison. I'm going to make good grades and pay my way through college. I absolutely refuse to let my debt sit around like a pet.

Part of my library in the prison project will be the purchase of every book in the Dave Ramsey store. I've been listening to his show this evening and a law graduate with $160,000 in debt needed to know what to do with his financial inheritance of one million dollars. He just didn't know how to approach the situation. I couldn't believe someone with that type of education didn't have a clue about finance.

June 9ᵗʰ, 2011 - Day 288

He said, "There are no good samaritans these days. When the wealthy give donations, they write that off on their taxes." It's not a write off, it's a write *over.* They simply take the place of their government, allocating their tax dollars.

One of the guys that's taking some of the Nations courses asked me if I was planning on writing a book. I told him I was working on three manuscripts and he seemed amazed. He explained to me that his son was friends with an editor at DoubleDay publishing and he'd send it to them for me if I wanted. He stated that I just needed to make sure that it is as clean and prepared as possible.

It was about 2:00 a.m. and I couldn't sleep, so I got up and started doing push-ups until I couldn't do any more. I think I did about 50 push-ups... I'm really out of shape.

June 10th, 2011 - Day 289

What is the definition of a patriarch? My definition of a patriarch is a man who is willing to sacrifice his dignity to feed his family and community.

I just finished watching a movie entitled *Keep of the Enemies* and it was based on true events. After watching the movie, I realized that I've got $26.00 on my prison account, and now that I look back, there have been many days I've had $26.00 on my prison account. I wonder how much it has cost me to keep myself in poverty.

I didn't know where this book would take me but I knew I could write it and save it and see what I had at the end. How relevant or irrelevant is something saved versus something not saved? Well, let's see.

If my parents taught me not to lie, shouldn't I have saved that? If they taught me to work, shouldn't I have saved that? If they taught me compassion, shouldn't I have saved that? If they taught me to forgive, shouldn't I have saved that?

How are prison, poverty, and a penny alike? Why did I go to prison so many times and never save what I learned? Why have I been in poverty so long and never saved it? Why have I earned a penny so many times but never saved it?

I read an article on nonprofits that said the laws had changed, and whether you earned $25,000 more or less, under the new law you had to file a tax return. The IRS said they'd contacted the National Council of Nonprofits and kicked off a get-out-the-change vote but they still had to revoke the exemption status of 175,000 non-profits.

I got some really good information at an entity called The Cooperation of Felon-Friendly Employers, where you can file an application with them and enter a database as a registered employer who offers jobs and wants the Work Opportunity Tax Credit for hiring felons at www.thenextstep99.com/.

Bob Gale's speech to the graduating class of the US Naval Academy in Annapolis in regards to leadership was extraordinary in my view.

June 11th, 2011 - Day 290

Sometimes I think I should just write books and lecture about what I know, but Mr. Blythe has raised my curiosity about import and export. So, I got my friend's book about import and export and spent the entire day reading about the adventures of a salesman. Blythe was telling me about how easy it is to become a millionaire, but from what I read, I just don't have the time for it.

Whenever someone tries to teach you something, there's nothing wrong with taking what you need or want and leaving the rest.

I just got finished talking to a black guy who has about 25 rental properties, but he said he had to sell drugs to get the money to start with at least three houses.

Meet the Press comes on tomorrow with the beginning of the presidential candidate reviews, starting with Rick Santorum. I don't know that much about him so this segment will be very informative.

I can't believe the craze over the Casey Anthony murder. The people outside the courthouse are running each other over to get to the 50 spectator seats in the courtroom. It's amazing to see what some people will spend their time on.

These idiots went to pull out another five-gallon bucket

of hooch from the ceiling but they dropped the bucket and it spilled. The smell was really strong. It made me sick to my stomach.

June 12ᵗʰ, 2011 - Day 291

Late last night I realized that I'm finally at a point where I don't have anything significant to write about anymore. So, that tells me that it's time to start developing the lesson plan for the PrisonProof Project. I understand a lot of people are going to disagree with my plan and that's okay, but I'm going to make mistakes and live my life the best way I know how. I also want to be an example of what you can accomplish if you put forth a little effort every day. I gave the business plan template and guide to Mason so I need to retrieve those and begin working on a rough draft of the plan and perfect it once I'm released. I've got to remember to catch *Meet the Press* at 4:00 p.m. on 590 so I can hear Rick Santorum answer some questions.

I just got back from the courtyard in the unit talking to another young man about getting his GED and writing a book while he's still incarcerated. He said he had problems motivating himself because of the uncertainty about the crack law due to his mandatory sentence. I told him that he's a diamond in the rough and he just couldn't see it. But once he gets his GED, he'll be able to get a sense of what I'm trying to convey.

It's been about 45 days that I've been debt-free and Dave was right about God's grace. I've already received a free book of stamps, and today my buddy told me that he needs me to come to the kitchen so I can tell him what I need free of charge. I couldn't believe it. Some of us are lucky enough to nurture God's grace.

I just finished reading Chapter 10: Cross-Cultural Challenges in *Beyond Opinion* and it was very good. I never knew that the intellectuals in our institutions of higher learning challenged each other's education and level of comprehension. It appears that there's a more expanded view in individuals who have studied other disciplines and in other geographical settings.

June 13th, 2011 - Day 292

I just finished talking to Dan, the Hedge fund manager. Dan explained to me that he got indicted for hiding 150 million dollar loss from the other investor, while the fund was originally worth $40 million. I thought a hedge fund was created through a C-corporation, but Dan explained that it is done through partnerships. Dan explained how trading on a margin account could really ruin your day and your life. He said bankers are kittens compared to broker-dealers, especially the ones on Wall Street. He said that, along with his degree in accounting, he worked at a couple of firms on Wall Street before opening up his own shop. Dan explained how the feds took all of his assets, closed his company, and seized his pension. He said he had a pension that required a $20,000 to $50,000 yearly administrative fee first to generate the pension on a yearly basis.

Dan said that he has taught at other institutions but doesn't know if he should continue because some guys have taken his class, invested their $40,000 stash hastily, and lost all of it. Then they wrote him back and told him that they lost everything. His conscience started to get the best of him and he had to stop teaching.

It's 9:11 and Mr. Blythe and I just finished watching the first hour of the republican debate. It was really interesting to see that no one chose to debate against each other. They all chose to debate against someone who wasn't there: President Obama.

I need to remember to look up a qualified, accredited, and sophisticated investor in Title 26 of the United States Code. Even my sole proprietorship will need to carry an umbrella policy because of defamation and like claims against me over my businesss.

I read an article in the NYT about a young Indian immigrant with a Ph.D. in Sociology of Religion. A reverend stated that he could not be effective in his field because he had no knowledge of theology or experience in the field.

Today I had lunch with an ex-cop who was also a union leader and a democrat-turned-republican. The democrats seem to have been the cause of him going to prison and he hates them with a passion. He asked me not to mention anything to anyone and I assured him that in my field of study confidentiality is a big tenet. The whole conversation came about because of a pack of ketchup that he squeezed on his shirt and pants. For some reason, the stain made him feel demoralized. He said he felt like he was the trash man.

I got into an argument with a Jewish man about whether or not it is in the best interest of employees of the Bureau of Prisons to learn the Spanish language. Of course he started preaching about how people should be required to learn English. If I was the president, I would tell all federal employees that if they pass a Spanish GED that their annual salary should be increased by $10,000 and it should be permanent.

The clerk that I work with explained how he was paid to blow up property and if they paid extra the timer could be set to go off when the individual was at the residence or place of business. He's about to be released and his parole extends to 2030, but if he gets arrested again, he'll have to return to federal prison.

I got a letter from China Daily informing that my free subscription has run out and to renew it. I should remit them $99 for a year and so forth. I will decline this offer, however it is a very good paper.

June 16th - 17th, 2011 - Day 295 & 296

I walked around the library and saw a couple more books that I had read: *The Case Against Lawyers* by Catherine Crier and one by Jay Ziskin, something about challenging the testimony of psychologists. Another book I found that I'm reading is *The Meaning of Everything: The Story of the Oxford English Dictionary* by Simon Winchester.

I saw a young man who I hadn't seen in a year or two. I asked him if he was in the Special Housing Unit the whole time and he said he was in the hole for 15 months. I read about him in the NYT because he had filed over 5,000 lawsuits in federal court and these people had big plans for this guy. He told me that he did it all for publicity.

He went on a hunger strike that got him force-fed through tubes being inserted into his mouth while being handcuffed and strapped to a chair. He said they videotaped force-feeding him and they begged him to come off of his 92-day refusal to eat. He said he was going to Hollywood because he's an actor and he'd been contacted by many publishers and screenplay writers. Apparently the warden wouldn't allow him to be interviewed by several periodicals once he filed paperwork against the institution. He told me that all of the staff were really crazy and funny, he enjoyed himself, and that he learned to intervene in a lot of cases even though they had been decided already.

June 18th, 2011 - Day 297

I just finished *The Trinity as a Paradigm for Spiritual Transformation* in *Beyond Opinion*. I simply like to believe that God exists in everything and everyone at all times forever. I do not believe that there is anything separate from God. God may have created separate entities to help relate to us and for us to relate to one another.

The political issue of the month is the right to work and I never knew how many states allow the right to work. If a state does not allow the right to work, it's because the unions require you to join their organization to hold certain jobs. I just found out that the state of Illinois is not a right-to-work state.

June 19th - 20th, 2011 - Day 298 & 299

I've discovered a way to submit my disability claim at present. I believe that in the past I was disabled because of my mental health and drug addiction, and that happened before I was incarcerated. During these months I met the eligibility requirements to file a claim for benefits. It may have been a short period of time, but I'm going to exploit this opportunity and see where it leads me.

1. TARP implications
2. Contracts
3. Profit allocation
4. Benefit of internship
5. Parameters of internship
6. Stipend
7. Why participate
8. Request for information
9. Irrevocable trust terms
10. Administrative cost
11. College education vs. trust

12. Manuscript copyrights
13. Case study

June 21st, 2011 - Day 300

I got a card from SIU-E informing me that my admission file was incomplete because of a few missing items. I needed an official copy of my GED transcript and the ones from Ozark Technical Community College. After a couple of hours of research, I got all that squared away.

There was a story in yesterday's paper about the Black Wall Street of 1922 in Tulsa, Oklahoma. A lot of young people really don't know about this story or what has become of those people.

The banker's bible, called *The American Banker*, needs to be in my library as well. The Glass-Steagall Act should've never been repealed.

I was in Bible study today and a guy suggested to me that I should enroll in medical school. I told him he's crazy to think I would enroll in medical school at the age of 40 and destitute. He then said don't worry about the cost, Obama will take care of it for me. At that moment he lost a little of my respect.

Some guys just came to my room to ask me about John Henson being the first black president of the United States. I thought this was absurd at first until they took me to the library, grabbed the encyclopedia, and let me read about him myself.

President Obama is planning to address the country tomorrow at 8:00p.m. about how we're moving forward on Afghanistan and Pakistan.

June 22nd, 2011 - Day 301

The President's speech today lasted about 15 minutes and seemed disappointing being so short.

Remember to do cash-based accounting according to Dave and during the first year, learn something about accounting each month. I need to get the book called *Entree Leadership* at the Dave Ramsey store.

I just found out from my counselor that I've not taken my yearly vacation for the year 2010. I'll be putting in a request for that vacation tomorrow morning.

June 23rd, 2011 - Day 302

Today I read an article in the NYT entitled, *Expert on Mental Illness Reveals her own Fright.* I believe that Dr. Marsha M. Linehan suffered a great deal when she was very young, but I admire her ability to overcome her demons and become a very good psychologist and professor. She is a gleaming light and example for me and my future.

This new wave of Social Entrepreneurs is really exciting, especially the ways in which they're being developed. I've never heard of an L3C which stands for low profit limited liability company. There are all types of new legal hybrids being created these days.

I just walked by my buddy's room and he's been staring at the wall for quite some time. I already know what he's going through but he'll have to accept that he's a convict now and his family is going to treat him a lot different. He's starting to realize that all the people he thought were his friends are not concerned with his well-being. A lot of people he may have helped on the outside will not reach out to him or his family. Mr. Kelly despises lawyers even though his son is in law school. They'll both look at each other with tinted glasses in the future.

June 24ᵗʰ - 25ᵗʰ, 2011 - Day 303 & 304

I just finished *The Role of Doubt and Persecution in Spiritual Transformation* in *Beyond Opinion,* chapter 12, and it was excellent material. I truly believe that trials and tribulations are good tests for everyone's soul. My title of a book dealing with visiting and lecturing at prisons will be called *Furnace of Adversity.*

I've started reading a book called *Soldier: The Life of Colin Powell* by Karen de Young, and so far it's quite unremarkable except for the historical accounts of war and politics.

I've noticed that when society's plans go well, there's no outrage or outcry when certain atrocities occur, but when the plans are not followed and something happens not according to plan, everybody loses their minds. 9/11 wasn't a part of America's plan, but it was a part of someone else's plan. If you want financial and social help in your country, all you have to do is attach America and we'll bomb you and start rebuilding according to plan.

If President Obama wants to get things done during his second term, he needs to get the house back under democratic control as soon as possible. This next presidential campaign is going to have to focus on registering more voters than this last presidential campaign.

I believe that I should make my next 10 to 15 years about being a professional student and deal with real estate later on in my life.

June 26ᵗʰ, 2011 - Day 305

After watching *State of the Union* this morning, it's obvious that President Obama will have to get involved in the debt ceiling negotiation to put a deal together.

I was at work yesterday and it was time to return back to our unit. I finally caught up with my supervisor, who was sitting in his secretary's office, gossiping about nothing. After I knocked on the door, I tried to explain to him what he needed to do with the project he had me working on. As I was explaining some changes he has to make in relation to the chart, he began to laugh and shut the door. He just elevated himself to the same level as that other asshole, Mr. Frolich, who took over accounts receivable when I worked at Unicor. I'm glad that I'm on vacation next week and they'll have to deal with the BS on their own. I shouldn't let myself get so worked up about my work in this prison because it's not really serving my best interest. If they don't care about their work then why should I?

I've got to start relaxing and not stressing about things that are clearly out of my control. I'm hoping Thursday's decision by the US Sentencing Commission will bring some needed relief to me and some other people incarcerated under some very bad drug laws.

I have a lot of reading to get in today since there isn't anything on television that I'm interested in watching.

June 27th, 2011 - Day 306

I've decided that I should have my first book be about not only my last year in prison but my first year out. I'm sitting here reading this book about the life of Colin Powell and its page count is 523. This is the area I want my first book to range, or about 600 pages.

I went to the barber shop yesterday and my barber asked me if I had seen the new show on BET called *Single Ladies* with Lisa Raye. I said I saw a few minutes of it. He told me about a scene where Lisa was on a date with a college professor and the topic of the evening was politics. A few minutes into the evening and she was asked her point of view on a certain subject. Apparently her answer had exposed her as not having a formal education and she was asked why. I think he said she felt her life experience was good enough. Her date came to her rescue as the interrogation continued.

I don't have to be the one that causes you to go toward education, but I'm an expert at laying seeds and all they need is a little water and some light to spring forward.

June 28th, 2011 - Day 307

Today Mrs. Spirits came to visit us in Bible study and she gave us our certificates for the study on Israel, Daniel, and the kingdom. She appeared to be a very strong-minded woman, and when she was leaving, she approached the door first but then stepped aside and waited for someone to get the door for her. In addition, she almost left her scarf. I forgot one of the guys got her some water in a little cup and I wanted to see if she would drink it.

I just so happened to turn my radio to the Mark Levine radio show and he was accusing President Obama of a crime of fixing the books. These guys on the radio are really an imminent threat to the security of this country. I believe they need to be censored or investigated for the crime of inciting a rebellion against the country. These radio show hosts realize that 75% of adults aren't educated enough to see through the false statements and misinformation they're being taught over and over every night. This guy is lying to the American people telling them the government is coming after their retirement funds 401K or 401(b), which is nonsense.

I think I should take another look at my convictions at the state level first and move to the federal court if necessary. I wonder if there's an avenue in the state for me to readdress my state convictions?

Chapter Eleven: George Moon

Professor Moon is a rock! He is a teacher, counselor, lecturer, and philosopher. It does not matter if you are eight years of age or eighty years of age, he would challenge you on any subject you brought up.

Mr. Moon was adamant about not reading periodicals that did not provide some semblance of substance. He will challenge you to read, to study, to listen, to contemplate, to write, and so forth. He is a self-educated, 70-year-old man with the recollection of history at his fingertips.

This man taught me how to read a book. He would say, "Have you read a lot of books, or are you well-read?" This man is among many who has spent a considerable amount of time helping me rehabilitate my thoughts and life strategies.

June 29th, 2011 - Day 308

I need to make sure that I subscribe to the congressional publication that prints every act of congress signed into law by the current president. In addition, I need to subscribe to the US Supreme Court publication of all the cases that are accepted in the instant term by the court.

I'll probably need to file a pardon sometime in the future in regards to my state charges in the past. The last law suit I filed should've been researched better.

Tomorrow is the big day in regards to the retroactive amendment dealing with crack cocaine. I hope the amendment is clean and doesn't have any disqualifiations so that everyone can benefit from it.

I haven't watched this much television in a very long time, however it is my vacation and I'm really enjoying the time off. I'll start back studying my Bachelor in Religious Studies next week when I return to work.

June 30th, 2011 - Day 309

It's 2:00 p.m. and we've just found out that the vote for the retroactivity amendment was unanimous. One of the guys put me on the phone so that I could listen as his girlfriend read from the released text from the US Sentencing Commission. A lot of the guys were standing around me, listening to my remarks about the new law, what I heard, and how it affected certain people. I really didn't notice until I turned around to get up and saw everyone staring at me.

I should get an immediate release in the first week of November of this year. I'm really glad I don't have to worry about the halfway house or the supervised release. I'm sitting here trying to write about what's going on and I can't believe I'm on my way home to see my mother. I wonder how long it will take for the courts to start contacting us about being released? It is time for me to start winding down my programming and other classes. In my book I want to make sure that I dispel a lot of myths about what an ex-felon may or may not be lawfully allowed to do or have.

FAMM (Families Against Mandatory Minimums) just sent out an email alerting everyone to the note with the unanimous consensus for retroactivity. I believe there's still going to be some disqualifications (criteria set by the commission to exclude certain inmates from receiving a sentence reduction) in the language.

I just ran across an editorial that said the republicans tried to bully the sentencing commission into not voting for retroactivity by threatening that they would make the commission pay for the release of inmates out of their own budget. I can't believe this nonsense.

I think I need to look into criminology instead of sociology. It would be a lot easier for me to parlay an education in criminology into an advanced degree in legal studies. I just found out that the new retroactive amendment is not available to people sentenced to the mandatory minimum or career offenders. I'm not going to let the guys know about this; I'll let them learn about it through another source.

It's 11:12 p.m. and Rico just got off of work on F4. This floor has the terminally ill or very chronically ill guys who really need help. Rico stopped by my room to ask me if I think he could get a sentence reduction with a 20-year minimum mandatory sentence. I just told him he'd have to wait until they release more information about the particulars.

July 1ˢᵗ - 2ⁿᵈ, 2011 - Day 310 & 311

I finished Colin Powell's unofficial biography and it was a real eye-opener in regards to leadership. It's time for me to start working on Nations again now that my vacation is officially over.

I'm pretty sure that there will not be a town hall meeting until they have a copy of the retroactive amendment to post for everyone's consumption.

I'm four months away from a possible immediate release and I'm thinking about submitting my social security disability in two months. I don't have any stamps to mail the application to submit a disability claim right now.

I think I should start a charitable trust that helps ex-felons to file petitions to have their civil rights restored once they're released from being institutionalized.

I want to name my private equity fund Greenwood or Greenwood Group.

In *Beyond Opinion* chapter 13, *Solidarity, Denial, and Self-Destruction: Hearts on Pilgrimage Through the Valleys,* was really nice. I believe that without grace, your mind or heart will always doubt, over and over.

July 3rd, 2011 - Day 312

One of the reasons I will take up criminology is to learn as much as I can so that I can develop a definitive guide for teenagers and young adults about the administration of justice in this country. I believe that this is a work that needs to be developed because the constitution is being watered down and the American people believe in a criminal justice system that doesn't exist anymore.

I've got to be able to deconstruct cults to be able to take the second exam of the course. Some of the guys are telling me that the exams are going to get harder.

I'm starting to feel as if I don't have anything else to write about. But really I should just pay a little more attention. My partner, Johnson-Bey, was telling me about a young man on the yard with his paperwork advocating that he should be going home. Johnson-Bey told him he needs to go sit his butt down and do his time. I told Johnson he should stop telling these guys that stuff because they can't handle it. It's not cool to just keep crushing other people's hopes just because you think that's what they really need.

My buddy, Ray-Ray, wants to talk to me about his fraud on the court claim but I've been avoiding him because I think my opinion will cause some damage to our friendship. I need to keep my mouth shut about the law now and go home to enjoy the rest of my life.

July 4ᵗʰ, 2011 - Day 313

I think I may have to interview a lot of sheriffs in various states so that any area my guide doesn't cover, the sheriffs may be able to expand on. I'll probably put all of the interviews on my web site and make sure the guide is about the fails. Some people may try to duplicate my idea, but the quality will never be on par with what I present.

I've learned that laying in bed studying and reading is not a good posture compared to sitting while reading and studying. It appears that sitting in a chair with a glass of ice cold water is very conducive to my learning.

One of the guys down the hall is named India because he is a 50-year-old native of India. India asked me earlier if I knew why the prisons are overcrowded and will always be that way. I told him it was because of many, many things. India said it's because every time someone leaves prison they bring one or two more back with them. I laughed so hard, but after a while I started thinking about what he said and it rings true as part of the problem. I need to look at these statistics and see what I come up with.

In the holiday we had two hamburgers, two polish sausages, corn on the cob, pie, and watermelon. We didn't get to eat lunch until about 1:30 p.m. but it was still a good meal and a good day.

July 5th, 2011 - Day 314

I can't believe that Casey Anthony was found not guilty for the death of her child. When I watched the verdict while passing by the television, I couldn't believe how cheerful everyone was about the outcome.

They've not held a town hall meeting about the new crack law amendment and the staff refuses to give us a copy of the information that they possess.

I received another letter from SIU-C asking for more documents but I don't have a clue which documents they are referring to. These people are not specifying anything in regards to what they need and I'm not able to keep calling them. I probably just need to let that application go and concentrate on SUI-Edwardsville, and if that doesn't result in an admission award then I'll move to another state and apply to another university. I probably should not make a rash decision while I'm upset and I really don't want to ask the staff to fax any more documents for me. I think they're really getting tired of the faxing.

We get paid next week and I really need a book of stamps, which will leave me with little remaining to spend. I haven't received any money in a while so it's getting kind of tight as far as resources go.

July 6th - 7th, 2011 - Day 315 & 316

My buddy, Johnson-Bey, asked me about a book he had selected from the library entitled *The Darkest Child* by Delores Phillips. I had read it a while ago, but I thought the book was very well-written.

A couple of hours ago my case manager, Ms. Hoskins, called me downstairs to inform me that my halfway house date is May 10th, 2012. I was smiling and she thought that I had already known about the date but I hadn't. I was smiling because I knew the crack law amendment would make that date a non-factor.

Kelly and I are studying for some course exams for Friday if we're able to take the test. I'll study all day tomorrow at work as well as tomorrow night and be ready on Friday to test.

There are a couple of guys who need me to type some letters to their lawyers or the clerk of court to get sentencing transcripts and other court documents to help file appeals and investigate for errors of law, especially procedural errors.

I called SIU-E and found out that some documents had to be re-submitted for various reasons.

July 9th, 2011 - Day 317

I just finished chapter 14 in *Beyond Opinion* entitled *The Church's Role in Apologia and the Developement of the Mind.* I, too, sometimes condemn or judge others for misconduct and catch myself doing so. The root word "apologia" means "to answer" and I'm starting to get a better grasp of the Christian Apologist. The answer to someone's question lies in the question or the origin of the question.

When individuals work with me on PrisonProof, I want them to sign a confidentiality agreement. I may have to structure it as a 10-year agreement.

Yesterday I watched a documentary called *News Wars* and I learned how bodies of law are created to support a position of great importance to our society.

There are about 30 different religious denominations being practiced in the chapel at the institution. I've got to remember to talk about all of them.

I'm starting to realize that I need to include other activities in my reading, writing, and studying. A lot of guys are not filing for financial aid because they believe that they can't get assistance, but that's not true.

July 10th, 2011 - Day 318

I met with my partner, Ray-Ray, in the chapel to discuss how he wanted to proceed with filing for a sentence reduction under the previous US Sentencing guideline amendment 70E, 711, and 713. Ray is a career offender, but I explained to him that their not extending the benefits of the 3582 avenue is a denial of his rights under the US Constitution.

I also found out that in the new amendment based on the Fair Sentencing Act of 2010, the commission has prohibited the judges from reducing our terms of supervised release. I also couldn't believe that Ray had at least 12 different drug convictions. I don't know how in the Hell he hasn't done more time than he has. Or maybe I don't want to know. Anyway, he has a lot of convictions related to all types of drugs. However, he still has the drug program, through which he could get 12 months reduced and another six months of halfway house.

My aunt Portia sent me $50 this weekend. It felt really good to go look at my account and not see $0.48 staring me in the face. I could make a good, large sum of money doing legal work, but I just don't want to anymore. I'm still interested in learning the law but just don't feel like holding someone's hand while I'm working. Or chasing some client around in the institution to get him to follow up on his responsibilities, like showing up on time.

July 11th, 2011 - Day 319

I went to work a little early today and ventured into the leisure library. I ran across a book that was a comprehensive guide to military and veteran benefits. The book was called *Military Advantage*. The first thing I noticed in the earlier 50 pages was that my mom was eligible for assistance and some benefits because she was over the age of 65. Before I contact her to explain some of these things, I'll finish reading the material.

Some Americans should be allowed to lease with the option to purchase. Once they've gotten to a balance of rent receipts for 30% down, they should be eligible to become full-fledged purchasers with a good, strong mortgage. People need to stop complaining and start bringing a solution.

Today was the first really hot day of the summer. I had to sit at my computer today with a staff member to make some changes to the re-entry catalog of programs and courses that are available at the institution.

I just came back from the diet kitchen, where I ate meat loaf and it was actually pretty good. The meat loaf in the regular kitchen was terrible, as usual.

I finished Ray's motion for appointment of council and dropped the guy from my list of pro bono people. I really don't want to do law work. I need to study for Nations.

July 12th, 2011 - Day 320

I spoke to one of the guys who has chosen to enroll in the BRS program at Nations and he had a few questions about the exams for the first course. I explained the format and that he should take one exam at a time. I told him that I planned on lecturing around the country about criminology and other things related to it. I explained that the Ph.D. in sociology was a personal accomplishment in addition to other things. I explained to him that a lot of people lead their lives based on a figurative or literal understanding of their faith, religion, or discipline. It is helpful sometimes to know if you're talking to or sitting across the table from a wolf or a sheep.

One of the guys was trying to get me to help him with his medical lawsuit but I really need to stop doing legal work and concentrate on my religious studies and my manuscript.

I went to the Catholic Bible study today and our guest speaker was the Catholic Bishop for the Lexington Diocese in Kentucky. His lecture on Luke was very educational and well thought-out. He said that his diocese has the most prisons to visit, which is 14 and growing.

I wonder what would happen to employment statistics if these prisons started to shut down. I remember one guard telling us that the only way to make money where he's from was growing marijuana. You can bet your money that the DEA and state task forces aren't paying them good old boys any attention.

July 13th, 2011 - Day 321

In yesterday's NYT I read an article entitled *Secularists Turn to Crowd on the Web to Finance their Projects.* I couldn't believe my idea for PrisonProof Project made the Science Times section.

I talked to Calvin today and he has a Doctorate in Theology. Calvin told me about a book he did his thesis on called *Christian Government Law* and we Googled it but couldn't find it. I think I'm going to go after the Doctorate in Biblical Law instead of Theology.

I received a letter today from SIU-Carbondale denying me admission to their school. The letter was signed by the associate director, Jonas Carl. I'll keep their letter with me for the rest of my life. It really shouldn't be a big deal because many thousands of students are denied admission for one reason or another.

One of the guys told me that he talked to his attorney and was told that everyone's paperwork is being processed now so that when November comes the judge can sign and send the paperwork to the Bureau of Prisons. Tomorrow morning I'll go to work and finish this re-entry project and be done with it.

July 14th, 2011 - Day 322

I received my halfway house package from the halfway house program, Substance Abuse Services in Marion, Illinois. However, I noticed when reading over the notes that the institution is coed. I went ahead and signed to accept the rules in anticipation of arriving on May 10th, 2012. I already realize that I'm probably going to be released in November of this year. I need to keep this resource as a backup plan for housing. The only difference is that if my supervised release officer puts me in the halfway house, he would have to write me up on a violation for me to return to prison. The halfway house could only make me leave.

One of the guys named Lester filed a claim on the internet looking for a lawyer. Lester told me that they called him immediately. As I was reading the newspaper clip of the news article of his suit, I had not realized it was him the clipping was talking about. Lester caught a bad staph infection and the jail he was in would not give him medical treatment.

I talked to my friend, Calvin, who suggested I read a book called *Christian Government Now* by Dr. David A. Pent at the Homestead College of Bible in Orlando, Florida. I had someone try a Google search and we couldn't find it, so armed with more information, I'll try again in a couple of days.

July 15th - 16th, 2011 - Day 323 & 324

I think I need to run some good columns so I'll probably need some good journalists. I also want to have the braille program for guys coming out of prison who got certified doing braille.

This next course is really hard because we have to identify the quote with a particular letter or a quote to a particular group of people. These next exams are not just fact-based multiple choice answers.

This is a time in my incarceration that I'm learning that patience and tolerance are key. I need to write a letter to the probation office and ask them if I'm allowed to return to any city within the Southern District of Illinois. I really don't care about the halfway house because the stupid case manager feels that she has something to hold over my head. I've written the probation officer for my district several times in regards to my future. Sometimes we need to know what is permitted under the law versus someone's opinion about our lives. I'm sure I'll get a quick response and support from the supervised release office.

I need as much information about what's ahead as I can get so that I'm not making decisions based on assumptions. I'm going to wait until I get a response about being released in November and then I'm going to send it, the halfway house acceptance letter, and my disability claim application via certified mail to the Social Security Office. This medical center does have social workers but they're disrespectful and snooty at best.

July 17th, 2011 - Day 325

There was a piece on CNN about missing children of color not being covered in the mainstream media. A group named "Peas in their Pod" was interviewed for their position on the issue and brought awareness of a couple of missing children of color.

I just finished with the conclusion of *Beyond Opinion* and I think that this book is really great and written perfectly. I enjoyed reading it and I look forward to reading more of his work and the work of some of his contributors.

Everybody is going to jam pack the TV room tonight because of the AMC premiere of *Breaking Bad*.

It's time for me to start getting rid of some stuff

because all I need to take with me is my paperwork. Once I hear something from the lawyer in a couple of weeks, I'm going to file my own motion for appointment of council. Some guys are really upset about the career offender and mandatory minimum that is stopping them from receiving a reduction.

I watched *State of the Union* and President Obama will make history again in his second presidential election. The republicans know that they don't have a candidate for president. Now, Rupert Murdoch and News International are about to be dismantled by the US and British governments. Fox News is going to get caught in this scandal one way or another. They arrested Reebok Brooks today and I wonder who's next. These individuals have made Scotland Yard look like some cheap prostitute and they're out for some red meat.

July 18th - 19th, 2011 - Day 326 & 327

I was listening to the Clark Howard show last night and he said that he vetted about 10 or 20 self-publishing companies. He said that iuniverse.com, Xlibris, and 1st book-something was where he referred people on his web site.

I think I want the introduction or prologue to be an open interview, a Q & A session.

This morning, one of the rastafarians wanted to know how he can get his state sentence run concurrent with his federal sentence. I told him that if it were me I would file a motion to modify my state sentence co-terminus with my federal sentence. I also told him that he should seek legal council before he makes that decision.

I tried to get the secretary to copy some information about getting your degree through Bible colleges. We were lucky to get copies of the catalog so that guys can enroll and pursue some form of education. However, this secretary would not copy the material because there were a lot of pages to be copied.

In 20 minutes I'm on my way to Catholic Bible study and to listen to some republican pundits plead their case against President Obama securing a second term.

July 20th, 2011 - Day 328

My subscription to the China Daily expired months ago - my free subscription - and they're still sending me the newspaper. I think that this is happening because they want to put the paper in circulation a lot more before they start to enforce their subscription rate.

I got my quarterly newspaper from the National Braille Association. I haven't paid my dues in a while but that's because I'm indigent.

My friend, Tracy from Baltimore, told me that I should watch a PBS documentary by a Harvard Professor named Gates called Tim-Buck-Too and it chronicles how Africans sold themselves into slavery. I can't wait to get to the chapel Friday, Saturday, or Sunday to watch this four-part series.

Everybody is walking around sweating very badly. The temperature is supposed to increase over the next couple of days and some people may start to collapse from the heat or dehydration.

I found out through one of the guys that his attorney wrote him and explained that the courts were working on immediate release schedules first and it would be a while before they would be able to reach everyone else. I think I'm going to go ahead and file my social security disability application as soon as I can. I do believe that I will be an immediate release in November.

A lot of the guys are coming to the career resource center and telling us that their case managers are refusing to help them with acquiring their social security cards, birth certificates, and photo identification. None of the staff is on the same page and they don't care that they're not competent or efficient with government resources. Until you ask them for some materials for inmates, then they say it's too expensive. I guess that's why the staff refrigerator was on sale.

July 21ˢᵗ - 22ⁿᵈ, 2011 - Day 329 & 330

One of the first assignments for the nonprofit will be to pay for the paralegal course offered at the University of Ohio for incarcerated people. I believe that these types of courses should be taken as soon as possible in a young person's life. Just sitting them down for a talk is not close to being adequate. They need something written to keep referring to.

I believe one of the avenues I should take is to create a sole proprietorship for my books with a trademark and issue a license to a nonprofit to use the trademark and copyright.

Last night I read something about a website that does a social background check called Social Intelligence which employers use to screen employees, but it was articulated in the article that this may be discrimination.

I was at dinner last night and we had Polish sausages for the meal. Every time I took a bite it felt like I had chewed and swallowed a rock. The guy sitting across the table, who was in for murder for hire, said it was bone chips. I said oh yea, I forgot about that!

I just filled out a cop-out to request assistance from the social worker to file my disability claim with the social security administration.

I got a letter today from SIU-Edwardsville informing me that I need to submit $300 as a security deposit for my on-campus apartment.

The school informed me that they will not process my application until I submit the letter. I'm going to write them back and request that my security deposit is taken out of my award letter since my EFC is 0000. Mr. Kelly assured me that this is their regular course of business. I'll take care of that first thing Monday morning.

I put in a request for a job change to work as an ICP (Inmate Companion Participant) but I'm starting to think that may have been a mistake. However, I'm sure that I can get out of it if and when I need to.

July 23rd, 2011 - Day 331

This morning I was sitting back reading my paper and watching a movie when I realized that the majority of my problems when I was a teen were really peer pressure. I didn't know how to defeat the strength of peer pressure because I didn't know how to use it against itself.

What I really needed was a pathfinder. I needed someone to show me the way. But sometimes our parents or community aren't there or don't know how to show us the path. There's another series that I want to create: *The Definitive Guide of the Pathfinder for Parents and Teens.* I might have to call it *The Definitive Guide to the Elements of Administration of Justice.*

The real name of the PBS series was *Wonders of the African World* by Harvard Professor Henry Luis Gates, Jr. and it is a three part series on VHS.

We've got chicken patties for dinner and some sort of cartoon for the evening institutional movie, which is really ridiculous. I don't understand why no one wants to see documentaries anymore.

I still haven't heard anything from the federal public defender's office about being released this November. I guess as I get closer I may hear something.

I just heard on 630AM radio that Amy Winehouse was found dead in her London apartment. They said that she has had a lot of problems with drugs and that's probably the cause of death. I think being born to a sick family or lifestyle is a death sentence.

July 24th, 2011 - Day 332

I watched a little bit of *State of the Union* and they're still crying about the debt limit. It seems the republicans kept coming up with ideas to avoid raising taxes but the White House just kept turning the proposals away. They've been negotiating for seven months now and there's been no progress on some basic tenets of an agreement.

I usually watch the program downstairs but some guys were watching a movie. So I went upstairs to the sports TV room. Moon had CNN on the big TV so I just watched a little with him. I think I'm just going to step into my room and study my religious courses with Nations for the rest of the day.

A few days ago I was listening to the Clark Howard show and he talked about how a destitute person or someone with no savings could start saving even though they felt that that their budget just couldn't do it. Clark told him to start by saving 1% of every check for six months, and continuously raise it by 1% every six months until he reached at least 15%. I love this strategy.

Listening to the Dave Ramsey show, he said that when you're selling your company you should value it at five times the net income and that you should yield at least a 20% return on your investment at a minimum.

I had to go to the diet kitchen because Ray caught me in the lunch chow line and told me he needed to talk to me about his daughter smoking weed.

His daughter is 19 and she's not in school at present. She didn't want to return to college but wants to go to nursing school. I told Ray that there's very little he can do over the phone but he needs to encourage her to go to the nursing school. I told him to ask her to send him literature about the vocational career. Ray's really got his work cut out for him with this young lady.

July 25th, 2011 - Day 333

In the Career Resources Center a white male of about 50 came to us for some help with his photo ID and social security card. However, his story evolved into talking about pain killers and why he was incarcerated and separated from his girlfriend. He explained to me how Roxycontin, *not* Oxycontin, is just as addictive – or more – as heroin. He said that all of the other pain killers just give you diarrhea.

I received a letter from the federal public defender's office saying that their office, the probation office, and the sentencing commission are putting together a list of people who would be immediately released in the month of November. Now that I've received this letter, I'm thinking about going to another college in another state. I'm really not interested in returning to the state of Illinois. I need to remember that community college is not a bad place to start. I probably should let my admission paperwork play out at SIU-E and SIU-C to see what happens. I could probably go ahead and start my social security disability claim now, too.

I didn't get my papers today even though they were delivered on time. I believe that Mondays are really busy for the mail room, so some of the mail gets put off until the next day. However, they've been pretty consistent with the paper overall for the last 18 months.

Sherman told me that some of the guys at FCI Miami were making money by charging 10% interest on any amount of the $390 spending limit made available for an individual on commissary restriction. I had to remember what the bad areas of the auditorium were called: blind spots.

I effectively stopped doing legal work because I want to relax these last few months. Kareem (one of the conscious brothers with 30 years) came to me last night and asked me to help him meet his deadline because of the unfairness of the Fair Sentencing Act of 2010.

I called the customer service center at the social security office and she explained to me exactly what I need to do to file a disability claim. First she informed me that I was not eligible for social security disability because I didn't have enough work credits. She then said that I *am* eligible for social security income. She said she needed the exact date of my release, a home address or post office box, and a 45-minute uninterrupted phone interview or we had to set up an appointment at the local office in the area of my release. The lady was very pleasant, she had a Hispanic accent and was very helpful with explaining to me what my options were. I also found out that Medicare and Medicaid had nothing to do with the social security administration. I think I may need to slow down on the social security claim until I get more information about whether one of these schools will admit me with residency.

July 28th - 29th, 2011 - Day 336 & 337

Today I read an article in the New York Times entitled, "Carmakers Back Strict New Rules on Gas Mileage by 2025." This article talked about achieving 54.5 miles a gallon by 2025. I believe that they could've achieved this years ago, but the billions of dollars of revenue would not be captured. Society's ignorance and complacency allows big a corporations to fleece them on products and services until they get caught at fraud, improper conduct, or outright deceptive practices.

I finally got a chance to read James Harris' article entitled, "Hitman." I couldn't believe some of the football training that he goes through. I didn't know that the New England Patriots had to cheat to win. However, they've picked up Chad Johnson. I'm glad the NFL lockout is over and now it's time to get back to some football.

July 30th, 2011 - Day 338

I couldn't sleep very well last night but I did wind up sleeping until 10:00 this morning. I just ate some rice I made last night and kept in my locker. The meat will spoil in the heated locker but one night will not hurt it too much. I've developed what they call in prison an, "iron gut." You get conditioned to low-grade food that's labeled *not for human consumption*. We've seen these types of labels all the time while working in the kitchen warehouse.

I got back to the unit at about 2:00 p.m. from getting my hair cut and watching part two of the documentary about Africa. They talked about Ashanti being a royal tribe that sold and traded other Africans that were prisoners of war and criminals to traders of the new world. They also talked about the Arc of the Covenant being at St. Mary's Church in Axum, Ethiopia – Africa. I really enjoyed watching these documentaries, especially the border countries who participated in trade. They said that once the patriarchy of Africa found out, they tried to stop the trade but were unsuccessful in their attempts.

I think I'm going to work on my manuscripts a little more on the weekends and some week days as my release date approaches.

There's a guy down the hall named Elvis and he's a really bad diabetic who has had another episode. The guards are all over the unit and he's probably on his way to the medical unit. His diet is absolutely terrible because he drinks soda and he eats candy and ice cream all the time. I don't really believe that he's going to make the next 60 days to his release.

One of my buddies named Flip (born and raised in the Phillipines) just came over to my room to return my NYT and he started to explain his strategies for trading in futures and commodities and that he wants to get into currency trading. I believe that you'd have to be really abreast with foreign policy and technology to be productive or profitable in these areas.

Chapter Twelve: Tyrone Johnson-Bey/Reylander Hughley

My partner and friend is the original gangster, turned teacher, counselor, lecturer, philosopher, and Grand Sheik of the Moorish Science Temple in Lexington, KY. This man helped me learn to master my thoughts; his firm insistence that I look to control my thoughts helped me while incarcerated and upon release. He taught me how to deconstruct and reconstruct a thought.

Johnson-Bey taught me that it was time to be loyal to myself and my family first. And on this path I found the power of a thought. Before I was released, Johnson-Bey sat me down and explained that he expected one thing from me. He wanted me to use what I have learned to help people like myself. Johnson-Bey is a contributor and supporter to President Barack Obama and a partner for life. May peace be upon you!

My main man Ray Ray is a cook at the Federal Medical Center in Lexington, Ky. Ray Ray and I worked together in the Diet Kitchen as cooks and we had fun eating food and helping a lot of men feel a little better. Ray Ray is from Indiana where his mother, daughter, and grandchild resides. He went out of his way to help me many times while I was incarcerated and trusted my thoughts when it came to criminal law. Ray Ray is a supporter and contributor to President Barack Obama and a partner for life.

It's early and I just finished watching *Good Morning America* because of one segment called Second Chance. They featured a young man who had been in prison, changed his life, and became an attorney. He was a kitchen worker at a restaurant while going to school three nights a week to finish college and get his law degree. I looked around to see if some of the guys were listening to the story but they'd all gotten up and just left. I guess they weren't interested.

While I was watching the show, I wondered what I could do to help guys getting out of prison when they don't have any money or any place to go. I want to create a financial institution to provide some type of loan or financing for ex-felons once they're released to start their lives over. It shouldn't be a loan; more like a line of credit with a certain amount with certain conditions. I think this is where my corporation called Greenwood would enter the picture. I've got to figure out something for the ones who need this line of credit but can't get a job to make the payments. Everyone should have to submit a budget to receive the line of credit, or some sort of personal business plan. I may have to create a private bank to accomplish this goal. One of the main reasons I want to publish this book with my ideas is because when and if other people build on them, it'll give me opportunities through mergers and acquisitions.

When and if I get married I plan on writing my wife one letter a month to express my loyalty and what I've noticed about our marriage, our family, and our future together. Maybe some goals we need to look at and bad choices to avoid in the future.

Kelly told me that I should use a debit card like the merchant card sponsored by Russell Simmons, but with this card you can only buy food or clothes. What about business loans? Business loans would be an answer for people who want to use the line of credit for significant amounts.

It appears that the government is about to come to an agreement on raising the debt ceiling. I've always known that this was politics as usual. However, these fights are a good tool for educating the citizens.

August 1st - 2nd, 2011 - Day 340 & 341

I got a letter from my aunt yesterday explaining some things to me about personality disorders and social security disability claims. I'm going through this process because a lot of the men here have these questions and are afraid to ask them. The institution staff will only help you in a limited capacity because their loyalty lies with the government.

I read in my Saturday NYT about Kevin Weiss, president and chief executive of Author Solutions, which owns numerous self-publishing companies, including iUniverse, Author House, and Xlibris. I need to look into Market Partners International, a publishing consulting firm.

I also believe that a ranch would be more secluded than buying old motels for housing in regards to ex-felons upon their release. It's just another option since there would be plenty of work for the occupants.

I'm going to file for disability because of my kidney disease, but my aunt is right: I will have to work to take care of myself. I really don't have a problem with this, though.

Mr. Shackelford just corrected some of the addresses on my list of colleges for the state of Kentucky. When I put the six schools out of Kentucky on my financial aid I'm sure it alerted them about my interest in their school. I've lived in Kentucky since 2003 and there shouldn't be a problem in regards to residency.

I need to remember to purchase *Reverse Mergers and*

Other Alternatives to Traditional IPOs by David N. Feldman, *The Story of America's Most Secretive Religion* by Janet Reitman, and *The Secret Life of Mary in the Catholic Church* by Jason Berry.

I need to keep in mind that I'm a primary case study element and I need to be released without one penny in my pocket. The fact that I've been released from prison two previous times should help me to develop a system in which an inmate in this type of situation could get back on his feet and begin to prosper.

I'm still trying to stop doing legal work but they will not stop coming. I just want to overload on a little NYT and football for the next 90 days.

August 3rd, 2011 - Day 342

This morning we were talking about the Affordable Healthcare Act and whether or not we should be allowed to purchase health insurance from state to state. I believe that Obamacare can be amended just like any other piece of legislation has been in the past. The republicans are going to try fruitlessly to overturn this law. The federal laws under HIPPA and COBRA allow you to carry prior insurance from previous employers, but you will be picking up the tab that your previous employer was contributing. I'm starting to realize that some conservatives are full of complaints and no solutions.

I just read in the paper that even in the private sector, a federal pension law prohibits pension cutbacks unless a company goes bankrupt. The federal government then takes over and covers many retirees' benefits up to a certain percent – I think it's 70% of the face value. However, these laws do not cover state and local workers.

I was thinking about opening my company account with $5,000 and securing a signature loan for the same amount, then taking the loan and applying at another bank for a $5,000 secured credit card and checking account. Then charge the card for the maximum amount of $5,000 and deposit $2,500 in each checking account. Then continue making deposits from my earned income to make monthly payments on both credit accounts.

After I complete this phase of the process, I should proceed to a reputable insurance company and insure both credit accounts in case I'm fired from my job. My initial deposit, which is used to secure those credit accounts, will subordinate the insurance policy or be outright excluded. Moreover, I would like for this policy to cover any line of credit that I open, and I don't know how feasible this proposition will be. I may have to enter into an umbrella policy in regards to the two credit accounts. I think this product may be called credit insurance. I may want to create an umbrella policy with credit insurance and identity theft insurance. Then open a credit account with "Ability One" – must check to see if they submit business credit reports to Dun & Bradstreet or another business credit reporting agency.

I started to read *What Caused the Civil War? Reflection on the South and Southern History* by Edward L. Ayers and I've decided to read it one section at a time. I need to work on my second manuscript.

Yesterday after mail call, a young man came to me with a letter from his attorney. It stated that his state case had been dismissed. He wanted to know if the letter was acceptable to the staff so that they could disregard the information in his PSI. I told him no, because the records office has to receive a court order of dismissal directly from the court. I told him to go to ISM and ask Mrs. Mitchell to call and request of the court clerk to send the order.

August 4th, 2011 - Day 343

Well, Mr. Kelly and I have just had a really good conversation about the article in the NYT entitled *New York Plan Will Aim to Lift Minority Youth.* I brought the article to his attention because it talked about Mayor Bloomberg and George Soros combining $30 million each with a city matching contribution for a rehabilitation program with an internship that leads to permanent employment. I wanted him to understand that he would be perfect to administer such a program. Mr. Kelly told me that he thought the program is a fluff and that you'd have to have a license to work for it. Mr. Kelly believes that to really make a difference in a convict's life he should have his or her conviction removed after the term of imprisonment is complete. He feels he should be able to have his license reinstated so that it's easier for him to be re-employed. However, this is a potential argument and the only way it'll come to fruition is through legislation.

My idea of education first is not feasible to Mr. Kelly because he said once they've gotten their degree what are they going to do? Where are they going to get a job? They can't get a job that requires a license. I understand this, but I'm looking for a remedy, not more complaints. I'm aware of the constraints on my civil liberty but the point in an incarcerated person's mind needs to be met with concrete choices for success.

The only thing that I need to keep in mind is that I'm conducting a project that's going to take years of research, many conversations, debating, arguments, information, and quiet observation. This is one of the reasons I want to look into criminology versus sociology.

I switched my job today from education to unit orderly and I feel a lot better. I can spend more private time studying and writing my manuscripts.

I've got access to several days of the NYT now and it's

nice. I've read a lot of good articles from the Sunday paper over the past couple of years.

August 5th, 2011 - Day 344

I woke up this morning at about 7:00, startled because I thought I'd overslept my dental appointment. I got up, took a shower, made some coffee, and was on my way downstairs to watch the news when I saw Beyonce in a video wearing a nice piece straight out of a Victoria Secret catalog. I eventually made it downstairs and watched a few minutes of CNN and strolled out to the unit courtyard.

Lester and I were talking about his son retiring from the service and all of the different opportunities that he has. I looked back towards the unit through the window and I could see the guard moving very quickly and telling everyone to go back to their cells. As I was walking back to the stairwell, I saw billows of smoke coming out of staff alley, however I didn't hear any smoke alarms going off. I made it upstairs and was looking out of the window where I could see staff from every department smoking and laughing at something going on inside the staff alley door. It just so happens that two guys who were on the alley saw what had transpired. They said it was a white guy who had been sent to the institution as a study was transferred from the psych unit to regular population a few months ago. They don't know what set him off, but all of the unit staff was on the staff alley except the unit manager.

Apparently this guy had a stick about four or five feet long and started destroying boards attached to the wall and eventually grabbed the fire extinguisher and started spraying it towards the staff members. They immediately left the hallway and locked the door behind themselves, severing the inmate in the staff alley alone. All the while the staff assistant was running toward the unit to see this spectacle. They might not give him another charge because he's mentally disturbed and was heavily medicated. Some of the guys told me that they had talked to him but he was incoherent and taking a lot of medications.

It's 10:00 a.m. and the unit staff is nowhere to be seen. I just got back from the dentist where I got my teeth cleaned. She did a wonderful job! One of the guys caught me before I went to the dentist to tell me the staff was looking for me because I had a package in the mailbox. It was my course material for the next two courses.

August 6th, 2011 - Day 345

As I was sitting here reading my NYT, I started to realize that being released from prison without any resources or support should not be a problem for an American citizen. I've come to this conclusion because of all the suffering that is going on in Africa and around the world. An American citizen's worst case scenario doesn't come close to the suffering experienced around the world. That's not to say that the suffering in this country is any less or unworthy of assistance. It just puts things into perspective.

My next door neighbor just got into an argument with the white guy named Kom. Kom was advocating the position that English is the national language of the country. I guess my neighbor was making the point that this is a country of immigrants. If a woman had AIDS and you know having unprotected sex will likely transmute the disease, do you go ahead and have sex with her to prove it so? This is what Cuba was doing by arguing against the ignorance of Mr. Kom.

I was returning from the law library because I agreed to type a letter for this guy a while back before I chose not to do legal work anymore. I just went through some hard times trying to get the resources to type the letter. I will never touch another typewriter again.

As I was coming through the metal detector, I was given a breathalizer by a rookie. I had to explain to him how the machine worked so that he could test me to see if I've been drinking alcohol. And I'm supposed to be relaxing these last 90 days or so.

I want to advertise affordable rental housing for ex-felons, people with terrible credit, and the outcasts of society.

It's 7:05 p.m. and I just finished watching *Source Code*. The plot reminded me of a teaching in my Siddha Yoga studies. Another thing that Siddha Yoga has taught me is that I shouldn't worry about planning for my release, I should be excited about not planning and enjoy watching the events unfold. Everything doesn't need to be planned.

I'm listening to the Clark Howard show and he explained to a gentleman that he should refinance his mortgage if he could recoup the closing cost by savings in the lower interest rate within 30 months. However, Dave says that you should be able to cover the closing cost with savings within 12 months.

Also I forgot about a good assist that is provided by your local congressman. Call them with your complaint and they send an inquiry called a congressional and the respondent party has to respond with their facts.

August 7th, 2011 - Day 346

We need different punishments for certain crimes. We need reforms in administration of justice and prison systems. It's 10:00 a.m. and Mr. Blythe from Jamaica and myself just finished watching *State of the Union*. The guests were Steve Forbes and Larry Summers, who had a debate about the economic policies of the Obama Administration and the downgrading of the country credit rating by S & P credit rating agency. I believe that it's very apparent that certain individuals and groups of people think that a black man can't run the country. However, not because he's incompetent, but because just his presence in the office is going to cause divided government. Some people would rather see the demise of this country's economic future rather than the success of Obama's economic policy.

Earlier this morning I went to my friend to get the business section of the Sunday NYT just to confirm that he took the paper out of the unit. About an hour later he came to see me, and not only did he take my paper out of the unit, he gave the paper away. He told me that he misunderstood my instructions to return the Sunday paper, which I find to be questionable because he returned the last paper.

I don't understand why someone would be willing to compromise access to something they desire to satisfy their ego to prove to someone else that something that you've said in the past is valid because what you've said has been written in the NYT. He asked me if I'm angry and I said no, getting angry is not going to change anything. Then he had the nerve to ask me if I still wanted the paper. He'll never see the Sunday paper again and I really shouldn't give him the paper at all. I'll think about it and take the appropriate action.

Sometimes I start having bad thoughts and start to get a bad taste in my mouth, so I eat a couple pieces of candy and everything is alright. I just walked past Kelly's room and I've not seen him reading the Bible in a few days... I think he needs a couple pieces of candy.

T-CREF is best for 403(b) or Roth IRA. Vanguard is the best choice for opening a Roth. Look for level term life insurance from very strong financial company rated A++. Get this book: Clark Harvard, *Living Large in Lean Times*.

It's 10:45 p.m. and Dionne Sanders just gave his inductee speech at the Pro Football Hall of Fame. It was quite extraordinary to say the least. It's really obvious that he loves his family, especially his mother. There's nothing else on TV and it's time for me to turn on the AM radio and go to sleep.

August 8th, 2011 - Day 347

I woke up this morning and was on my way to my call-out to see the unit counselor. I got lucky and left the unit the exact time he was coming through the main corridor. I asked him if he wanted to see me and he asked me if I was still interested in a job. I told him that I was comfortable where I was and that I had someone for him. So I went and got lucky to find Mr. Sherman and told him about what had just occurred. However, he informed me that he's on his way to F4 in a couple of days. He seemed very happy about the move and I just left it at that.

For some reason I was contemplating what to purchase with the credit card I'm using to build credit. It just came to me that tax lien certificates are income-producing assets. The county or state collects the interest payment, and if the payments aren't made, they'll foreclose on the property for me and pass me a good, clean title to it. With my earned income, this passive income will help me build a strong balance sheet. I wonder what other type of liens the county and state have for sale? I'm only really interested in real property and business. Another source of income could be tax liens. I need to do more extensive research in this area, but this is another low-cost income-producing asset that may be available to me.

I got an information package from Union College in Kentucky, but they require ACT or SAT scores if you're a freshman or transfer student with less than 31 credits from a regionally accredited university.

August 9th, 2011 - Day 348

It's 3:07 p.m. and I just got off of the phone with SIU-Carbondale and the admission director, James Carl, told me that my application was denied because they didn't think that I'd be able to complete the academic workload of the university. I wish I had a thermometer to check my temperature right now. I'll never forget his name and I hope to God he never forgets mine. Another thing I'm pissed about is that I should never have listened to some of these guys. I should've stuck to my plan about attending the community college first. I need to establish a good academic record.

Today on CNN the Federal Reserve chairman, Bernanke, said that the interest rates set by the Fed were going to stay extremely low because of the bad economy until mid-2013. This means it's time for me to get an international finance manager. Mr. Blythe is telling me a lot about international finance but I don't have the educational foundation to put the pieces together. However, I have a clear understanding of what professionals I need to help me build a company. I'll also probably need to get an export/import broker or agent to work with us to find good quality products to export or import. I would want them on a salary or commission basis; I need good people and I need them to stay.

I asked Baker today if he wanted to go in with me with a $50,000 investment, but I told him to think about it. I don't know if he'll move forward with it but if he doesn't it's really not going to stop me from completing my goals.

August 10th, 2011 - Day 349

I spent $54 today at the commissary and it made me sick, but I'm tired of asking people for stuff until I get to the store. I need to get back to my budget of $5 a week and stay there.

I'm at work handing out toilet paper at two rolls each. Some of the guys noticed they're only supposed to get two rolls but I'll give the old timers more anyway. We don't need strict control of the paper, just a little discretion. Some guys don't even come and get toilet paper. I went to the dentist an hour early so that I could make it to the store because I had to work tonight until we're released to chow.

This is the second day in a row my paper has not shown up. I'll be paying the mail room a visit tomorrow morning to investigate exactly what is going on. I don't believe that the problem is with the NYT.

It's been a while since I've listened to the Dave Ramsey Show. I'm going to have to find a job immediately upon my release. Dave has a lot of people on Twitter asking him about investing in gold and he doesn't support that decision. I believe I need to be listening to the show a lot more because I've been thinking about using debt too much to get ahead.

August 11th, 2011 - Day 350

One of the reasons I want to tell Mr. James Carl, the Associate Director of Undergraduate Admissions, that his method of denying admission with a blank denial is unreasonable is because when they're trying to get you to apply for admission or secure a housing deposit, at the end of their notices it always says that if you've got any questions, please call this number. However, the letter from the director denying my admission didn't have the line informing you to call if you've got any further questions.

I was talking to Smear, one of the guys from Indiana, today about his Facebook page. What he's telling me is really exciting and I'm starting to get really interested. I think I'm going to go ahead and pay to have the page set up so that it will be established when I'm released from prison.

I didn't pay any attention to how Facebook changed the world until I saw what happened in Egypt. I want to start the Facebook page in prison and as I transition I can start an art gallery and expand on my thoughts and reach for more help as I grow being a free man.

The name of the company that's helping me with my Facebook page is Connect-4-You and it's an outfit out of Virginia. I went to go and meet Smear but he wasn't where he was supposed to be. I'm going to take that as a sign that I need to wait to build the Facebook page.

I got my Wednesday paper today so now I'm missing my Tuesday and Thursday NYT.

August 12th - 13th, 2011 - Day 351 & 352

It's 11:56 and I'm still up revising my introduction for the Facebook page I'll be setting up in a couple of weeks. I've done a little more investigating into the Facebook page mechanism and I might be able to deal with its parameters. I hate taking photos and I've got to get up tomorrow and go out to the yard to take photos. It feels really good not having to go to work every day, though, and being able to watch a little football.

It's 10:00 a.m. on Saturday and Mr. Smith just came and explained to me what he was being told by the halfway house representative that came a couple of days ago. He told me that the room the guys were sent to was not large enough to hold the men and there was standing room only. The people that came to give the presentation were only prepared to answer questions about Kentucky or Tennessee and had no advice for the men from other states. Moreover, Mr. Smith said that normally the halfway house charges the government $100 a day for their clients and they're not responsible for your medical or transportation. Mr. Smith has not received his official date to be released to the halfway house. My official date of release is May 10th,

2012 and I have not been scheduled to go to this pre-release class. What a joke!

Yesterday I ran across a book entitled *The Forgotten Man: A New History of the Great Depression* by Amity Shlaes. This will be a good prelude until my other books come in.

I just found out that the owner of Connect-4-You sent out an email telling everyone that the Facebook pages of inmates are being taken down in large numbers and for unknown reasons. I think this is a prime example of why I should wait until I'm released.

Earlier today I was outside taking photos for the Facebook page and Big Tex (an avid Dallas Cowboys fan) was outside with me. He's about to graduate from the 500-hour residential drug abuse program. He was telling me about an experience where the staff gave them papers with guidelines about who's selling the drugs and who's getting the cell phones in the prison. They were supposed to walk the compound and the rec yard, compile the information, and return the questions for consideration.

August 14th - 15th, 2011 - Day 353 & 354

I ran across an interesting article in the Weekend Arts section of the NYT that did an exposé on a Harvard professor named Randall Kennedy. He's written a new book entitled *The Persistence of the Color Line* and it's an overview of the Obama presidency. I wonder how many professors at Harvard are African American and what they have published?

"I am willing to make personal loans on the security of character." I read this in one of the books I'm reading.

Yesterday, on an impulse, I was going to get my bio posted on writeaprisoner.com because they offered a lot of good services, employment opportunities, housing, and more.

Ms. Sanborn came in today with a lot of paint to make over her classroom for the non-residential program. I'm filling in for Tank this morning so that he can go to the rec yard and act like he's exercising when he really isn't.

I've got to remember to stop acting on my impulses because it's causing me to make some weak choices. Sometimes I'll implement a good plan and allow myself to deviate from it because of impulses.

I decided to send the pictures that I took to my mom and Portia because they send me many when they can.

My NYT is all of a sudden no longer coming on time like it has for the last 1 1/2 years.

August 16th - 17th, 2011 - Day 355 & 356

I ran into Mr. William Hawkins, who I met in Greenville when I first reached federal prison in 1996. I asked him about some of the old guys and he told me that some got relief on their cases and some were still locked up at different institutions. He told me that the best hustler I've ever seen in my life named Preacher was in Fort Worth, TX and he wasn't doing so well. Preacher would've never left Greenville if it wasn't for his poor health. I'm sure he went to Springfield Medical Center and got his medical problem taken care of as soon as he could.

I need to remember to get a book called *Think Outside the Cell* by Joseph Robinson, ISBN 978-0-9791599-0-9.

I remember one night Dave said to refinance the house at the current market value and the deficit becomes an unsecured subordinate loan to the borrower. I wonder at what rate of interest and for what length of time?

It's Wednesday at 4:00 p.m. and I want to remember to go to NOLO.com (booksellers) to learn more on forming a nonprofit. Instead of just the 50 books for each state, I can create 50 LLCs that do their own research and development.

We saw an unusual event today, being that a bus came in with inmates and it usually doesn't come until Thursday. Earlier tonight I found out from staff and inmates that this medical center has been designated for sex offender rehabilitation. Now I've really got to be careful who I let into my circle.

I need to remember to add to my plan to have your child do an essay for money on a different criminal law every week until you've covered the entire state and federal criminal code.

August 18th - 20th, 2011 - Day 357 to 359

I've been sitting out in the courtyard here in the unit all day. We talked about businesses and starting them from scratch and our long-term goals we've set. One of the guys was back on a violation; he had been kicked back into the system from the halfway house in St. Louis. I've always been told that the halfway house in St. Louis is the worst. They say it looks as if it's in the middle of Afghanistan. However, he shocked me when he said he was about to be accepted into the military. He said as long as you're 45 years of age or younger, no drug trafficking or murder, the Army will accept you. When I receive my sentence reduction in November, my first stop will be the recruiter's office.

I just saw two guys hugging each other because one of them appeared to be going to work. I really didn't need to witness that at all. Anyway, I think there's going to be a lot more of this at this institution.

It's the 20th and Mason just told me that I should try and get the military recruiter to come to the prison to see me. I probably should just write him a letter and ask him to come and visit me.

I have not written in this journal for a few days but that's okay. I've been talking to a few guys that have been in the military and they all say they'd return if they were allowed. Moon seems to think I should apply for officer school as soon as possible.

August 21st, 2011 - Day 360

I woke up after a good sleep and went to watch *State of the Union* with Candy Crowley, the CNN reporter. Candy had two guests who were governors and they helped me realize a couple of things. The Bush era tax acts are money that has been spent. Medicine is an obligation to spend that can be reformed. The medicine part and inability to negotiate drug prescription prices is in effect money spent because the republicans will not allow reform. The wars over the last 10 years is trillions of dollars already spent. Social security is an obligation to spend that can be reformed. Medicaid is an obligation to spend, not money already spent. America's trade account has been expended, not an obligation to spend.

When the US Treasury borrows money, they don't borrow it from other countries. The money is borrowed from the federal reserve and they sell bonds or treasuries to recapture the paper currency and control inflation and deflection. China does not purchase US debt with Chinese money, the treasury will not accept shipments of China currency. China accumulates our debt by accepting payments in the trade account. The US does not give China cash money in any transactions in regards to sovereign debt. I think that all of their conversations about this country's debt is a facade and people that are uneducated can't see the omitted information and factors.

I'm sitting on this bed and there are a lot of bugs on it and flying around... I don't understand where they're coming from. I've got to go to the barber shop today and I'm probably going to try and finish watching Professor Gates' Africa Documentary. Tomorrow is my birthday and

I've decided to end this part of the project at this point. I've decided to send my manuscript home to my mother.

I'm seriously considering the military as my next move.

August 22nd, 2011 - Day 361

Today, I'm 41 years of age and I've got nothing but bad news. Counselor Jennings let me talk to the Army recruiter and they refuse all people with drug convictions. The Marines will do a case by case, but you must be 28 years of age or younger. I tried to call the Navy and Air Force and they either didn't answer the phone or the line was disconnected. That pipe dream collapsed quickly.

I remember robbing a fast food restaurant in the 1990's and just the idea of it saddens me. I robbed the store with a water gun held inside a paper bag. I left the store with about $1,000 and almost got caught by a state trooper. When I walked into the store I was a coward and I had just decided again to put my life on the line. I robbed that store thinking I was going to make out with a lot of cash, but in actuality, after 17 years of contemplation, I realized I walked out empty-handed and empty-headed.

Epilogue

Receiving & Discharge

It's November 1, 2011—the morning of my release. I woke up this morning at about 5:00 a.m. I was well-rested and a lot of the guys were happy about my being released. I made myself a cup of coffee and started making my rounds. I wanted all the guys to be assured that I was not going to forget them and that I would be in touch when I've had about six months to set up my office and start school. I went to the kitchen and ran into everyone at the same time, it seemed. I started to get a little nervous while saying goodbye. Being incarcerated for so many years means you become indoctrinated to a way of life and change can be scary and emotional at best.

I had to turn in all of my bedding and uniforms the day before and it was a great relief just to get that done. I went to all of the places that I had worked because of the "Merry-Go-Round" process. You essentially go to all of the departments in the institution. The heads of these departments will then check their records to see if there's unfinished business you have with them and sign off. This process is also another way for you to say your goodbyes. I didn't have to go to Unicor, but I wanted to so that I could say goodbye to a lot of the guys I would miss when I'm gone. I also found out that I'd be going home via airplane and this was really unexpected. The business office gave me enough money for the plane trip, food, and a taxi to the halfway house.

The night before my release I had to take my release clothes and other items I planned on taking with me to the Receiving and Discharge Department. They inventoried the items and bagged them for me to take possession of the next morning.

While I was putting my clothes in the bags they

provided, another very young black gentleman walked into the room. He had cornrows and looked like he hadn't shaved in a couple of weeks. I found out his name was Carl. After talking to the youngster, it came out that he had just gotten in off of a transfer. When he arrived, the people who inventoried his clothing told him he didn't need any of it since they had clothing for him – they were aware of impending release because of the crack law.

He had a lot of paperwork with him and asked whether he was still fighting his case or filing a lawsuit. He said he had filed a grievance and wanted to see it through, even though he was about to be released in the next couple of days. He was really angry at the system and some black men because he felt that if you didn't stand and fight every battle with the administration, you've capitulated to the system. The angrier he got the more his glasses slid down his nose, and being a short man took away from his command of your attention. He wasn't a threatening person but he was frustrated in a way that could easily spill over into his life when he is released.

All I did was listen because I just didn't want to get into it right then. I had too much on my mind in regards to finding ways to help the men I've made promises of assistance to. I could see he was still young and reckless and he had some fight in him. But he was challenging the justice system in small battles and never winning the war within himself.

That evening, back in the unit, I spent much of the night going to different units saying my goodbyes to guys that I've been doing time with for more than 10 years. I went back to the unit to watch a little television and try to relax so I could be mentally prepared for the next morning. I wanted to be surprised and happy about being released... and it was really a big surprise.

The next morning, after meeting some guys for breakfast and taking a walk around "central park" (inner walk area in prison), I headed to Receiving and Discharge. When I arrived, there were two other men who were getting released with me because of the new changes to the crack law. One gentleman was a black man about 45 to 50 years of age and he had been down for about 20 years. He had depended on the staff to give him some presentable clothing, but he was disappointed when they gave him something very old and small.

Carl wasn't happy that he was being released. It seemed to me that he felt they owed this release to him. To some extent I do believe that the system owes in regards to the draconian federal drug laws that started in New York City. Senator Rockefeller was adamant about locking up as many minorities as possible. Anyway, we parted ways and I went back to the unit to read my New York Times and relax. It was about 3:00 p.m. and the day was still young, so my newspapers served as my outlet when I needed to get away from the television.

I made it to R&D kind of early the morning of my release, but the officers were expecting me and there were two other men already in the caged bull pins. Even though we were being released that morning, the officers still treated us as prisoners, like we were either transferring or going on a medical trip. The officers didn't put shackles or handcuffs on us but they locked us in the bull pin.

A few minutes later we realized why they had locked us in: they were still processing other inmates, specifically female inmates. The guys and myself chatted a bit about being locked up and it turned out that the white guy had been down for about ten years on a crack cocaine case. He had his family send in clothes and he seemed pretty satisfied with their selection. He said he was from West Virginia and he had to go back there to do his supervised release.

The female officer called the taxi company and requested two cabs, one to go to the bus station and the other to the airport. We chatted a while, waiting for the cabs to arrive, and each of us was very happy to be released and elated that our term of incarceration had come to a close, even though supervised release was still outstanding. The first cab arrived for the other two guys headed to the bus station but my cab hadn't come just yet. I wished the other guys well and watched them leave with really big smiles on their faces. I was a little disappointed that I waited almost 45 minutes for my cab to arrive. The female officer called the cab company back to reconfirm the request for the taxi to the airport.

About 30 minutes later, the officer from the mail room showed up with a check for me from Southern Illinois University Edwardsville. The check was the return of my housing deposit that I had submitted with my admission application. The money was returned because, as part of my being admitted into the school, a condition that I not receive resident housing was required. However, this was not a surprise to me because I'd been made aware of this decision a few days earlier.

Anyway, right at the moment the mail room officer touched the door to return to the mail room, the perimeter guard truck called in the arrival of a taxi. That's what I call grace! Another point in my life that I needed to realize that I am not in control and I need to let go and let GOD. It's a very hard thing to do and even harder to realize.

We rode through Lexington and everything looked new, as if I hadn't seen it before. I had been out to the University of Lexington Medical Center about a dozen times, but this time everything just looked and smelled so different. The taxi driver was a young lady. She didn't seem afraid but wanted to hold a conversation about anything except where she just came to pick me up. I had to stare at the meter for a little while to figure out how I was being charged for this ride. We got to the airport in about 15 minutes and, as soon as I got out of the taxi, it started to overwhelm me.

When I walked into the airport, everyone knew what they were doing except me. Everything was computerized and I felt like I was on another planet, even though I taught computer class for years. When I finally got some customer service and went to the right checkout counter, there was no representative, just a computer check out. At first I was afraid but I told myself, *Why don't you try calming down and reading the screen?* Afterward I realized I was panicking because I was free, not because of the computers. As soon as I calmed down, I walked up to the computer and checked myself in. Not long after that, I boarded my flight to St. Louis, Missouri.

The Flight

I went to the first security person and I noticed the people in front of me showed the man a photo ID and their ticket. So, when I got up to this person, I showed him my ticket and my prison ID. He didn't look at me at all, he simply looked at my ID, looked around, signed my ticket, and let me pass through.

Next I got to the actual check through and immediately I was asked to take off my shoes and step to the side. I noticed that no one else was asked to step to the side and take off their shoes. In hindsight, I realize that when the first security guy looked around he was signaling his colleagues and that's how I got tagged.

Once that was done, I moved on through the terminal, trying to understand what I was reading on these signs and checking my ticket every now and then to look at the same numbers I looked at five seconds before. Eventually I found my way to my terminal and I finally saw the tarmac where my plane would be arriving. It dawned on me that I had never been on an airplane aside from con air in handcuffs and shackles.

After about an hour of waiting, the plane arrived and

the receptionist starting boarding individuals according to the status that they had paid for. Everything was the same as con air except that it was all a lot smaller. The plane was really small and I had to bend down to get into it. The cabin was really small and everybody was crunched in the plane. I knew not to drink any juice or eat anything until I get off of the plane. The ride was really nice except for the landing because we hit the ground a little harder than I wanted to.

I arrived at Chicago O'Hare to catch my next plane to St. Louis. I thought I'd have some time there to eat and board the next plane with a little time to spare for sightseeing. However, I didn't know how long it was before the next plane would arrive, so I skipped getting something to eat and kept moving to find the terminal where I would be boarding. As soon as I found my terminal, the boarding receptionist was calling last call for boarding on my flight. I couldn't believe this craziness! If I would have stopped to use the bathroom, I would have missed my flight and I would have been *really* nervous then. I wonder what I would've had to do to get back on schedule and get to the St. Louis airport?

Anyway, I made the flight and I sat next to this older woman who was really pleasant. I could tell by the rings she had on her fingers that she was probably a widow because she had on her late husband's wedding band. As soon as the flight took off, she went to sleep. When we started to get closer to St. Louis, she woke up and we started to talk about the guy on the front page of my New York Times. It just so happened to be Herman Cain. She was not a fan of the republican and she wanted to know how I felt about this politician. I told her he's got too much baggage and he should not have tried to fight his history because the press will make you look like a villain.

The Metrolink

We landed in St. Louis and it was time to make a decision: Did I want to catch the taxi straight to the halfway house or go to my sister's house and surprise my mother and family? I decided to get on the metrolink and go to my sister's house.

I followed the arrows to get to the metolink boarding area and found a machine that allowed me to purchase tickets. When I arrived at the machine there were a few women standing in line to buy boarding passes. I watched them get their passes but I still could not figure out how this vending machine worked. One of the nice ladies asked me where was I going, so I explained and she advised that I buy a two hour ticket, so that's what I wound up buying.

I put my $5 bill in the machine to purchase this ticket for $2.75 but the change that came back to me was all coins. I asked the lady where in the world my dollar bills were. She explained that the coins are dollar coins. I felt stupid, like I was from another country. The machine gave me my tickets and I walked out onto the boarding dock to get on the train, but there was no one to take my ticket. So I followed everyone else to get on the train and I wondered when someone was going to come and punch my ticket. The doors closed and the train started to leave the airport. I thought the door had a scanner above the entrance that must've scanned my pass so I was okay. Everyone was dressed so weird and all the young people had earrings in places all over their faces. This was a real strange thing to witness but some of the older guys told me that I'd see some really strange things because I'd been locked up for 17 years.

I didn't know where to get off of the train to get to University City so I walked up to the conductor behind locked glass doors and asked for directions. The conductor was a young black man and he said that I should get off of the train at the Delmar substation stop. So that was where I got off.

I started asking for directions to Crest Avenue and got all types of directions. I was getting a little nervous; I didn't have a problem getting lost but I was on the clock. The US Probation Office was expecting to hear something from me in the very near future. So I decided to start walking until I got to a business and I would ask them for directions.

I arrived at the housing department for Washington University and the secretaries went on MapQuest and found exactly where I needed to go. The secretary was a beautiful black sister and she went out of her way to make sure I didn't get lost. I ended up getting lost anyway and wound up passing my turn. I walked up to an older black lady waiting on her bus and she started directing me to the other side of town. I didn't want to talk to her anymore because she made me feel really stupid in regards to interpreting directions. But I felt that the lady at the university knew what she was talking about, so I decided to head back in that direction.

I started heading back but decided to check with the people taking orders in the pizza joint. So I walked in and asked and they explained, after arguing with each other for a few minutes, that I just missed my turn about two blocks up the street. I thanked them and, feeling really relieved, I walked briskly in the right direction and saw the street where I was supposed to turn.

Sutter Avenue was a street that happened to be set back just enough for someone to miss it if they're not from this area. I walked with a different stride because I knew I was about to surprise my mother and sister. Some of the guys told me that I shouldn't do this because she might have a heart attack and I really gave that some consideration, but I went ahead with my plans. I arrived at Sutter Avenue and I knew that I was close to the house because I could feel I was going in the right direction. I kept walking up the street and I ran into this youngster and asked him where Crest Avenue was; he said it was the next street up. I continued up the street and walked past a young girl tying her shoes and scared the Hell out of her. I smiled and kept on with my journey. Finally, I arrived at Crest Avenue.

Crest Avenue

I wanted to make sure I surprised them so I observed the people standing on their porches. I started walking down the street, paying close attention to the addresses on the houses and knowing every step brought me closer to seeing my mother. I finally arrived at the correct address and ran to the front door. I wanted to just walk into the house but I chose not to because I might be walking into the wrong one and that would be a very bad thing. So I walked up the steps and knocked on the door. No one came at first but I stood there and knocked a little longer until I heard someone unlocking the door.

Angel opened it, looked at me, and broke into tears. She ran to me and gave me a really big hug and she couldn't believe she was looking at her brother who she hadn't seen in so many years. She read my mind and she wanted to surprise our mother. So she went and got a chair and I sat down in the living room. She then went and got my mother, who came downstairs with her hands over her eyes and sat in the chair.

Then there was a knock at the door and a young girl came into the house. It was Christine, Angel's daughter. I turned to get a look at her and it was the same little girl I scared when she was tying her shoes. Momma took her hands off her eyes and looked right at Christine; she didn't even notice I was sitting there. She just happened to gaze in my direction and asked my sister, "Is that John, Angel?"

She jumped up to give me a big hug! She made me step back so she could see me and then hugged me again –

she just couldn't believe that I had actually arrived at the house. They all sat down and I started to explain my experience at the airport and metrolink, getting lost trying to find the address, and how much I enjoyed every minute of it. My momma wanted me to take off my sweat suit because I was making her hot just looking at me sweating in long johns with sweatpants and a sweatshirt. I needed to take some of those clothes off and start relaxing.

Final Thoughts

Over the years I have found that being able to communicate a thought is paramount in presenting your views or ideas. Writing this material opened up doors in my mind to venture into and explore the capacity to be a student of life.

Men like myself have a history of communicating with silence, aggression, loneliness, lies, deception, abuse, acts of fraud, impatience, and an unforgiving recklessness towards our women and ourselves. However, we all have the capacity to change and help others change with insight into the errors of our ways being put into the light of day. Over the years I have come to accept that integrity is the secret to maintaining youth and success.

About the Author

John Leroy Hunt was born at Christian Welfare Hospital in East Saint Louis, IL on August 22, 1970 to Dwight L. Hunt and Jessie M. Hunt. His father was a Vietnam veteran who died in May of 1998. As is the case with many African Americans, his family originates out of Greenwood, MS and is spread out all over the US.

Mr. Hunt started writing because he believed that if an individual had the capability to read and write, they should be able to have a diary at least. A diary is a good start for an amateur writer to expose their weaknesses in grammar while simultaneously exposing inner strengths and weaknesses. Mr. Hunt started writing while incarcerated in federal prison to be an example to other inmates that their life was not over and that the court system could not take away their mind and education.

The author is working on two additional books to complete his three-book memoir set. The second book is primarily essays explaining the informal education he received while incarcerated at several different correctional institutions. The third book is composed of short stories about the major turning points in his life and how he had to deal with the consequences.

He lives and works in St. Louis, Missouri and has no kids or pets. Surprisingly, he lives in an extended stay hotel, works in a fine restaurant, and studies in the field of Hotel and Restaurant Management at St. Louis Community College at Forest Park in St. Louis, MO.

John L. Hunt's forthcoming book is entitled *A Puzzling Education in Essays.* It will be released in 2013.

The Violent Cycle: Crime, Abuse, and Trauma Connected
Jennifer-Crystal Johnson

I'm the editor of this book by Mr. Hunt. Because of my history and some of the clients I've worked with, I've begun to take an active interest in the US recidivism rate and hope to be able to confront some of the issues criminals face. And why are they labeled criminals? Because they're in prison. There are plenty of people breaking the law every day who either don't get caught or are in complete denial of what they're doing.

Any human being can be influenced into criminal behavior in one way or another. There's peer pressure, desperation, anger, revenge, and a range of other things that can easily lead to criminal behavior. Believe me... I've had some of my own vengeful thoughts. I never acted upon them (unless you count writing about it), but I have definitely had them. While some get caught, others do not. However, those who are in a criminal lifestyle are more likely to be arrested one way or another, and the longer they stay in said lifestyle, the more likely they are to get caught.

Of course, this influences those around them. If a man is living a life of crime, his mother will worry. If he has a wife and children, or even a girlfriend and children, they're subjected to that lifestyle and all of its side-effects. Criminal behavior often has violent tendencies and history as well. Even if the crimes themselves aren't considered violent (i.e. drug abuse), there's a good chance that the emotional ups and downs caused by living this kind of lifestyle will affect others in the family and the community.

It has already been determined that people influence each other and that families are a large part of that influence. Because I do know this to be true, I decided to do some research on how people can be affected from early childhood in regards to criminal behavior and activities. According to AnnaFoundation.org, 83.3% of convicted killers suffered severe physical or emotional abuse as children. Likewise, over 80% of women in prisons and jails have been physically or sexually abused. So, the cycle continues.

Because people inflict trauma on each other, the victims are likely to turn into perpetrators and victimize someone else. This rings true for people even if they're bullied in school; just remember the Columbine shooting. Those kids were harassed and abused in school to the point of believing the abuse was accurate, and eventually all they wanted was revenge. Even if they don't victimize someone else to the extent of being convicted of a crime, victimization can still happen. A great deal of self-training, education, and reconditioning thought processes is required to break this cycle. Reconditioning oneself to control emotions is also absolutely necessary to minimize future incidents of violence and abuse. Do you control your emotions or do they control you?

This reconditioning can be read about in a number of books available. The only person who can control you is you, even when it doesn't feel that way. But once you are able to recognize that feelings can be controlled and even used for good and to your advantage, this process becomes less daunting and more doable. The more you know yourself and learn your conditioned responses, the more you can do to change those conditioned responses. Just think of Alexander DeLarge in A Clockwork Orange; his conditioning is forcefully reset by psychiatrists who re-train him to vomit when he sees violence or hears classical music. This treatment was performed because of his sociopathic, violent nature and his damage to the community inflicted by him and his gang of thugs. Though this is a fictional tale, the conditioning aspect can be applied to anyone. Re-training your brain can be done, even though not everyone believes this. However, the more you study yourself, your own thought patterns, and the nature of psychology, the more you will realize that it is, in fact, doable.

Any kind of trauma – be it childhood abuse, molestation, domestic violence, death in the family, or another kind of trauma – can and usually will cause some form of post-traumatic stress disorder, or PTSD. The symptoms of this disorder are many and the causes are many, which is exactly why there are so many sub-categories of PTSD. A soldier wounded in battle can't be lumped into the same category as a battered spouse, for example. Similarly, a domestic violence victim can't be lumped into the same category as a rape victim who was assaulted by a stranger. They tend to exhibit different symptoms, even though some of them may be the same.

One common symptom, though, is addiction and substance abuse. According to a report by NCADV, women who have been abused are 15 times more likely to abuse alcohol and nine times more likely to abuse drugs than women who have not been abused. So, a woman is abused or assaulted, suffering from PTSD, and simply wants to dull the unexplainable pain inside... so she starts drinking. A lot. And it's okay... alcohol is legal. Right?

Alcohol has been linked to numerous criminal behaviors ranging from domestic violence to beatings, shootings, stabbings, rape, and other assault. Alcohol has been a factor in over 60% of homicides and 75% of stabbings. What's more, alcohol has actually recently been linked to a reduction in the brain's ability to heal emotionally on a molecular level.

According to a September 2nd press release, a study was conducted on mice, one group having been given the equivalent of double the legal limit on a regular basis and the other being given no alcohol. They were then given a slight shock every time a specific sound played, and later, the sound played without the shock. The group of mice that had not been given alcohol eventually stopped fearing the sound, while the group of mice with alcohol in their systems continued to fear the sound no matter how much time went by.

This leads doctors and researchers to believe that people with anxiety disorders such as PTSD are less likely to be able to heal themselves emotionally if they have chronic alcohol problems. This finding is extremely important because people with anxiety disorders and PTSD are drawn to alcohol to help them relax and unwind. If they knew that it was hindering their healing and recovery from PTSD or anxiety, they may find the strength to stop depending on alcohol to relax. On top of that, the study will eventually lead to researchers developing medication that is specifically designed to protect the areas of the brain that alcohol affects so they can heal.

The cycle is destined to repeat itself over and over if people remain uneducated about their own afflictions and problems, or if they simply choose to ignore what their problems are and pretend they're fine because of their pride or a fear of being judged. But isn't it better to feel a little judged by peers or family and become a better person than to wait until it's too late and be judged by an actual judge and sentenced to prison time?

There is a connection between trauma, abuse, rape, and any other crime that hurts another person and the prison population itself. Because the prison population has already committed their crimes, chances are that there were witnesses, people who were victimized, or even people who have witnessed prior crimes even if the perpetrators weren't punished for them.

According to some statistics, victimless crimes account for about 86% of the prison population, which should be a good thing, right? The problem with this statistic is that some of the most unpunished crimes are by people of means and people who sexually assault their victims. One in four women will be sexually assaulted in her lifetime; this doesn't even account for the number of domestic violence disputes or molestation that go unreported and unpunished.

Children who witness or experience trauma are more likely to be perpetrators if they're men and victims if they're women, though there are exceptions to this.

I've seen some of the effects on children who have witnessed and been abused emotionally. One of them has had a lifelong problem with stealing. And sure, it starts small at first. Stealing candy from the cupboard... stealing a toy from a friend.... But before you know what's happening, they're stealing from the student store or the local gas station. Then what? The cycle is perpetuated, once again.

One major aspect to all of this is mindset, self-discipline, and mental conditioning. People can learn and unlearn things if they put their minds to it; though it does take some education, study, and will-power, it is possible. After having gone over the contents of this book several times, I saw a real issue with people – labeled as criminals – feeling a lack of confidence or hope that they can make anything better of themselves besides what they already are. Of course they would never admit this. They simply continue playing the criminal "badass" and go on doing the same things over and over again. ("If you want something you've never had, you've got to do something you've never done." - Dr. Neecie Moore in Encouragement for Your Journey)

This belief that nothing can be done or that change is too hard means the recidivism rate will continue to remain the same (or get higher) and criminal behavior will be attributed to genes, personality, or upbringing. A great number of people feel that these are traits that cannot be changed or developed into something else. I disagree. I firmly believe in mind over matter and growth over being trapped, which means that every single inmate in this country could change if he or she applies him or herself to change and education toward change.

A criminal lifestyle isn't necessary to be wealthy or to maintain your status. Unless the status desired is a "street" status, but to be perfectly honest, this is a status only other criminals respect, not people who are successful in the world outside of crime, drugs, violence, and death. Successful people in the world of jobs, business, vacations, and love have achieved their goals without resorting to criminal behavior.

Why not you?

The human brain is an amazing thing that is constantly changing, evolving, and developing. As you learn new things, your mind begins to change physically, and the more you learn, the more powerful your mind becomes. Thus the saying: "Knowledge is power."

Now, the question is this: would you rather perpetuate the cycle, inadvertently creating more criminals as you go? Sometimes criminals who do not yet understand the full weight of their decisions, like young kids (whose innocence should be protected in the first place)? Or would you rather begin again with a new life? Clean, moral, with a job or by starting a business? The workload might be heavier, but the results are often priceless.

The only person who is responsible for your actions is yourself. Though hardships might be easy to blame, that's a cop-out. An excuse to behave badly because the goodness of life seems infinitely far away. Everyone has problems of one kind or another. So ask yourself: would you rather be a part of the problem or a part of the solution in the bigger picture?

If you're ready to start learning and becoming a better person, all you have to do to start is read. Read and apply what you're reading to your life. Learn from what you read. Two excellent books on this topic are *The Talent Code* by

Daniel Coyle and *Mindset: The New Psychology of Success* by Carol S. Dweck, Ph.D. You can begin there and start to break the cycle.

Internet Sources:

The Anna Institute. Gary Wheeler. January, 2001. The Anna
Institute. December 12th, 2012.
<http://www.theannainstitute.org/wchac-ststs.pdf>

National Coalition Against Domestic Violence. Gretchen
Shaw. NCADV. December 12th, 2012.
<http://www.ncadv.org/files/SubstanceAbuse.pdf>

DARA. December 12th, 2012.
<http://alcoholrehab.com/alcohol-rehab/crime-and-substanc
e-abuse/>

EurekAlert. Tom Hughes. September 2nd, 2012. NIAAA.
December 20th, 2012.
<http://www.eurekalert.org/pub_releases/2012-09/uonc-hdr
083012.php>

PBS.org. Mary Dickson. 1996. PBS. December 20th, 2012.
<http://www.pbs.org/kued/nosafeplace/articles/rapefeat.htm
l>